VERISIMILITUDES

VERISIMILITUDES

Essays and Approximations

By James Gallant

ODD VOLUMES

OF

THE FORTNIGHTLY REVIEW

LES BROUZILS 2018

ODD VOLUMES

OF THE FORTNIGHTLY REVIEW

www.oddvolumes.co.uk

Editorial address:
Le Ligny
2 rue Georges Clémenceau
85260 Les Brouzils
France.

ISBN 978-0999136508

For Christine: generous patron, demanding critic, excellent cook.

When the Way was lost there was virtue; when virtue was lost there was benevolence; when benevolence was lost there was rectitude; when rectitude was lost there were the rites.

> The rites are the wearing thin of loyalty and good faith, and the beginning of disorder.

—XXXVIII

When the empire is ruled in accordance with the Way,
The spirits lose their potency.
Or rather, it is not that they lose their potencies,
But that, though they have their potencies, they do not harm the people.
—LX

—Lao Tzu, *Tao Te Ching*,
translation by D.C. Lau. Penguin Books, 1963

CONTENTS

FOREWORD

Verisimilitudes collects short prose written over the past twenty years or so. The first section, nearly half of the book, comprises essays with related concerns published mainly by *The Fortnightly Review*. ("The Humiliating UFOs" first appeared in *Raritan*.)

"Reviewing *America, Land of Faeries*" in the second section, appeared in *The Georgia Review,* and "Lancôme of Paris Has a Gift for You," in *Riding Light Review.* "Won't You Come Home, Bill Bailey?" was the opening chapter of my novel *The Big Bust at Tyrone's Rooming House: a Novel of Atlanta*, published by Glad Day Books.

I am grateful to Denis Boyles, editor at *The Fortnightly Review*, both for inviting me to write my column, *Verisimilitudes: Essays and approximations*, for his publication, and for his assistance with this collection.

James Gallant
Atlanta, 2017

I

THE HUMILIATING UFOS

I.

As an undergraduate I got serious about Aristotle way too early. The *Metaphysics* was an exhausting study, but I had understood it more or less, and was in awe of it, when a professor of mine remarked offhandedly that if I knew Kant I'd realize the whole Aristotelian structure was built on sand. This offended me profoundly, personally.

Even when I found out later what Kant was saying about metaphysics and the limitations of human knowledge, my admiration for Aristotle lingered beneath the "secular humanism" *de rigueur* in the humanities at the time. His epistemology might be dubious, but his vision of Nature as totality spoke to the intuition we come into the world with, that the many are in some sense one.

Of course, the moment we begin elaborating this intuition difficulties set in, and the elaborations in the mythology, philosophy, and theology of the pre-modern world were often far more fantastic than Aristotle's. The following is an excerpt from a hymn to Enlil, chief of the ancient Sumerian gods:[*1*]

> *Without Enlil, the Great Mountain,*
> *No cities would be built, no settlements founded,*
> *No stalls would be built, no sheepfold erected...,*
> *The sea would not readily produce its bountiful treasure,*
> *The fish of the sea would lay no eggs in the canebrake,*
> *The birds of heaven would not spread nests over the wide earth.*

1 ** Quoted from Samuel Noah Kramer's, *The Sacred Marriage Rite.*

In heaven the rain-laden clouds would not open their mouths,
The fields and meadows would not be filled with rich grain…
The cow would not throw its calf in the stall,
The ewe would not bring forth the…lamb in its sheepfold,…
The beasts, the four-legged, would bring forth no offspring,
Would not want to copulate.

Strange, that the divine blessings should include not only rains which assure plentiful crops, seas full of fish, and sexual desire in farm animals—but also city- and sheepfold-building we accomplished Nature-conquerors would usually see as our ingenious responses to practical need. For ancient holistic mentalities, though, *all* things—including environmental challenges and ingenious responses to them—issue from a common matrix. For the Sumerians with their Enlil, as for the Greeks with their culture-bringing god Prometheus, craftsmanship and skills are gifts to humanity, as they really are in some sense whether we venture to explain this or not, and whether we are grateful.

Underlying the vision of the world propounded in the hymn to Enlil, as well as the metaphysics of Aristotle, is a sense of involvement with, and dependence on, Nature uncommon in modern societies, but not in early modern Europe. In *The Order of Things*, Michael Foucault discusses the "similitudes" of sixteenth century European thought which propound the unity of Being: *convenientia* (adjacency— things commonly found in one another's presence are assumed to be related metaphysically); *aemulatio* (emulation—a person born under a specific astrological sign will act in accordance with its dictates, and vine leaves mimic the daily transit of the sun across the sky);

analogy (qualitative similarities between the physiognomies of animals and humans, or the sun and gold, expressive of occult relationships); and *sympathies* (cucumber shoots with water, or fire with the air into which it rises and dissipates as heat and smoke).

Foucault understands perfectly, without approving, the totalistic thrust of such thinking. Here, "space bristles with relationships, with strange figures that intertwine and in some places repeat themselves. Sympathy and similarity are everywhere; the work of the mind is to decipher them." This "deciphering" eventuated in grand, and to modern eyes absurd, constructions like the Great Chain of Being, and the microcosmic man who unites in his being all elements of a Creation that included angels and demons of various description long since devolved into Christmas card illustrations and Halloween costumes.

That the cosmos "bristles with relationships" was equally evident in the beneficence of Enlil, the primal substances and forms of Greek metaphysics, Neoplatonism's hierarchies of spirits, and the similitudes of sixteenth century thought. But in the vision precipitated by the modern natural sciences, humanity occupies a little island of lucidity and technical competence enveloped by a sea of *je ne sais quoi*: the "homeless" condition Heidegger described, compounded of about equal parts lucidity and immodesty. Yes, the human world is obviously part of something larger, but since articulating this relationship lies beyond the reach of our methodologies, it is as if this were *not* the case, and finally we forget about it altogether until reminded forcibly, perhaps by a natural disaster.

There could be no more eye-opening reminder of this "something more," as William James called it, than being visited by entities from other planes of existence discounted by our epistemology: gods, angels, dybbuks, elves, monsters, demons, etc. There may never have been a time when we were *not* visited by such entities. Whether we have always identified them properly and given them the attention they warrant, is another matter.

In and around Point Pleasant, West Virginia, in November, 1966 there were multiple terrified witnesses of a murky gray or brown creature six to seven feet tall which had large, bat-like wings, and bubble-eyes mounted in its shoulders. Dubbed "Mothman" by a local newspaperwoman, it stood upright, shuffled along on legs resembling a human's, and stared at people hypnotically with luminescent red eyes. It could rise straight up from the ground like a helicopter, and chase cars at speeds up to a hundred miles per hour, reportedly without flapping its wings.

In 1966 and 1967 there were in this same area also a number of sightings by credible people of strange lights and UFOs in the night sky, and odd people were turning up in the streets. Meanwhile, both locally and nationally, there had been a rash of baffling "animal mutilation" cases: farm animals discovered dead, either butchered elaborately, or with throats slit neatly, blood removed but never spilled on the ground where they lay. In folklore, such anomalies augur tragic or epochal events, and in December 1967 the Silver Bridge between Point Pleasant and Gallipolis, Ohio collapsed into the Ohio River, killing over forty people.

That the atmosphere of strangeness was causing people to "see things" was certainly possible. "Mothman" might have been something other than the demon from Hell many locals felt him to be—perhaps a sandhill crane, a university biologist named Smith suggested, although the Ohio River Valley was not usually a habitat for that bird. (Mary Mallette of Point Pleasant who'd had a personal encounter with Mothman looked at a picture of a sandhill crane, and said, "I wish Dr. Smith could have seen this thing.")

Or perhaps Mothman was a member of an elusive species of giant owl for which cryptozoologist Mark Hall proposed the name Bighoot; or a terotorn survived somehow from the Pleistocene Age, a bird known to have had a wingspan of up to twenty-five feet. (Birds as large as small airplanes—never identified—had been seen over Illinois in 1948. The Wyandot Indians feared the carnivorous, blood-sucking Thunderbird associated with wind and storm, said to have carried off children and old people, and blighted crops.)

The beauty of the cryptozoological take on anomalous creatures people claim to have seen is that, while not dismissing them as hallucinations, it allows for an agnostic suspension of judgment that can last indefinitely, without people being inclined to ponder what the hermit Mark of Chersonesus told the Christian Neoplatonist Michael Psellus in the eleventh century about the air, the earth, the seas, and the bowels of the earth being chock full of demons; or the medieval Sufi mystic Ibn al' Arabi's observations on shape-shifting spirits both luminous and earthy which, depending on the will of God, present themselves to humans in sublime or terrifying guises.

In December, 1966, a year before the collapse of the Silver Bridge, author John Keel, a student of anomalies interested in the Mothman sightings, visited Point Pleasant. There he became alarmingly enmeshed personally in the local strangeness. Odd lights began following him around "like dogs." Dark presences hovered over his bed. Once, checking into a motel at random, he found a reservation had already been made in his name. He, like others in Point Pleasant were receiving peculiar phone calls, and visits from olive-skinned men in black attire who seemed ill-at-ease in their bodies and curiously unacquainted with the conventions and language of ordinary life. Keel's personal experiences in West Virginia solidified his belief in what he had come to think of as "ultraterrestrials": entities that "operate outside the limits of our space-time continuum," but can invade and influence our common world.

Patrick Harpur refers to such entities collectively as "daimons." He includes under this rubric fairies, trolls, Bigfoot, the Himalayan Yeti, the Abominable Showman, sea monsters of impossible dimensions, phantom animals, and UFOs and their crews: expressions one and all, Keel thought, of a timeless, sinister, something-or-other demanding our acknowledgement, and relishing our disturbance of mind. Like Mothman, these entities have always been palpable in a locale for a time, then vanish without having been captured or identified conclusively. They may leave behind some kind of material evidence, as if to prove their reality. For Keel, Mothman belonged in the same category with the Garuda and Roc of mythology, and the winged birdman whose aerial acrobatics over the beach at Coney Island were observed by many in 1897.

Even more problematic for modern intelligence than Thunderbird or Mothman, since further observation and research cannot be expected to rescue them from make-believe, are those other "ultraterrestrials," the deities of ancient polytheists.

What is likely to be said in our time about the old gods is that they personified seasonal cycles, or maybe "inward" truths. (A visit from Athena was a bright idea, the great lover was a devotee of Aphrodite, the warrior of Mars.) A discussion of ancient Sumerian civilization in a contemporary book for young people includes the statement that Sumerians, like kids afraid of the dark, imagined "forces and beings… always present [that] continually affected human life, whether for good or evil." Since the seventeenth century, says the author, we have tried "to banish or at least suppress" such fantasies.

The Sumerians were no dummies, though, judging from Samuel Noah Kramer's studies which attribute to them the first writing, the first bicameral congress, the first code of laws, the first schools, the first historical documents, and the first moral ideals. Odd, they should have been so theologically-challenged! Kramer writes, "The Sumerian theologian assumed as axiomatic the existence of a pantheon consisting of a group of living beings, manlike in form but superhuman and immortal, who, though invisible to mortal eyes [Kramer seems very sure of this] guide and control the cosmos in accordance with well-laid plans and duly prescribed laws. Each of these anthropomorphic beings was deemed to be in charge of a particular component of the universe"—sky, wind, storm, ocean, rain, rivers, mountains—not to mention "cultural entities such as city and state, dike and ditch, field and farm; even implements such as the pickax, brick mold, and plow."

Even more insufferably, these deities "plan and act, eat and drink, marry and raise families, support large households, and are addicted to human passions and weaknesses." In these respects the Sumerian gods resembled the Homeric gods Edith Hamilton wrote about with barely restrained contempt in *The Greek Way*. They were simply not "edifying," she said, although they had helped free humanity from the remote, inhuman gods of earlier peoples, and in so doing foreshadowed the later glories of free-thinking, individualistic Greek philosophers, historians, sculptors, and champions of democracy. (These latter worthies in Hamilton's praise of them bear a striking resemblance to American intellectuals of her generation devoted to science, art, and the humanities, and proud of having transcended those dreary, superstitious, witch-hunting Puritan ancestors of theirs.)

Obviously neither Kramer nor Hamilton could conceive of the gods of mythology as anything other than projections of ethnic psychology, fictions, or dream images. Their interest in them was merely antiquarian, and given the Western scientific paradigm's crisp distinctions between real/unreal, objective/subjective, happened/did not happen, how else were they to be conceived? Ernst Cassirer's study of the archaic myth-making mind in *Philosophy of Symbolic Forms* (1923-1929) creates the impression that the mentalities of those who created the myths must have resembled ours not much more than chimpanzees'. Bless their hearts, they could not discriminate between wish and fulfillment, dream and reality, image and thing.

None of these scholars imagines that entities based in other planes of being could ever have appeared in our midst—although countless world myths and theologies treat such manifestations matter-of-factly. Socrates, accused by the Athenians of not believing in the gods, although his belief in spirits or demigods *was* acknowledged, remarks in Plato's *Apology*, "If the demigods are the illegitimate sons of gods, whether by the nymphs or by any other mothers, of whom they are said to be the sons—what human being will ever believe that there are not gods, if they are the sons of gods?"

It is usual in modern discourse to see the ancient gods as "anthropomorphic." Judging from what we read about them, their behavior certainly did very often resemble ours. In order to go about their business in the world unobtrusively, they might disguise themselves *as* human beings. Odd, that their resemblance to us did not seem to detract from the Sumerians' and the Greeks' respect for them. How was it that in so many unrelated regions of the ancient world people claimed to have had dealings with these shape-shifting beings who, except for their extraordinary powers, resembled us? These entities could appear spontaneously and disappear quite as readily, scare the daylights out of people, convey advice and prophecies, intervene in wars, and influence weather and crops. If these entities had *not* been palpable at times, would the idolatrous peoples condemned so roundly in the *Bible* ever have created images of them? (Attempting to invoke the presence of a god or spirit with just any old image that came to mind might have been counter-productive!)

The Homeric hymns to Demeter and Aphrodite describe epiphanies. Demeter disguised as a ragged old woman meets with the daughter of Keleos. In the *Iliad*, Athena visits Achilles on the battlefield, Aphrodite removes Paris from danger in a cloud, and Apollo whisks Aeneas off to his temple on the Acropolis to save him from Diomedes. When King Priam approaches the Greek encampment hoping to retrieve the body of his dead son Hector, Hermes appears to him in the guise of a young man, and guides him in and out of the camp safely. In the *Aeneid*, Venus disguises herself as a huntress to give advice to Aeneas. While such literary epiphanies were presumably fictional, they reveal that the idea of a god or spirit assuming physical or quasi-physical form did not offend the ancient sense of plausibility.

There was very general belief in the pre-modern world that subtle-material entities from other "dimensions" or "planes"—Harpur's "daimons," Keel's "ultraterrestrials"—could manifest in, and influence, the physical world. Their home base might be called Olympus or the "astral realm" or "faerie." ("You must call it *something*," W.Y. Evans-Wentz remarks in his *The Faerie Faith in Celtic Countries*.) The Syrian Neoplatonist Iamblichus (fourth century AD), echoing remarks attributed to the prophetess Diotima in Plato's *Symposium,* says that gods, formless themselves, require subtle-material daimons to execute their commands on Earth. Closer to our own time are those witches who claimed to have experienced materializations of demons, and rural British people's transactions with *faerie*, conceived as a realm little people and animals parallel to our world, imitative of it, and capable of interacting with it somewhat as the Olympian pantheon did.

No doubt a wealth of superstitions and tall tales would emerge in the wake of epiphanies, but had they not sometimes actually occurred would the Sumerians and the Greeks ever have created impressive statues of their gods and goddesses, and built temple-homes for them staffed with cadres of priests and priestesses? (At her temple in Uruk the effigy of the Sumerian goddess Inanna was treated to meals served with elaborate decorum at regular intervals throughout every day.)

Nothing in polytheism is more difficult for the modern Western mind to negotiate, Sumerian scholar A. Leo Oppenheim remarks in his *Ancient Mesopotamia* (1964), than the idea of a "plurality of spiritual dimensions." This difficulty had precipitated, he believed, a wealth of dubious anthropological speculation: "For nearly a century [Western thought] has tried to fathom these alien dimensions with the yardsticks of animistic theories, nature worship, stellar mythologies, vegetation cycles, pre-logical thought, and kindred panaceas" that yield "lifeless and bookish syntheses and smoothly written systematizations decked out in a mass of all-too-ingenious comparisons and parallels obtained by zigzagging over the globe and through the known history of man." The problem fundamental to these speculations is, of course, that they view the "plurality of spiritual dimensions" from the standpoint of the belief in a one-dimensional universe most scientists and intellectuals embrace—except, of course, for those physicists interested in "string theory" and such which I, for one, do not pretend to understand.

Years ago, teaching a university course in mythology, I was becoming increasingly impatient with modern interpretations that represented the old gods as metaphors for natural forces or the cycle of the seasons, projections of the Archetypal Unconscious, etc. Joseph Campbell's psychologizing of the gods once caused me to throw one of his rambling, incoherent books out an open second story window, startling an elderly Ohio neighbor trimming his rose hedges below.

One day a colleague mentioned Erich von Daniken's *Chariots of the Gods* (1968) that he had just read. He described its thesis: Von Daniken had taken the anthropomorphic view of the old gods one step further, proposing that not only were they *like* human beings, they *were* highly intelligent humanoids: ancient astronauts, descended to Earth from somewhere in space. They brought to humanity civilizing knowledge, and created architectural wonders such as the pyramids whose construction would have exceeded the capacities of primitive humans then roaming the Earth. (In a memorable moment on the old Johnny Carson "Tonight Show," Cornell astronomer Carl Sagan remarked that just because Von Daniken couldn't figure out how to build the pyramids didn't necessarily mean that this would have been impossible for the Egyptians.) Wowed by the spaceships and acumen of the newcomers, the more primitive earth dwellers saw them as an entirely different order of beings, the gods.

What excited me about Von Daniken's thesis when I first heard about it was simply that it made the gods seem as real as ancient peoples had obviously thought them to be. A breath of fresh air coming in through the window out of which I had thrown Joseph Campbell!

Von Daniken continued to amplify his argument in later books, and Zecharia Sitchin also wrote on myths from this standpoint in popular books such as *The 12th Planet*, 1976; *The Wars of God and Men,* 1985; and *When Time Began, 1993.* Sitchin proposes that in aboriginal times, the Babylonian Anunnaki (literally, "those who from heaven to earth came," the Elohim or "Sons of God" in *Genesis*) "splashed down" in the Persian Gulf. The Elohim were astronauts dispatched to Mesopotamia to mine gold necessary for an environmental rescue mission on their home planet. Sitchin's ancient world comes furnished with rocket science, space-ports, a hovering manned space station, "Mission Control" at Nippur, and sophisticated genetic experiments in Africa for blending the hominid nature with the constitution of the sky people, resulting in the oddly mixed humanity familiar to us.

Intent on the theme oft repeated in mythology that the gods came from the sky, both writers make much of stories and images of gods disguised as birds, or riding in chariots propelled by giant birds. An ancient clay figurine found in Turkey resembles a modern shuttlecraft with a god-astronaut ensconced in a snug cockpit, and Mesoamerican archaeology has turned up images of bearded gods in the presence of what bear a certain resemblance to rocket-ships. (Sitchin suggests that Sumerian Inanna, originally the goddess of Aratta who later became the goddess of Uruk as well, may have commuted by air between her two cities.)

The projection of spacecraft, astronauts, environmental crises, genetic experimentation, and commuting into the aboriginal world is certainly an arresting gambit. Sitchin's learning is extensive, and he presents his vision so authoritatively as virtually to preclude objections. But the amount of conjecture required by what both he and von Daniken propose forces classification of their works as a kind of learned science-fiction. Robert Carroll in his online "Skeptic's Dictionary" lumps them together with Immanuel Velikovsky, author of *Worlds in Collision* (1950), as the "holy trinity of pseudo-historians." Von Daniken and Sitchin, "weave a compelling and entertaining story out of facts, misrepresentations, fictions, speculations, misquotes, and mistranslations."

Both authors have enjoyed wide popular followings at times, though. Having read some of their books, the best explanation of this is, I think, that their sweeping visions allow people, without relinquishing modern realism and scientism, to envision their lives in a cosmic context. "Doctrines which heedlessly run off from the [human, rational] subject to the universe," Theodor Adorno writes, "are more easily brought into accord with the world's hardened condition, and with the chances of success in it, than is the tiniest bit of self-reflection by a subject pondering itself and its real captivity." Maybe so, but stoical acceptance of the world's "hardened condition" can be very tedious; and, lest we forget, the truth is, *we are in the universe*. We respond to "doctrines" and imageries that remind us of this—even absurd ones, perhaps.

Is it possible, though, that our kinship with the cosmos can become explicit? The pre-modern world certainly thought so. A host of ancient myths *say* that gods, or spiritual entities of one sort or another, came to us out of other dimensions, presented themselves visibly and audibly in various shapes, offered counsel, scared us silly, delivered prophecies, rescued us from danger, made off with us into their own realms—even made love to us.

There is one phenomenon today sufficiently common and overwhelming in uncanny immediacy as to suggest a parallel with earlier humanity's experiences of other planes of being: the UFO.

II.

Carl Jung acknowledged in his 1959 essay, "Flying Saucers: a Modern Myth," that UFOs might pose a challenge modern epistemological orthodoxy, because while they behaved "not like bodies but like weightless thoughts," they could also register as physical realities on photographic film and radar screens. The strangest possibility he could envision—it would "open a bottomless void under our feet"—was that the UFO might be a "materialized psychism." Jung was drawn to metaphysical positions that relaxed barriers between mind and matter, but the term "materialized psychism" emphasizes the subjective aspect of the UFO experience. Modern man is experiencing a longing for belief *(-ism)* powerful enough to float a mysterious figure in the skies?

The trouble with this speculation is that not everyone who has a UFO-related experience seems to be hungering for revelation, and, indeed, many people who have had "close encounters" with UFOs would rather not have. An encounter with a UFO is usually something that just happens—often to people whose families and friends describe them as not given to wild imaginings. Harvard psychotherapist John Mack who has studied alleged UFO "abductions" at length remarks that "unless we are prepared to consider the whole universe…as but the play of consciousness we would be hard pressed to explain UFOs…in depth-psychological terms."

Mack thinks, as others have, that it may be impossible to account for the UFO without an appeal to ontology. Keel and Harpur classify the UFOs and their crews among "ultraterrestrials" and "daimons." Salvatore Freixedo, a onetime Jesuit, says the question is no longer whether UFOs are "real," but "which reality they belong to," because they are evidently not from other planets, but rather "other levels of existence or mental/physical dimensions." (He, like Keel, emphasizes their demonic aspects.) Ivar Mackay of the British UFO Research Association concluded that minor spirits intermediate between God and the Creation in the Kabala were more illuminating where UFOs were concerned than the "postulates and dogmas of a few generations of scientists."

Astronomer J. Allen Hynek a scientific advisor to the U.S. government's early study of the UFO, Project Blue Book (1951), had originally pooh-poohed the suggestion that the UFO might be an occult reality, and made his disagreement with Keel and his kind explicit. Later, though, he came around to their point of view. When he did, he could not publish his conclusions in scientific journals that would not hear of them, and resorted instead to writing articles for *Playboy*.

Jacques Vallee, an astrophysicist, a onetime associate of Hynek's, and a longtime UFO investigator, describes in an online interview a UFO ascent from earth two Californians witnessed, after which they found at the launch site some molten metal and a pile of sand. Analyzed by a geologist friend of Vallee's, the metal turned out to be ordinary brass. The sand was odd, it contained no quartz; it was not stream sand, beach sand, or the residue of mining, and might have been produced by grinding various kinds of rocks together. There was no reason to suspect either material had extraterrestrial origin.

Surely, though Vallee's interviewer said, sighting of the UFOs by the Californians, followed by the discovery of the sand and brass, would suggest that the UFO had been *physically present*? In some sense, yes, Vallee replied, otherwise, human beings, themselves physical, could not have perceived it. However, the UFO "has the ability to create a distortion of the sense of reality, or to substitute artificial sensations [imaginings] for the real ones, so that while *something* of a physical nature occurs in a UFO encounter, it may not be exactly what people think." What is verifiable, Vallee said, is that a UFO concentrates a "tremendous quantity of electromagnetic energy in a small volume," heavy doses of which have been known to induce visual and auditory hallucinations, fainting, and strange behaviors. In short, if a reality from of another "dimension" invades our spaces in a UFO-related experience, the imagination may have a role in its formulation.

How this might occur is suggested by an experiment G. N. M. Tyrrell describes in his studies of spiritualism. As an experiment, a spiritualist once willed himself to appear before an acquaintance in a distant place, and this occurred. However, the phantasm witnessed by the friend represented not the sender's present appearance, but rather that of years before. The percipient's memory had contributed to the apparition which was, in part, a work of the imagination. It would be possible, then, that an incursion of "other dimensions" in our familiar world of the kind that once caused people to envision fairies or gods might now be causing them to see "aliens" in space ships. As for the brass and the peculiar sand—"daimons" and "ultraterrestrials," as if to confirm their reality, have often left behind physical evidences of their presence.

However, from the beginning of the UFO flap in the late 1940s, to the present, the most common hypotheses have been that the UFO is either a sophisticated spaceship from a distant planet— if not Russia—or a misunderstood natural or human-made aerial phenomenon. Otherwise, it must express mental derangement.[2*]

In his *Revelations* (1991) Vallee, whose personal efforts across decades to determine if the UFO was a physical reality of any ordinary came to naught, surveys the dense jungle of private and public agendas, government propaganda and disinformation, conspiracy theories, and fraud that have enveloped UFOs—a tangle so dense that even if the "smoking gun" proving UFOs to be high-tech flying machines from planet Goofy were to turn up now, maybe no one would believe it. While it seems increasingly unlikely that this will ever happen, the authority of the Western scientific paradigm virtually guarantees this quixotic quest will continue among dedicated students of the UFO, who these days are mainly amateur enthusiasts, trained scientists generally being disinclined to sully professional reputations by associating themselves with this murky field of study.

But taken seriously, as usually it is not, the idea that UFOs and their crews are "daimons" or "ultraterrestrials" would bring welcome relief from the torturous half century-old quest for proof that we are being visited by nuts-and-bolts flying machines from space. The wealth of empirical data gathered on UFOs worldwide has only intensified their mystery. People have witnessed them as majestic light-radiating structures a la Stephen Spielberg, shy aerial saucers, derby-shaped structures, triangles, cigars, or cylinders. Shortly before one UFO "abduction," a miniature illuminated UFO resembling a child's top hovered

2 ·Brenda Denzler relates the history of U.S. government research into UFOs in her *The Lure of the Edge* (University of California Press, 2001).

at the bedside of the abductee. Some UFOs observable to the naked eye show up on radar, some don't. People who have had "close encounters" report UFO crews as fairy-tiny, giant-tall, large-headed but small bodied, headless, boyish, grim, friendly or hostile. They have tiny, or immense, feet. They come in gray, blue, or green. They cause illnesses, or effect miraculous cures. It is as if, Harpur remarks, UFOs and their crews were "specifically designed to refute any theory we might hold about them."

But "daimons" or "ultraterrestrials" have *always* been shape-shifters capable of sudden, prankish appearances and vanishings—as are "aliens." Historically, such entities tended to favor remote wilderness areas, and highways at night, as do the UFO-related "aliens." Such entities have often been associated with lights that wink in and out of visibility. Fairies pointed wands at people to incapacitate them; some UFO-related "aliens" have similar equipment. Both daimons and UFOs disturb the human experience of time. (A person who danced with the fairies and believed he had been away from his normal life a few minutes might discover that decades had passed.) While a UFO close-encounter is in progress, watches will stop, and people involved may not be able to account for what they did during a period of hours or days, or how they came to be relocated from point A to point B. Conversely, a complex UFO experience may seem to unfold outside time, and when the experiencer returns to normalcy, time will seem to have stood still.

Historical daimons, as if persuade people of their physical reality, deposited material evidence of their presence. "Aliens" debarked from UFOs leave behind footprints small as children's, and others fifteen inches long. John Keel describes footprints at UFO sites that "look like the prints made by ripple-soled shoes." The spacing of the footprints tends to be peculiar, starting arbitrarily somewhere and leading nowhere.

Some New Jersey people who observed a flying disk discharge flaming metal over telephones lines retrieved a piece of honeycomb-like metal they placed in a jewelry box where it disintegrated swiftly, like fairy gold turned to ashes. After observing a UFO landing, and communicating with pint-sized aliens in 1964, a farm worker in Newark Valley, New York, found at the site a ruddy, jelly-like substance impossible to scoop up, regardless how he tried. Several days later it simply melted away. Precursors of the UFOs, mysterious flying boats resembling dirigibles later developed were seen in the skies over the United States during 1896-7. They dropped to earth newspapers, shoes, and peeled potatoes.

In a 1961 incident, mention of which is seemingly obligatory in studies of UFOs, a saucer-shaped flying machine, chrome in appearance, touched down before a sixty year-old Wisconsin chicken farmer who noticed through a window of the UFO an alien working at what appeared to be a flameless electric grill. A crewman held out a jug to the farmer and, without speaking, conveyed the idea that he needed water, which the farmer supplied. The alien reciprocated with a stack of pancakes. The farmer ate one. He said it tasted like cardboard. (The others, federal investigators determined, were ordinary buckwheat.)

Classified information leaked by military personnel includes reports of fighter jets being destroyed while giving chase to UFOs. There have also been reports (or at least rumors) of debris and alien corpses retrieved from crashed UFOs and stored at Wright-Patterson Air Force Base in Dayton, Ohio. A woman who had worked there spoke on her deathbed of having catalogued thousands of pieces of junk from crashed UFOs. A meteorologist who visited a friend employed at Wright-Patterson reported seeing tiny space suits that had been removed from alien corpses. (These outfits might conceivably be the contemporary equivalents of fairy paraphernalia found about Irish countryside in the nineteenth century that included a minuscule jacket with a velvet collar lightly greased from wear, pockets singed as if by a tiny pipe, and cloth-covered buttons too intricate for human manufacture. (There was also a long, narrow miniature shoe in the style of a gentleman's from the previous century which scientists at Harvard believed to have been fashioned of mouse skin.)

The psychosomatic effects of "close encounters" with UFOs—temporary paralysis, lengthy hangovers, headaches, elusive ailments (or sudden cures), nightmares, abrupt changes of temperament and outlook—have parallels in the occult experience of the past. UFO abductees' conviction that they are involved in a program of genetic modification that is to merge alien and human natures recalls the folklore of fairy "changelings," amours between fairies and mortals, and the mixed-parentage demi-gods of mythology. Fairies had a vampire-like need of human or animal substances to sustain or invigorate themselves. "Aliens" are sometimes interested in the blood of menstruating women; and simultaneous UFO-sightings and farm animal mutilations caused John Keel to wonder if the UFO had sometimes been a cover for the more critical business of gathering biological materials.

The evidence that the UFO, or what it represents, can influence the material world is likely to be convincing for anyone but the Western scientific paradigm's most dogmatic faithful. UFOs produce explosive sounds, deposit metal fragments, bend tree branches, and alter growth patterns in plant life. Microorganisms in soil near UFO "landings" are reduced in significant numbers.

Whatever happened in the now famous episode at Roswell, New Mexico in July 1947, it left some very odd material in its wake. Military sources at a nearby base had initially reported a crashed UFO. Later, government sources replaced the original announcement with word that an experimental weather balloon had fallen from the sky. UFO investigator Philip Imbrogno interviewed in 1993 a retired electrical engineer, who, with specialists in other scientific fields, had been flown a New Mexico in the summer of 1947. The engineer was conducted to a field where five tents stood, each protected by a uniformed guard. The tent to which he was admitted contained pieces of a heavy-looking, dull silver-colored metal. "When I picked up the larger pieces," he told Imbrogno, "I was surprised to find they had no weight at all. It was as if I had nothing in my hand—I couldn't even feel it resting on my skin. I had to grab it with both hands and squeeze it to make sure it wasn't some kind of illusion. Some of the pieces were very thick and they looked like they weighed a ton, but they were lighter than a feather....The metal would not bend or crush even with more than three thousand pounds of pressure, and it would not react to a metal detector."

All of the evidence that UFOs can work influence in the physical world notwithstanding, Cornell astronomer Carl Sagan in his *The Demon-Haunted World* (1995) treats this evidence as existing only the mind of its beholders, and deserving classification among timeless fantasies of gods and demons "come down from heaven to haunt us, to offer prophetic visions, and to tantalize us with visions of a more hopeful future." He lumps the UFO together with other forms of contemporary irrationality. Responding to a UFO enthusiast who criticized him for ignoring 4400 cases from 65 countries in which UFOs had left behind physical evidence, Sagan remarks that "not one of these cases, as far as I know has been analyzed, with results published in a peer-reviewed journal in physics or chemistry, metallurgy, or soil science, showing that the 'traces' could not have been generated by people." (Of course, what would obviously prevent most scientists from spending time and energy on UFO traces, and submitting articles about them to peer-reviewed journals, is that to do so would be professional hari-kari, as Hynek had discovered.)

Vallee refers to "hundreds of cases" in which soil disturbances produced by UFO "landings" had been observed, measured, and photographed. Of such disturbances Sagan remarks that there are ways of disturbing soil other than landing a UFO. "Humans with shovels is a possibility that springs readily to mind." As for the curious discolorations, and cup-shaped indentations, found on the skins of people claiming to have been abducted by UFOs, "there are well-known psychiatric disorders in which people scoop, scar, tear, cut and mutilate themselves." Sagan's response to the mysterious little metal gizmos, function unknown that have been removed surgically from the flesh of people claiming to have been abducted, is breathtakingly level-headed: None, he remarks, has revealed "unusual isotopes" suggestive of "unearthly manufacture." If a simpler, more prosaic explanation of a UFO-related anomaly is *conceivable*, then, as far as Sagan is concerned, that *is* the explanation.

His conviction that the natural sciences deliver any and all truth amounts to a religious faith. Scientific colleagues of the Victorian-era English chemist and physicist Sir William Crookes who embraced that faith once dispatched Crookes to debunk spiritualist super-star D.D. Home. (Home, among other feats, was said to have levitated, floated out one open window in a room, and then back through another.) Crookes conducted his investigation and returned with a report that Home was on the level.

Impossible! said his colleagues.

"I never said it was possible," Crookes replied, "I said it was true."

Patrick Harpur, who relates this story, remarks that "for as many as believed in the reality of psychic powers [of spiritualists like Home] there were more who believed it was all trickery, even to the extent of disbelieving their own eyes."

Sagan's dismissal of the UFO recalls the typical scientific response to things people have reported seeing falling out of the skies: red rain, grease, stones, frogs, charcoal, a fibrous substance like blue silk, a dark stuff smelling of burnt meat, a fine yellow powder that was not pollen, blood mixed with gobbets of flesh, a putrid buff-colored substance resembling soft soap, dried fish of the chalwa species, jellyfish, an olive-gray powder comprised of black and white hairs. The usual scientific responses to such droppings amused Charles Fort, the early twentieth century investigator of anomalies. A frequent explanation was that a "whirlwind" had scooped up stuff in one place, carried it through the air, and deposited it elsewhere. Whirlwinds had been known to do this on occasion; however, Fort was disturbed to see this explanation hauled out of the hypothetical closet and dusted off to account for droppings even when no "whirlwind" had been reported anywhere in their vicinity. If odd things falling from the sky were not seen as the work of whirlwinds, they might be explained as misperceptions: People only *thought* they had seen such stuff fall from the sky. It must have been on the ground all along, *because such stuff does not fall out of the sky*. Commonly, Fort observed, scientists simply crammed reports of these anomalies into the overflowing drawer of The Unknown where they could be blessedly forgotten.

Fort, who thought scientists' belief that certain things were impossible had often prevented or warped investigations, did not think everyone who reported strange things falling out of the heavens was hallucinating; and he did not find compelling in many cases the hypothesis that things falling from the sky had been blown from somewhere else. While insisting that such events should not be explained away or ignored, and that to do so was not at all scientific, Fort had no explanations for them himself. Sometimes, though, he ruminated whimsically about a hobgoblin prankishness in Nature which took aim at "cloistered minds that [find] repose in the concept of a smug, isolated little world free from contact with cosmic wickedness, safe from stellar guile, undisturbed by inter-planetary prowlings and invasions."

Fort would have had a wonderful time with scientific responses to the prankish UFOs, had he lived to see them.

The uniformities in tales of UFO "abductions" described in the case studies of John Mack, Budd Hopkins, and David Jacobs are remarkable. In many of these cases, Jacobs observed, it is as if the same videocassette had been plugged into various minds.

In a typical abduction, a person is "beamed up," or otherwise elevated, into a hovering UFO, and laid out on an examination table. There, he or she encounters a Chief Examiner who communicates telepathically through large, dark, mesmeric eyes. There is a supporting staff of trolls clone-like in appearance and behavior. The examinations recall the torments of Hell in medieval woodcuts: a tube inserted down the throat, a catheter up the urethra, a large needle through the navel. Steel implements probe women's reproductive organs. Eggs are believed to have been extracted from women, sperm from men. Apocalyptic visions of ecological or nuclear catastrophe appear on screens. Banks of transparent, aquarium-like vessels contain alien embryos. Abductees are apprised of their involvement in a project of cross-breeding to fuse alien genetic material into humans', or vice-versa. An abduction may entail a more or less straightforward sexual encounter with an alien. There have been cases in which a female abductee pregnant after an abduction discovers months later she is no longer carrying a child, and believes the embryo has been removed from her body in a later abduction.

Paradoxical as ever, the "aliens" who have taken the trouble, or had the fun, of invading the human sphere and disturbing people's lives, seem to covet privacy. They tell abductees that they will not remember what has happened to them, or warn against revealing what has happened, should they remember. Sometimes what abductees recall, rather than their abduction, is an impressive "screen" image of some kind— a gigantic owl or monster at a window, or perhaps a vision of the Virgin Mary—its purpose, apparently, to divert attention from the main event.

Author Whitley Strieber experienced his personal abduction as an "overwhelming, devastating, and total assault on the deepest sense of being and worth." It left him convinced that "if there aren't demons out there, there might as well be, because these guys [aliens] are indistinguishable from demons....To look into their eyes is to be less. Forever." Investigator David Jacobs describes the painful psychological aftermath of abductions as "a combination of Post-Traumatic Stress Disorder and the terror that comes from being raped." The physical consequences of abductions have included headaches, fear of hospitals and hospital equipment, urological-gynecological symptoms, and sexual dysfunction. Brands are sometimes found on the skin of abductees. There may be miniscule metal implants in their nasal canals, or elsewhere on their persons.

Attempts to explain abductions as nightmares, or the delusions of mentally disturbed people, have been unproductive, Harvard psychiatrist John Mack writes in his *Abduction* (1994). Abductees have come from every social class, every level of intelligence and education, and they do not generally seem more neurotic than anyone else. While a UFO abduction is dream*like*, abductees generally insist they were not dreaming; others would prefer to believe they had been, but the aftereffects of their experiences argue the contrary.

About a third of people claiming to have been abducted have a conscious recall of what happened, according to psychiatric social worker John Carpenter. The other two-thirds may have partial recall, or simply feel they have experienced something extraordinary, and the stories of their abductions emerge during hypnosis. The dependability of hypnosis as a research tool is, of course, questionable. Does fantasy mix with memories in such dreamy states of mind? May the therapist interested in abductions be providing suggestions that would encourage his patient to imagine one? And if the patient is aware of the therapist's interest in abductions, might he or she not contrive one to gain the therapist's sympathy and interest?

John Mack responds to such questions in the appendix of a revised version of his 1994 book. The abduction experience by its very nature does not lend itself to observation and measurement of any ordinary kind, he points out. The analyst must, therefore, give due attention to the subject's character and motives, the consistency in the story he or she tells, and the affective responses generated by it. Mack avoided leading his hypnotic subjects into abduction narratives by suggestion and, as he says, what patients had described without prompting surpassed anything he could have imagined. In his experience the memory of an abduction lay so close to the surface of consciousness that a patient had only to be relaxed before the story came spilling out. As for the trustworthiness of memory in the hypnotic state, Mack found hypnotized patients generally more candid about their experiences than they were in conscious recollections that tended to filter embarrassing details.

Do UFO abductions really happen? As much the foregoing will have suggested, the answer depends on what one means by "real." Like other UFO "close encounters," they are not, it seems purely subjective events, but involve the psyche's influence by powerful objective forces or entities. Mystification—at times simple nonsense—seems to be essential in these visitations. While aboard a UFO, one abductee is instructed to enter a tank containing what looks like water (although it is not), to submerge in it and breathe normally. This turns out to be possible. Then the abductee is told to get out of the tank. The point of this exercise is unclear. In another incident, a youthful female abductee David Jacobs interviewed was told by her abductor to memorize a list of boys' names because "there's a war and I'll need to know those names."

"What are you doing?" one abductee asks her medical examiner. "You know what we are doing," comes the reply. "Why me?" she asks. "You are very special to us," says he.

An abductee aboard a UFO is placed at an electronic control panel with columns of buttons, and told to operate it. The abductee says he doesn't how. "Do it anyway," says the abductor.

It is as if an abduction were the work of Kafka or the Marx Brothers, if not a Zen master. "Daimons," Patrick Harpur writes, "not only leave red herrings, they *are* red herrings, leading us up blind alleys where we come face to face with mystery." Is that the *point* of them? To disturb the cloistered minds Fort spoke of who regard themselves as occupants of a "smug, isolated little world free from contact with cosmic wickedness, safe from stellar guile, undisturbed by inter-planetary prowlings and invasions"?

People who have UFO-related experiences are often described as level-headed, sensible sorts. Precisely! says Harpur. Those *would* be the people daimons would go after. A "close encounter" will tend to disturb complacency and pride, and open closed minds to new possibilities. An abduction is a kind of humiliation that undermines the ego, forces a realization of ignorance and dependence. Mack, noting that the preponderance of abductions have occurred in the United States, remarks that perhaps the medicine is being administered where most needed.

In her 2007 *They Know Us Better than We Know Ourselves,* Bridget Brown focuses on the humbling aspect of the abduction. Her book, based on interviews with eleven supposed abductees, as well as the case studies by Hopkins, Jacobs, and Mack, argues against abductions having anything to do with "other dimensions." Instead, they are hallucinations or fantasies revealing the masochism of abductees. The abduction scenario is a metaphorical rendering of the helplessness induced by the hypnotist who elicits the tale, or by hostile cultural or political forces at work in the abductee's life. The abduction reenacts "power relations" and involves "inchoate individual and collective feelings of anxiety and disempowerment."

In other words, what abductees *say* about their experience cannot be taken at face value. One of Brown's pet expressions, "reading between the lines," epitomizes her methodology. The fact that she is interpreting a kind of experience she has obviously not had herself does not prevent her from presuming to understand it better than people who have had it. Her assurance that what these people *say* they have experienced they *cannot have*, resembles the usual scientific response to strange objects falling out of the sky Fort contemplated, Sagan's *a priori* skepticism about the UFO, and the assurances of modern scholars that the childlike minds of early peoples who claimed commerce with entities from other planes of being could not distinguish between fact and fancy.

Brown is right, though, about humiliation being a main theme in abductions—indeed, in UFO encounters of every kind. When UFO crews behave like kidnappers and rapists, *we* are the victims. When UFO crews are practical jokers, *we* are the butts. When UFOs perform their aerial acrobatics, *we* are uncomprehending, slack-jawed observers. When UFO crews come on like Zen masters brandishing paradoxes and blarney, we are the baffled novices.

The analogy between the UFO experience, and the historical experience of "daimons" and "ultraterrestrials" is suggestive, and seems to square better with what we know about UFOs than more down-to- earth approaches. The lesson of the UFO may be that those content with the little island of intelligibility on which the sciences have marooned us will be reminded forcibly of the sea of their unknowing.

Hard to say, though, who the teacher might be! Abductee Whitley Strieber thought the violence of abductions might be a response—he didn't say *whose*—to the modern refusal to acknowledge the reality of gods and ghosts. Vallee has speculated that in the UFO we might be witnessing a meta-logical challenge—he didn't say whose— to the Western scientific paradigm. If in the interest of producing a spiritual revolution, he writes, "you wanted to bypass the intelligentsia and the church, remain undetectable to the military system, leave undisturbed the political and administrative levels of society, and at the same time implant deep within society far-reaching doubts concerning its basic philosophical tenets, this [the nonsense of the UFO crews] is exactly how you would have to act."

If the UFO is not a projection of a longing for revelation, as Jung had speculated, a personal experience of one certainly may resemble religious awakening. A physicist doing field work in a region where UFOs had been sighted saw one himself, and a year later could not mention the moment in public without experiencing a rush of emotion. Although he believed an advanced technology of some kind must have been involved in what he'd witnessed, this interested him less than his sense of a "relationship, a cognizance, between us and the UFO intelligence." The Japanese UFO researcher Junichi Kato, who with his study group has had numerous encounters with UFOs, describes similar telepathic communion: "Sometimes it feels as if there's something right in front of me, something I can touch. Occasionally I receive a symbolic sign or image quite vividly. Basically the feeling is very exciting and I am most grateful for it.... It feels like seeing someone you have been longing for very much. Sometimes I receive a great impression, as if a chord is struck deep inside me."

Writers like Strieber, Vallee, Keel, Freixedo, and Jacobs have emphasized the shocking, sinister aspect of humiliations administered by the UFO crews. It is not impossible, though, to envision them as bad-tasting medicine that benefits patients. Mack found analogies between UFO abductions, and the opening stages of initiation rites in primitive societies which isolate initiates from their families and communities. In this isolation, initiates experience harsh abuses to dissolve ego-states blocking access to some form of wisdom, or a new life stage. A number of the abductions Mack studied had promoted spiritual development, he thought. ("Scott," who believed he'd been abducted repeatedly since childhood, had come to think that "getting through the trauma part" had opened him up to "the real stuff, the spiritual behind it." "Sheila," was trying to come to terms with her recognition that there are "greater powers…how insignificant we are as human beings," and felt her abduction enabled her to cross "some barrier.") Abductees sometimes felt their abductors had their best interests at heart. Strieber during his personal ordeal had the intuition that his abductors, though vicious in their attacks, sought "communion."

Sacrifice, a theme essential to the sacred, is the "antithesis of production…accomplished with a view to the future," Georges Bataille wrote. Peoples less able to ignore the cosmic context of their lives than those of us in modern urban societies squandered the "first fruits" of the harvest, or a head of livestock, acknowledging in sacrifice that what they had produced with their own labor, considered metaphysically, were gifts of the gods or God. Gifts exact gratitude and reciprocity, and a failure to reciprocate them may inspire hostility. One of the purposes of sacrifice must always have been to ward off divine resentment at being ignored.

There is a curious resemblance between ancient sacrifice and the "cattle mutilations" sometimes associated with UFO sightings. When people preoccupied with their own "productions" fail to make offerings and express gratitude, do cosmic messengers come on like butchers and take what is due them forcibly?

A farmer once spied a troop of aliens trying to corral his dog. The aliens noticed the farmer. “We come in peace,” said one, “we only want your dog.” The farmer watched the aliens insert the dog into their UFO which then took off.

The event might have been apparitional, but the farmer never saw his dog again.

Works Contributory to this Essay

Bridget Brown, *They Know Us Better Than We Know Ourselves* (New York University Press, 2007).

Ernst Cassirer, *Mythical Thought (*Vol. 2 of *The Philosophy of Symbolic Forms* (Yale University Press, 1968).

Erich von Daniken, *The Return of the Gods* (Element Books, 1997); *Odyssey of the Gods* (Element Books, 2000).

Brenda Denzler, *The Lure of the Edge* (University of California Press, 2001).

W.Y. Evans-Wenz. *The Fairy Faith in Celtic Countries* (Career Press, 2004).

Charles Fort, *The Book of the Damned* (Holt, Rinehart, and Winston, 1941).

Salvatore Freixedo, *Visionaries, Mystics, and Contactees* (IllumiNet Press, 1992).

Edith Hamilton, *Mythology* (Mentor Books, 1943); *The Greek Way* (1930, W.W. Norton and Company, Inc.).

George P. Hansen, *The Trickster and the Paranormal* (XLibris Corporation, 2001).

Patrick Harpur, Daimonic Reality, *A Field Guide to the Other World* (Viking Press, 1994).

Budd Hopkins and Carol Rainey, *Sight Unseen* (Atria Books, 2003).

Philip Imbrogno, *Interdimensional Universe* (Llewellyn Publications, 2008).

David Jacobs, *Secret Life: Firsthand Documented Accounts of UFO Abductions*, (Simon and Schuster, Inc. 1992).

Carl Jung, "Flying Saucers: a Modern Myth," in *Civilization in Transition* (Princeton University Press, 1964).

John A. Keel, *The Mothman Prophecies* (Tor Books, 2003); *The Complete Book of Mysterious Beings* (Doubleday, 1970).

Samuel Noah Kramer, *History Begins at Sumer* (Doubleday Anchor Books, 1959); *The Sumerians: Their History, Culture, and Character* (University of Chicago Press, 1963); *The Sacred Marriage Rite* (University of Indiana Press, 1969).

John E. Mack, *Abduction* (Charles Scribner's Sons, 1994).

Carl Sagan, *The Demon-Haunted World* (Ballantine Books, 1996).

Zecharia Sitchin, *The 12th Planet 1976; The Wars of God and Men 1985; and When Time Began, 1993* (all from Avon Books).

Whitley Strieber, *Communion* (William Morrow, 1987); and *Confirmation* (St. Martin's Press, 1998).

G. N. M. Tyrrell, *Science and Psychical Phenomena* (University Books, 1961).

Jacques Vallee, *Dimensions* (Contemporary Books, 1988); and *Revelations* (Anomalist Books, 1991).

MATERIALIZATIONS

I.

The séances of "physical" mediums in America and England during the last half of the nineteenth century promised marvels, and often delivered them: mysterious spirit rappings and light orbs, unearthly music and voices, furniture that moved or levitated without human contact, musical instruments that appeared to play themselves. In dubious experiments, loaded guns being provided, invisible hands lifted them and fired at targets with deadly accuracy.

Strangest of all were the temporary "materializations" of bodies or body parts. Spirit-hands, described variously as fleshy and warm, or corpse-cold, would appear before "sitters" (a *séance*, in French, is a sitting), shake hands with them, touch them, and perhaps take up pencils to write messages.

Investigators with unimpeachable scientific credentials attested that physical mediums had sometimes materialized complete persons with mobile eyes, legs that moved, personalities, and conversational powers. These figures might appear dressed in clothes made of what appeared to be woven fabrics. Oxford philosopher H.H. Price, always suspicious of fraudulent mediums, witnessed the materialization of a girl who had died at age six. He felt the girl's pulse and heard her breathing. Asked if she loved her mother present at the séance, she said yes, before falling silent and fading away.

Charles Richet, winner of the Nobel Prize for Physiology in 1913, was among scientists who gave materializations serious attention. "I shall not waste time in stating the absurdities, almost the impossibilities, from a psycho-physiological point of view, of this phenomenon," he wrote in *Thirty Years of Psychic Research* (1923). "A living being, or living matter, formed under our eyes, which has its proper warmth, apparently a circulation of blood, and a physiological respiration, which has also... a will distinct from the will of the medium—in a word, a new human being!"

But facts were facts, and Richet's list of scientists who had examined the most gifted physical mediums for trickery "not once, but twenty, a hundred, or even a thousand times"—and found none— included Alfred Russel Wallace, a colleague of Darwin's who wrote on various aspects of evolutionary theory, and physicist-chemist Sir William Crookes." (Price, Crookes, Richet and Wallace were all fellows of the English Society for Psychical Research organized in 1882 for the study of what was once described as the "lesser known faculties" of the human mind. A glance down the "Contents" page of F.W.H. Myers' monumental summation of SPR research, *Human Personality and its Survival of Bodily Death,* 1903, suggests what those faculties were: Genius, Sleep, Hypnotism, Sensory Automatism, Phantasms of the Dead, Trance, Possession.)

Crookes, like Richet, recognized a marvel when he saw one, and wouldn't turn his back on it just because he hadn't an explanation. He spoke of "a hitherto unknown force" responsible for the "very remarkable phenomena which at the present time are occurring to an almost incredible extent." Richet characterized the attitude of his scientific contemporaries who refused to look into materializations: "I do not want to see or to study these things, for I know beforehand that they are not possible. Therefore... you have all been taken in by imposters."

Imposters there *were*—a lot of them—on both sides of the Atlantic. Word of what happened at séances got around, and con-artists came out of the woodwork. Moreover, genuinely gifted "physical" mediums, whether to compensate momentary loss of powers, or to spice performances, might not be above chicanery. The English medium William Eglinton, a remarkable fellow by all accounts—he not only materialized complete human bodies, but levitated and flew about séance rooms—was accused of deception several times. The gifted but prankish Italian peasant woman Eusapia Palladino seemed to enjoy toying with the earnest representatives of the Society for Psychical Research studying her, by mixing crude and obvious tricks with astounding displays of occult prowess. The problem for investigators was to distinguish the one from the other.

Richet described a typical sequence of events at the séance of a "physical" medium. There might be, first, knockings like someone at a door seeking admittance, or table-movements. Perhaps a book would levitate, or sitters would feel the touch of an invisible hand. Materializations were rarer, and likely to come later in a session, if they happened.

When complete human figures materialized, there would be "a first stage in which [the presences] are invisible, a second in which they begin to be visible but are still more or less amorphous, and a third stage in which they take on the semblances of living organisms surrounded by veils which at first mask the imperfections of form, but become thinner as the underlying form becomes more dense." Early on, miniature two-dimensional figures like photographic images might be visible. Richet once observed "a white, opaque spot like a handkerchief lying on the ground... [which then] assumed the form of a human head level with the floor, and a few moments later it rose up in a straight line and became a small man enveloped in a kind of white burnouse."

Commonly the medium would have withdrawn behind a curtain or door, seeking a freedom from external stimuli that would encourage a trance state before a materialization began. In that case, "sitters" would not have observed the developmental stages in a materialization, and when the materialized figure then emerged from the medium's private space the question would arise whether he or she were just the medium in disguise. To dispel suspicion, the hands and feet of the medium might be secured, but the best proof of an authentic materialization would be the sight of the medium and materialized figure *together*.

In the 1870s, the English teenager Florence Cook had often materialized her "control" spirit Katie King who claimed to have been in life Annie Morgan, hellion daughter of seventeenth century pirate Henry Morgan. Sir William Crookes, who studied Cook and Katie at length, wrote in an 1874 letter to Richet of having "absolute proof" Katie was not just Cook disguised. During a séance at his home, "Katie... having moved among us, retired behind the curtain and a moment later called me, saying, 'Come into the cabinet and raise my medium's head.' Katie stood before me in her usual white robe and wearing her turban. I went towards the bookcase to raise Miss Cook, and Katie moved aside to let me pass."

On another occasion, Crookes had seen Cook "dressed in black velvet, apparently asleep.... Raising the lamp I looked round and saw Katie standing close behind Miss Cook. She was clothed in flowing white draperies. Holding one of Miss Cook's hands and kneeling down by her, I raised and lowered the lamp so as to see Katie's whole figure, and to convince myself that it was really Katie. She did not speak but moved her head. Three times I examined Miss Cook carefully to be sure that the hand I was holding was really the hand of a living woman, and three times I turned the light on Katie and regarded her attentively."

Although Crookes had gone about proving Katie's independence of Cook with empirical thoroughness, he became the object of ad hominem attacks by skeptics. His numerous scientific achievements notwithstanding, he was said to be gullible and short-sighted; and since he had at times housed the pretty teenager Cook with his wife and ten children, hadn't he just fallen in love with her? The joke going around was that the next "materialization" was going to be in a maternity ward.

At a séance at Mr. Luxmoore's home in 1873 which American journalist Epes Sargent describes in *Proof Palpable of Immortality: being an account of the materialization phenomena of modern spiritualism* (1875), Cook was bound fast to a chair behind a curtain when barefooted Katie appeared in a loose white dress with long sleeves and a hood. She answered questions of sitters about conditions enabling materializations. Asked to write something, she seated herself and did so. She kissed one fellow audibly, although he "felt no pressure of the lips." To demonstrate her independence of the medium, she asked Mr. Luxmoore to pull back the curtain, and those present saw the entranced medium still fastened to her chair.

Katie was, excuse the expression, *really something*. She could materialize for hours. She kibitzed with sitters, touched them, kissed them. Gifts people gave her would vanish when she did, but reappear with her later. A male sitter once presented her a gold ring. She put it on a finger and uttered the fathomless double entendre, "Now we are engaged."

On one occasion, she cut a swatch from her dress and presented it to a sitter, then repaired the dress by waving a hand over the cut. The swatch survived her disappearance, as in folktales gifts received in Fairyland sometimes survive people's return to terra firma. (American anthropologist W.Y. Evans-Wentz in his 1911 *The Fairy-Faith in Celtic Countries* noted other similarities between séance anomalies and experiences with Celtic "little people": objects that moved without human contact, mysterious rappings and aerial music, manifestations and vanishings.)

Katie once allowed sitter George Trapp to examine her bare arm. He found it to be warm and beautifully shaped, but unnaturally smooth like marble or wax. There was something else odd about it: no bone at the wrist. He mentioned this to Katie. "Wait a bit," she said, before continuing around the circle of sitters. Returning to Trapp later, she offered him her arm again, and the bone that had been missing was now in place.

Katie was chameleonic. Sargent noted that people had seen her on various occasions as an "apparition of ravishing beauty," or a woman with a "massive face" and "stout and broad across the waist"; she was fair-skinned, or resembled "a woman of the Levant"; she had large blue eyes with long lashes, or brown eyes; she was a "gentle and graceful young woman," or a girl of "roguish, infantile, defiant vivacity." In one materialization, her skin was dark at first, then became light. One of the numerous photographs Sir William Crookes took of her depicts what was conceivably a botched or incomplete materialization: Katie is life-sized, but has a glassy-eyed, doll-like appearance. One bent, crossed arm is dusky. The other, white, ends in four curved fingers resembling animal claws.

Disappearances of materialized bodies were as uncanny as their emergence. Crookes once held Katie King's hand tightly, resolved not to let it go, but "little by little the hand seemed to dissolve into vapour, and it thus disengaged itself from my grasp." Sitter George Trapp made some jesting remark offensive to Katie, and she struck him in the chest with a clenched fist. When he seized her wrist in response, it "crumpled in my grasp like a piece of paper or thin cardboard, my fingers meeting through it." A fellow who grabbed Katie bodily in a fit of passion or curiosity saw her legs and feet vanish first, then the rest of her.

Richet mentions a Dr. P. Gibier having witnessed the materialized "Lucie" collapse "like a house of cards." Reaching down to touch the last spot of Lucie on the carpet, he felt nothing.

Richet, while convinced of the reality of materializations, was reluctant to embrace the "anthropomorphic hypothesis" that disembodied spirits were their sources. ("We may allow it a place, strictly provisionally, but on this delicate matter it is advisable to take the scientific ground here adopted.") French astronomer Camille Flammarion agreed, allowing only that materializations involved some unknown "psychic force" of the medium.

Spirits or no spirits, materializations clearly involved mediums' psychosomatic life. Before a materialization occurred a semi-transparent, white stuff known as "ectoplasm" could be seen flowing from mediums' bodies. There are Victorian-era photographs of it to be found online. One taken in 1921 shows the seated, entranced Norwegian medium Einar Neilson vomiting the stuff profusely into his lap. The medium Mme. d'Esperance likened her personal experience of venting ectoplasm to having "fine threads... drawn out of the pores of my skin." Arthur Conan Doyle in the second volume of his *The History of Spiritualism* (1926) mentions Judge Peterson's observation of a "fleecy cloud" issuing from the side of the medium W. Lawrence; and Richet had seen a "liquid or pasty jelly" coming from the mouth or breast of the medium Marthe Beraud. ("Under very good conditions of visibility," he wrote, "I have seen this paste spread on my knee, and slowly take form so as to show the rudiment of the radius, the cubitus, or metacarpal bone whose increasing pressure I could feel on my knee.") He once saw emanating from Eusapia Palladino a rod of ectoplasm with a hand at the end of it, "a living hand warm and jointed, absolutely like a human hand."

John S. Farmer, biographer of Victorian medium William Eglinton, described one of his subject's materializations: "His breathing became increasingly laboured and deep. Then, standing in full view, by a quick movement of his fingers, he gently drew forth, apparently from under his morning coat, a dingy white-looking substance." The stuff slipped down Eglinton's left pant leg to the ground where it expanded and "commenced to pulsate, move up and down and sway from side to side," before rising up into a vertical form. Eglinton then parted the ectoplasm to reveal the bearded face of a materialized figure taller than himself. The ectoplasmic link between the medium and the figure now "severed or became invisible, and the spirit walked round the circle and shook hands with the various sitters."

Ectoplasm, subtle and evanescent, was difficult to study, but a Polish medium Mike Dash mentions in *Borderlands* (2000) once captured in a test tube a small quantity which proved in chemical analysis to be "an unsavory concoction of human fatty matter, leukocytes (white blood cells) and cells from the mucous membranes." Spirits might be making esoteric use of human substances, but the substances themselves were unremarkable.

II.

Spiritualism's influence in America and England during the last half of the nineteenth century, and into the early decades of the twentieth, is generally forgotten. At a time when scientism and materialism were undermining traditional religions, spiritualism, promising empirical evidence of the afterlife, had acquired millions of adherents.

Only a few years after the Fox sisters began hearing mysterious knockings in their family's rural home near Rochester, New York, and discovered that the spirit could answer questions yes or no to by knocking once or twice, people in thirty-six American states were hearing them. Knockings and mediums multiplied as if by contagion. People everywhere were gathering in séance circles hoping for communication with departed relatives and friends.

The *Spiritual Telegraph*, one of the numerous spiritualist newspapers that sprang up, noted that Boston séances attendees in the 1850s included doctors, clergymen, lawyers, judges, merchants, and city officials. Emma Hartinge Britten, a medium and itinerant lecturer on spiritualism, estimated in *Modern American Spiritualism* (1870) that a quarter of the American population was now in the fold. This struck her as mysterious, there having been "no regular system of propagandizing."

"Physical" mediums were associated with knockings, materializations, and the other anomalies discussed in the first portion of the present essay. "Mental" mediums' specialty was putative communication with the spirits of deceased persons. Messages ostensibly transmitted from the "other side" (the metaphor "downloaded" is almost irresistible) could represent with uncanny accuracy the character, interests, style of expression, and sense of humor of persons unknown to the mediums in life.

Some very intelligent people thought communication with spirits of the deceased occurred. James Hyslop, a Columbia University philosophy professor, had long since abandoned the fundamentalism of his Ohio farmer father without ever losing interest in the question of "survival." He arranged for sittings with renowned Boston clairvoyant Leonora Piper, and was convinced after a dozen of them that he had been communing with his deceased father, brother, and uncles. The only alternative he could imagine was that Mrs. Piper possessed an "omniscient telepathy" that could access detailed retrospective knowledge of persons' lives. (Richet had acknowledged the extraordinariness of Leonora Piper's powers, but did not think more than that need be said of them; and Mrs. Piper, announcing her retirement as a professional medium in a *New York Herald* interview, admitted her own uncertainty about the source of her clairvoyance.)

Alan Gauld in *Mediumship and Survival* (1982) envisions the possibility of a "super ESP" that might provide certain persons detailed knowledge of "any living or recently deceased person in the whole of the Western world."

Frederic Myers in *Human Personality and its Survival of Bodily Death* made a distinction between "supernormal" and "supernatural." Supernormal powers were resources of the "Subliminal Self"—the Subconscious or Unconscious of modern psychology. A "super ESP" would be supernormal, not supernatural. Debunking the supernatural having been nearly mandatory for Victorian-era scientists and intellectuals, the fellows of the Society for Psychical Research tended to favor "supernormal" over "supernatural" hypotheses. The poet William Butler Yeats once remarked, "If you psychical researchers had been about when God Almighty was creating the world, he couldn't have done the job."

G.N.M. Tyrrell (1879-1952), a member of the Society, was a physicist who had worked with Marconi in developing early radio technology before turning his attention to paranormal phenomena. He mentions Myers' "supernormal" and "supernatural" distinction in *Science and Psychical Phenomena*—but only to disparage the latter term as antiquated. Anything once regarded as "supernatural" could probably in that enlightened age be dealt with as a manifestation of the "Subliminal Self."

Tyrrell, while agnostic about the supernatural, was fascinated with mental mediumship. In *The Personality of Man* (1947) he dwells at length on messages received in automatic writings between 1901 and 1932 by five reputable mediums in different locations: Mrs. Piper in the U.S.; Mrs. Leonard, Mrs. Verrell and her daughter Helen in England; and Mrs. Holland in India. The presumed sources of the messages were three deceased SPR men—Myers, Sidgwick, and Gurney—all of whom had been seriously interested in the "survival" question in life, and were evidently still interested in its relationship to embodied life. There were cross-correspondences among the messages received by the various women. In some instances messages received by one medium were complete only when placed side by side with what another had received.

While mental mediumship interested Tyrrell, he gives short shrift to physical mediumship in *The Personality of Man,* describing it as having been "for ages the happy hunting ground of tricksters and charlatans." He abhors its "sordid sensations" that were irrelevant to the "survival" question. (Camille Flammarion agreed: "The greater part of the phenomena observed—noises, movement of tables, confusions, disturbances, raps, replies to questions asked—are really childish, puerile, vulgar, often ridiculous, and rather resemble the pranks of mischievous boys.... Why should the dead amuse themselves in this way?") Much that happened at the séances of physical mediums *was* undoubtedly "puerile" or "sordid." One Victorian photograph shows ectoplasm shooting from the vicinity of a medium's vagina. The hyper-skeptical SPR medium-debunker Frank Podmore wrote in his 1902 *Modern Spiritualism: a History and a Criticism* that if the physical marvels weren't just trickery, it was certainly conceivable that they might be the work of demons, rather than benevolent spirits.

In any case, it was absurd of Tyrrell to says, as he does in *The Personality of Man*, that physical mediumship was of little interest. Had conscience allowed, he probably would have been happy to ignore the physical mediums altogether. He is simply turning his back on them, and phenomena associated with them, when he writes, "I am not aware that any case of *complete* 'materialization' [of a person] investigated by critical observers has resulted in a favorable verdict." Richet and a number of other "critical observers" *had* produced such a verdict.

The best explanation of Tyrrell's inclination to ignore materializations and the other marvels of the physical mediums, apart from the fact that he found them distasteful, was that he could make no sense of them—as he freely admits. He cannot deny that at least some of was said to have occurred at the physical séances really had, but the idea of a connection between these occurrences, and the mental states of mediums and/or sitters, makes him squirm intellectually. To admit such a connection would disturb the conventional modern distinctions between objective and subjective, physical and psychological, fact and imagination, which are sacrosanct for him. "Mental" mediumship did not disturb them, since it involved telepathic communications between the spirits of persons present and absent, or living and deceased, that were purely subjective in nature.

When Tyrrell stoops to speculate about how anomalies at the séances of physical mediums might be explained, he does so within the safe confines of the modern dualisms, musing at one point that perhaps "in the neighborhood of a living human body in a particular state [*not*, of course, the mind or imagination in a "particular state"] the movement of objects and various other physical effects are brought about in some unknown way." Tyrrell had obviously heard of ectoplasm, but never once mentions it in *The Personality of Man.* No doubt it struck him as "sordid." He does mention having heard of shysters regurgitating cheesecloth. Maybe, he writes, there is "some as yet unrecognized matter" emitted from the person of the medium which exerts "the necessary mechanical forces, etc." Ectoplasm had not only been "recognized," but, alas, its emission seemed connected with the mental states of mediums and/or other "sitters."

At one point he surmises that a physical force of unknown character might be at work in the marvels at physical séances—or even "something deeper." His idea of "something deeper" is that "the scheme of space, time, matter, and causality might be only a *department* of nature, and another order of things behind it may occasionally show through." One gathers that if and when it were to "show through," it would be independent of, and perceptible by, minds functioning as they do ordinarily. But another "order of things" did seem to have shown through at the séances of the legitimate physical mediums, and its manifestations were evidently dependent on meditative mediums and sitters gathering in dimly-lit rooms, and perhaps holding hands to heighten collective psychic energy.

There is an analogy between Tyrrell's inability to come to terms with physical mediumship, and his torturously ingenious view in *Apparitions* (1953) of haunting ghosts and postmortem manifestations.

People had witnessed apparitions mistakable for actual persons moving about in rooms or along garden paths in broad daylight. Tyrrell's view is that they were in no sense physical presences. Faithful to the dichotomy between physical and psychological realities, he represents apparitions as "supernormal" products of the subliminal mind.

His understanding of apparitions resembles that of Oxford philosopher H.H. Price, who writes in "Paranormal Cognition, Symbolism, and Inspiration," that something first happens "at an unconscious level of our personalities. We…receive a paranormal [i.e. supernormal] impression of some kind." The paranormal impression conveys to its recipient what Tyrrell calls an "idea-pattern," the nucleus of an apparition, which the imagination of the recipient then fleshes out in "waking mental imagery…a vision or a voice, a visual or auditory hallucination." The hallucination is not in any sense a physical presence. It resembles a daydream.

Tyrrell dwells at length on "crisis apparitions," which are more readily accounted for as intra-psychic telepathic phenomena than many ghosts. In crisis apparitions the source of "paranormal impression," the "idea-pattern," is a person in some serious trouble who is communicating long distance, knowingly or not, with percipient, usually a closely related person. The "idea-pattern" communicated by the troubled person awakens the visual or auditory imagination of the percipient to produce an hallucination that may represent the distant crisis quite realistically, or only metaphorically. In any case, the relationship between agent-sender and the person who experiences the apparition is intra-subjective, and resembles in that respect the putative relationships between "mental" mediums and the spirits of deceased persons.

While crisis apparitions depict remote scenes, apparitional figures may appear in familiar settings. A few days after the death of Unitarian minister Dr. Harris, American novelist Nathaniel Hawthorne saw him seated in a chair at the Boston Athenaeum reading a newspaper, as had been his wont in life. Tyrrell, like Myers, believed the perception of an apparition always to be the work of the percipient's "subliminal mind" that did not involve the physical eyes. Not surprisingly, then, when a ghost appears in a room, some people there might see it, while others would not. The "subliminal Self" of a certain person or persons would respond to the *inspiration.* Others would see nothing.

In Tyrrell's characterization of Myers' position on ghosts, an apparition like Dr. Harris would have been "pasted" into an ordinary scene of life. The idea of the "pasted" apparition troubled Tyrrell. If the apparition did not involve the physical eyes and was a product of the subliminal mind, a sort of dream image, how could the senses be operating as they did ordinarily in wakefulness to articulate its setting? That would amount to saying that the waking and sleeping minds can operate simultaneously.

Tyrrell proposed what he regarded as a better interpretation of the situation: Not only is the apparition a work of the imagination responding to some paranormal inspiration, *so is the setting in which it appears*. In other words, the entire experience is phantasmal. He envisions a "complete machinery in the personality for producing visual imagery exactly like that of normal perception up to the range of a complete environment, and for making everything [in the environment of the apparitional figure] appear as natural and as fully detailed as normal sense-perception can do." That would indeed explain how one can witness a ghost—a dreamlike figure—moving about in a familiar room, and it would preserve the dichotomy between what is subjective and what is objective. Somehow, though, it does not inspire a "Eureka!" response.

Neither does Tyrrell's speculation in *Apparitions* about ancient people's belief in mythical creatures like Pan the goat-man, the Chimera, and the Hydra. He thinks these figures were probably more than just make-believe. People had undoubtedly *seen* them, but what they had seen were, like ghosts, projections of the subliminal mind; and then, "collective idea-patterns" having taken root in popular traditions, "anyone suitably sensitive going to the places... Pan was especially supposed to inhabit would then see and hear Pan with exactly the same reality that a person going into a haunted house [expecting to encounter a ghost]" may actually see one. Here again, by insisting apparitions are dreamlike projections of the "subliminal mind," Tyrrell clings to his distinction between objective and subjective realities.

What makes this construction of the apparitional situation less than compelling in many cases is that humans both ancient and modern have experienced apparitional figures (fairies, angels, phantom animals, djinns, UFO-related "aliens") as capable not only of visibility or audibility, but of working physical influences. The mind-boggling phenomena at the physical mediums' séances were cases in point. Celtic peoples, well aware of what the "good people" could do to their persons and property, tried earnestly to avoid trespassing on their precincts. Big Foot, UFO-related "aliens," and the phantom panthers of the Ohio-Indiana border will leave footprints—sometimes very odd footprints—that start somewhere, go a little distance, then stop, as if the apparitional figure had taken flight or simply dematerialized. John Donne remarked in a 1627 sermon that angels with no more substance than "froth is, as a vapor is, as a sigh is," can, if so disposed, reduce rocks to atoms. William A. Christian in *Apparitions in Late Medieval and Renaissance Spain* writes of the numerous apparitional figures that had appeared to people in nineteenth century Europe, walked with them, touched them, and left behind objects with sacred significance. If apparitions are merely the psychological projections of those who witness them, it is difficult to explain the physical effects associated with them.

Tyrrell acknowledges, reluctantly, in *The Personality of Man* a few reports of people who believed they had been touched by specters. A woman who saw a ghost at her bedside had reached out and grabbed "something soft, like flimsy drapery." Tyrrell writes, "There may be, for all I know... *physical* [italics mine] apparitions.... On that point I express no opinion; but if there are, they are phenomena of a totally different kind from the apparitions we are dealing with here"—and as if that were all that need be said on the matter, he turns his attention elsewhere. But "physical apparitions" exist, as rather evidently there do, Tyrrell's worldview is questionable.

As one would expect, poltergeists were problematic for him, too. Those, also, he dismisses with an offhand remark: They "lie outside my present terms of reference, and in any case form a very small proportion of those collected by the Society for Psychical Research."

Carl Jung in a lecture before the English Society for Psychical Research in 1919, "The Psychological Foundation of Belief in Spirits," had argued that primitive humanity's "spirits" and "souls" were actually "autonomous complexes," highly charged elements of personality split off from conscious identity that yielded visual or auditory phantasms. A ghost or a fairy was not to be regarded as being in any sense a reality independent of consciousness.

The lecture must have pleased many members of the Society, since it squared with their preference for "supernormal" as opposed to "supernatural" explanations. But a year later Jung was having second thoughts. He had rented a cottage outside London that proved to be haunted. There he experienced strange rappings, sounds of dripping water, bad smells, and the horrifying apparition of a woman's face on the bed pillow next to his. These and other later experiences, both his and his patients', prompted him to add a footnote to the 1948 republication of the 1919 remarks: "After collecting psychological experiences from many people and many countries for fifty years, I no longer feel as certain as I did in 1919 [about these matters]. To put it bluntly, I doubt whether an exclusively psychological [i.e., "supernormal"] approach can do justice to the phenomena in question."

If the apparition *is* in some sense a physical presence, its perception may still depend on states of the subliminal mind. Emanuel Swedenborg, the eighteenth century visionary, wrote in *Heaven and Hell* that the spirits of deceased persons were palpable for him only when he was "withdrawn from the sight of the body, and the sight of his spirit had been opened." The opening of the "sight of the spirit" occurred for him in trance states induced by restraint of breathing. Sometimes, though, no special preparations had been necessary. He might be walking in a city street talking with friends when it happened. Then he would have to shift attention back and forth between the two forms of awareness that accessed two levels of being.

A man who lived near Ireland's Tara Mountain told American anthropologist Evans-Wentz, "The souls on this earth are as thick as the grass, and you can't see them, and evil spirits are just as thick, too, and people don't know it"; but the "old people" with "second sight" or the "third eye" had seen them about the mountain hundreds of times. An "Irish mystic" remarked to Evans-Wentz that when fairies became visible "the physical eyes may be open or closed," but "mystical beings in their own world…are never seen with the physical eyes."

And by the way, what are house cats looking at so earnestly in thin air when we see nothing?

Apparitional figures capable of acting in the physical world, visible to some people but not necessarily to others, abound in world religion, folklore, and literature.

Angels materialized as men before Abraham and Lot. St. Augustine writes in *On the Trinity* of angels taking "created materials distinct from themselves and using them to present us with convincingly real symbolic representations of God." Spanish Jesuit Martin del Rio in *Disquisitiones* (1599) speaks of angels, fallen or otherwise, compounding of air "things that can be touched and felt (*papalia*)." Robert Kirk, in his seventeenth century study of elves, fauns and fairies, *The Secret Commonwealth*, describes the "good people" as consisting "of matter in a state unknown to us." They have "light, changeable bodies... somewhat of the nature of a condensed cloud," "chameleon-like bodies [that] swim in the air." Marsilio Ficino, the fifteenth century Platonist wrote of ancient Egyptian priests animating idols: Having "invoked the souls of demons or angels... [they] introduced these into their idols by holy and divine rites, so that the idols had the power of doing good and evil."

Where materialized figures capable of acting in the natural world are concerned, the resurrected Jesus is an interesting case. After the Crucifixion, he appears disguised as a gardener before Mary Magdalene in *John* 20, shares a meal with the disciples in *Luke,* and invites doubting Thomas to touch his wounds. The body of the resurrected Jesus in St. Paul's interpretation (I Corinthians 15) was a "spiritual body" (*soma pneumatikon*), not a physical being of an ordinary kind.

What, though, is a "spiritual body"? William Lane Craig, a contemporary American philosopher of religion and Christian apologist, remarks at his website that in modern liberal Protestant theology the Pauline "spiritual body" is typically represented as a paradoxical "unextended, immaterial, intangible, mass-less entity." Emanuel Swedenborg had noticed the same tendency in eighteenth century theology for which, as he wrote in *Heaven and Hell*, the soul was "like some volatile kind of pure ether which, on the death of the body cannot help dissipating."

Such nearly complete divorce of spirit and body parallels, and probably reflects, the divide between psychological and physical realties in conventional modern epistemology. No wonder, Swedenborg wrote, that a person who reaches the other side and discovers that he (and presumably she) can still see, hear, speak and touch, is bewildered. "He still yearns, wishes, craves, thinks, ponders, is moved, loves, and intends as before." It is as if a person had simply traveled from one place to another, taking with himself "all the things he possessed in his own right as a person" After this initial bewilderment there was likely to follow astonishment "that the Church does not know anything about this condition after death, and consequently does not know anything about Heaven or Hell."

As Craig points out, the reduction of the spiritual body to the vanishing point precludes taking literally the Gospel stories of Jesus's worldly behavior after the Resurrection; but if the spiritual body of Jesus were conceived as resembling that of fairies or the materialized Katie King, whatever the differences, this would not be necessary.

If one holds fast to conventional modern subjective-objective, imagined-real, psychological-physical dichotomies, making sense of what happens in "close encounters" with UFOs and "aliens" is as difficult as understanding the behavior of the resurrected Jesus, the materializations at séances, and the interactions of Celtic folk with "little people."

A direct, impressive personal encounter with either a UFO or "aliens" is likely to yield spontaneous regression to something like primitive belief in aerial spirits. To wit, thousands of people in Arizona saw flying over their state on March 13, 1997 an enormous V-shaped, soundless or gently buzzing pattern of lights, its width estimated by some observers at a mile. Some saw the lights mounted to the arms of an immense, chevron-shaped object that blocked the view of stars as it passed overhead. Bill Greiner was driving a truck loaded with cement down a mountain north of Phoenix when he saw the lights. "I'll never be the same," he said. "Before this, if anybody had told me they saw a UFO, I would've said, 'Yeah and I believe in the Tooth Fairy.' Now I've got a whole new view, and I may be just a dumb truck driver, but I've seen something that don't belong here." The responses of other Arizonans were similar: "I have never forgotten that experience and hope never to see another thing like it for the rest of my life." "They [the lights] left such a disturbing impression that I still think about them from time to time." "This was a life-changing experience." "It was the most awesome thing I've ever seen." "We have never seen anything like this." And: "For sure it was not of human origin."

Jacques Vallee, one of the most persistent, careful, and imaginative twentieth century students of UFOs, concluded early on that these presences in the skies were less likely to be nuts-and-bolts spaceships than aerial wonders of the kind found in the legends of Magonia, the land beyond the clouds in French folklore. (Magonian spirits were said to travel through the air in "cloud ships," a term that describes rather well the appearance of many UFOs.)

Vallee and Chris Aubeck have collected in *Wonders in the Sky* (2010) five hundred examples of aerial anomalies dating from the second millennium BC least likely to have been simply misunderstood natural phenomena: chariots drawn by dragons, ghost ships, anomalous lights, armies on the march, multiple suns or moons, etc. Vallee surmised not only resemblance, but identity of kind, between the "aliens" people met up with in "close encounters," and the shape-shifting elves, djinns, dybbuks and demons of folklore. Author and occultist John Keel agreed. "Aliens," he thought, were not "extraterrestrials," but "ultraterrestrials," beings that had always shared the planet with us that could not only assume perceptible forms, but influence the physical world.

Salvatore Freixedo, a onetime Jesuit, expressed in a private conversation with Vallee, his grim evaluation of UFOs and aliens as manifestations of powers that manipulate our reality and our destiny for their own purposes. "Using our naiveté and our lack of critical judgment in the presence of 'miracles,' these entities…play with our emotions in order to be worshipped as gods….We are manipulated by someone or something unknown, a power which accords us little respect, and uses us for its own ends in the very same way we use animals."

Father Seraphim Rose, an American-born Eastern Orthodox priest, concurred. In "aliens," he writes, "the multifarious demonic deceptions of Orthodox literature have [simply] been adapted to the mythology of outer space, nothing more."

Views of UFOs and aliens like those of Vallee, Keel, and Freixedo are not, of course, the ones generally found in popular discourse. The usual idea, derived from the same dichotomies between subjective/objective, and psychological/physical realities that yielded Tyrrell's position on apparitions, is that UFOs—if "real"—must involve space travel, high-tech hardware, and exploratory humanoids from outer space. After a number of people, including airline pilots, saw a UFO hover for some time above O'Hare International Airport in Chicago in November, 2006, the question for local media was whether extraterrestrials had blown into the Windy City; and a BBC special that Public Broadcasting was airing a few years back, while acknowledging all that was baffling about UFOs, reverted again and again to the notion that the "extraterrestrials" must possess technologies far in advance of ours.

Popular books on UFOs and "aliens" based on the conventional assumptions about them leave a reader with uncertain impressions. Anecdotes of freakish, dreamlike experiences the authors believe "really happened" fill these books. But how can experiences be both real *and* fantastic? If the authors have an explanation—it is not always clear that they do—it will usually not have been integrated with the anecdotal material. The reader is left to conclude that these strange events must have happened in the same way that anything does in the ordinary course of human affairs.

These books would be less puzzling if their authors had woven into their anecdotal material psychological and philosophical considerations like those entertained in the present essay, but doing that would create complications and cast doubt on the conventional understanding of how the world works, so it does not happen.

There are wonderful illustrations of the problem just described in studies by Budd Hopkins and David Jacobs of the "alien abductions" being widely reported in the later decades of the twentieth century. Abductees' convictions that their bizarre experiences were not merely nightmares had seemingly been confirmed in some instances by what were ostensibly the consequences of examinations by alien doctors: internal bleeding, skin markings, on the skin, fear of hospitals, and sexual dysfunction. Mysterious little metal implants, purpose unknown, had been found in the nasal canals or elsewhere on the persons of some abductees.

In more than a few cases, pregnant women believed alien doctors had removed embryos from their bodies, a subject that first came to the attention of Budd Hopkins, a pioneer in abduction studies, while researching the case of abductee "Kathie Davis," the principal subject of his *Intruders: the Incredible Visitation at Copley Woods.* Kathie and members of her Indiana family had had more than one UFO-related encounter before a physician confirmed with positive blood tests and urinalysis that she was pregnant by her fiancé in the 1970s. When she thought she had experienced a miscarriage, her doctor confirmed that she was, indeed, no longer pregnant, but after examining her could not account for the lack of evidence she had ever *been* pregnant. The fetus had simply vanished. Kathie had always felt that her child had survived somehow, and while under hypnosis relived emotionally the supposed removal of the fetus from her body by an alien doctor.

After publishing *Intruders*, Hopkins learned of "hundreds" of women who believed that they had undergone similar experiences. He investigated personally two cases in which fetuses had disappeared in the seventh month "without any of the serious, even dangerous, symptoms that usually accompany such late miscarriages." A doctor attending one of these women had heard the heartbeat of the fetus more than once. The woman awoke one morning sensing that she was no longer pregnant. During the "D and C" cleaning procedure which follows miscarriages, her doctor found the placenta, but, as in Katie's case, no trace of the fetus.

Odd things can happen during gestation, Hopkins allows. Doctors will attribute vanished fetuses to "missed abortion, fetal 'absorption,' or unreported miscarriages." Still, it seemed curious to him, and it *is*, that memories of abductions should accompany so many interrupted pregnancies.

This motif in abduction tales jibes not only with other reports of aliens' interest in human sexuality and reproduction, but recalls folklore stories of "changelings" (fairies who steal human babies and perhaps leave their own defective offspring in place of them); tales of women "taken" by fairies to become wives and mothers in Fairyland; and amours between humans and fairies or deities. Seventeenth century Franciscan Ludovico Sinistrari, an advisor to the Tribunal of the Holy Inquisition in Rome, wrote that "to theologians and philosophers it is a fact that from the copulation of humans with the demons human beings are sometimes born." St. Bonaventure and St. Thomas Aquinas labored to understand how such births might be possible; and scholarly eighteenth century Pope Benedict XIV speculated that the "sons of God" said to have mated with the "daughters of men" in Genesis 6:4 were "those demons who are known as incubi and succubae."

Hopkins, in *Sight-Unseen*, a book he co-authored with Carol Rainey, wrote, "It is absolutely critical to know if the extraterrestrials exist and are, as the reports indicate, experimenting with humankind—or if the reports represent some profoundly radical new mental aberration." I.e., either aliens are technologically advanced little extraterrestrial explorers and experimenters, *or* the delusions of crazy people. Harvard psychiatrist John Mack in *Abduction* (1994) observed that the abductees he studied had come from every social class, every level of intelligence and education, and were not for the most part either mentally disturbed or strongly imaginative; and neither Hopkins nor David Jacobs (author of the 1993 *Secret Life: Firsthand Documented Accounts of UFO Abductions*) thought the experiences many abductees reported were simply delusions. Therefore, given the conventional subjective-objective dichotomy to which Hopkins and Jacobs are faithful, they have no alternative but to conclude that abductees' tales about alien embryo-theft, and baby labs aboard UFOs, are to be taken literally.

Really?

Yes, really. In an interview about his 1998 book, *The Threat: What the Aliens Really Want and How They Plan to Get It*, Jacobs, an American history professor at Temple University, stated his belief that the "aliens" are "here on a mission…a breeding program, which accounts for the reproductive activity that we see, and a hybridization program…an integration program in which ultimately these hybrids, who look very human, will be integrating into this society. And who will eventually, I assume, be in control here because they do have superior technology and super physiological [sic] abilities." Jacobs' speculation about "alien" organization in "The Abductors" chapter of his *Secret Life* makes it sound like that of a smoothly running corporation: "The technology and science that the aliens possess suggest that they have logical thought processes with a great capacity to learn and understand." They are just like us, only better! "The achievements they have demonstrated depend on cooperation among the aliens, and this would probably entail a hierarchy of work and divisions of labor; the differentiation of tasks that abductees report suggests this as well… a hierarchical structure not only of work but of command and knowledge."

To envision aliens stealing human embryos as a contribution to their project of world domination requires about as great a stretch of the imagination as assuming that fairy "changelings" were realities. But assuming for the sake of argument that aliens are, in fact, copping embryos, one need not necessarily conclude with Hopkins and Jacobs that the aliens' purpose would be species-modification. Adopting an epistemology less realistic and naturalistic than theirs, and assuming that in abduction experiences, as in other encounters with entities from other dimensions, "ultraterrestrials," etc., the human mind is not functioning as it does normally, the significance of embryo thefts (real *or* imagined) might well be symbolic and hortatory rather than biological and imperialistic.

A Welsh scholar remarked to Evans-Wentz during the latter's studies of the fairy-faith, that God deploys spirits with uncanny powers "in times of great ignorance to convince people of the existence of an invisible world." Whether or not God does that, there is substantial evidence, both ancient and modern, that the "invisible world" refuses to be ignored. Personal experiences of materialized figures like Katie King, fairies, poltergeists in haunted houses, ghosts that move about in rooms, UFOs and "aliens" compel awareness of the invisible world's reality—make of that what we will.

MADAME BLAVATSKY, THE SPIRITS AND THE ELEMENTALS

Madame Helena Petrovna Blavatsky, and Henry Steel Olcott, an American lawyer, collaborated in founding the Theosophical Society at New York in 1875.

The Russian Blavatsky, in her forties at the time, had spent most of her mature life traveling the world in exploration of esoteric spiritual practices. Supposedly she had studied with both an Egyptian magician and a New Orleans voodoo doctor, and when she left Paris for New York in 1873, it was at the behest of Tibetan monks in the Himalayas. The monks, alarmed by the sway of materialism both East and West, hoped to create a lay society, with chapters worldwide, for the study ancient Asian spirituality. Blavatsky was to be their agent in New York.

Not only in New York but all cross the United States, spiritualism was the rage at the time. Emma Hartinge Britten, an English-born medium and itinerant lecturer, estimated in her 1870 *Modern American Spiritualism* that a quarter of the American population were in the spiritualist fold. (A correspondent to the journal, *The Spiritual Telegraph,* reported that three of six traditional churches in Newton Falls, Ohio, had closed, their former memberships, having gravitated to spiritualist meetings providing what appeared to be empirical proof of the afterlife.)

The Tibetan monks had serious reservations about American spiritualism. Koot Hoomi, a monk who oversaw the development of what came to be known as the Theosophical Society, described spiritualism as an “insane and futile superstition”; and Blavatsky told Olcott that her assignment in America had been “to show the fallacy of the spiritualist theory of spirits.” However, spiritualism’s challenge to materialism seemed to the monks promising raw material where their project was concerned. Blavatsky once said that they regarded spiritualism "as an evolutionary agency."

The monks could not have been involved directly with the development and management of the society they had in mind without abandoning their retreat and discipline. So they sought the collaboration of lay people like Blavatsky sympathetic to their cause. Blavatsky had studied with them. How extensive those studies had been was unclear to Olcott and others who knew her well. At any rate, it was clear that the monks had not regarded her as a candidate for adept status in their order. Koot Hoomi referred to her as a "devoted" woman in whom "a vital cyclone is raging much of the time." Olcott in *Old Diary Leaves: The True Story of the Theosophical Society* described her as having "none of the superficial attributes one might have expected in a spiritual teacher; and how she could, at the same time, be philosopher enough to have given up the world for the sake of spiritual advancement, and yet be capable of going into frenzies of passion about trivial annoyances" mystified him. "Karma forbid that I should do her a feather-weight of injustice," he wrote, "but if there ever existed a person in history who was a greater conglomeration of good and bad, light and shadow, wisdom and indiscretion, spiritual insight and lack of common sense, I cannot recall the name, the circumstances or the epoch."

Blavatsky, a master of humorous self-irony, once confessed that, like other geniuses, she was "cracked."

The basis for Blavatsky's relationship with Olcott, which began in New York and continued later in India, was their shared interest in occult spirituality. They first met at séances of the Eddy brothers in Vermont in 1874. Both were in their forties. Olcott and his wife had divorced. Blavatsky was unattached—basically un-attachable, Olcott thought. In *Old Diary Leaves* he said that he had never been in a relationship with a woman so utterly devoid of sexual attraction, and he thought the source of rumors about her wild romantic escapades in youth had probably been her own bravado. She once described herself as "an old woman whose…features even in youth never made her appear pretty; a woman whose ungainly garb, uncouth manners, and masculine habits are enough to frighten any bustled and corseted fine lady of fashionable society out of her wits."

As Blavatsky was composing *Isis Unveiled: A Master-Key to the Mysteries of Ancient and Modern Science and Theology* (1877), Olcott sat across a table from her in New York correcting her imperfect English. Her scanty philological background had scarcely prepared her for writing this densely learned work, but in trance-like states she was seemingly yielding her pen hand to mentalities other than her own commanding a wider range of reference. Variations in Blavatsky's handwriting accompanied these shifts in authorial intelligence. "If you had given me in those days any page of the *Isis* manuscript," Olcott wrote, "I could almost certainly have told you by which Somebody it had been written." He could also tell when these other authors were *not* in play, because then "the untrained literary apprentice became manifest and the... copy that was turned over to me for revision was terribly faulty, and after having been converted into a great smudge of interlineations, erasures, orthographic corrections and substitutions, would end in being dictated by me for her to re-write."

Blavatsky claimed the Somebodies that commandeered her pen in inspired moments were the Tibetan monks with whom she was in regular telepathic contact. In later years when she was in India, A.P. Sinnett, an English journalist who befriended her, observed that if the monks wished to communicate with her, an airy little bell would tinkle, audible not only to Blavatsky but to anyone in her presence. She would then go off by herself and fall into a brown study to receive a message. She could transmit messages to the monks by the same telepathic means.

With the exception of her obeisance to the Mahatmas, Olcott wrote, Blavatsky was a person unwilling to "controlled by any power on earth or out of it." Even as a child she had been fiercely independent and willful. Achieving submission to the will of the monks had cost her years of effort she told Olcott, and he doubted that anyone had ever aspired to selflessness "against greater obstacles or with more self-suppression."

Once when she and Olcott were working together on her writing in New York, she was at their work table, Olcott at a distance thinking his thoughts, when he heard her say, "Look and learn." He glanced her way and saw rising from her head and shoulders a mist that presently "defined itself into the likeness of one of the Mahatmas.... Absorbed in watching the phenomenon, I stood silent and motionless. The shadowy shape only formed for itself the upper half of the torso, and then faded away and was gone, whether re-absorbed into H. P. B.'s body or not, I do not know." Blavatsky sat statue-like for two or three minutes, then asked if he had seen anything. He told her what he had seen, and asked for an explanation which she refused to provide, "saying that it was for me to develop my intuition so as to understand the phenomena of the world I lived in."

Once during the composition of *Isis Unveiled*, Olcott thought Blavatsky had misquoted an author. The author's book was not at hand, but Blavatsky materialized the volume out of thin air, and it survived long enough for the accuracy of the quotation to be checked before melting away.

On another occasion, a cold winter night in New York with snow on the ground, they were working together when Olcott, who had had "saltish food" for dinner, remarked that it would be pleasant to have some grapes. Blavatsky agreed. But the stores were closed at that hour, so buying grapes would have been impossible, even had they been in season. Blavatsky asked him to adjust lower the gas light over their work table. As he did so, the light went out. By the time he had succeeded in relighting it, Blavatsky was pointing to a bookshelf from which hung "two large bunches of ripe black Hamburg grapes which we proceeded to eat." Blavatsky said that "certain elementals under her control"—nature spirits—had produced the grapes.

Over the years Olcott was to witness a host of wonders involving Blavatsky's "elementals." Having once observed a lack of towels in her quarters, he had purchased some for her which were unhemmed. Blavatsky was sitting at a table "plying her needle," when suddenly she gave a kick under the table and cried, "Get out, you fool!"

Olcott asked what that was all about.

She said a "beastly little elemental" wanting something to do had tugged on her dress.

Well, if so, why not let it hem the towels? Olcott suggested.

Blavatsky's first response was that she didn't want to give the elemental the pleasure of knowing it had dictated her behavior, but she finally agreed to Olcott's suggestion, and told him to place the towels, needle and thread in a glass-fronted bookcase at the far end of the room. He did so. Fifteen or twenty minutes later the two of them were discussing some point of occult philosophy when Olcott heard "a little squeaky sound like a mouse" beneath the table where they sat. Blavatsky announced that the "nuisance" had finished with the towels. Olcott went to the bookcase, opened it, and removed a dozen towels hemmed "after a clumsy fashion that would disgrace the youngest child in an infant-school sewing class."

Olcott remarks in *Old Diary Leaves* that he had seen such wonders produced frequently enough over the years so "they actually excited at length but a passing emotion of surprise"; but they had aroused his suspicion that the basis for "Eastern fables" like that of Aladdin with his magic lamp and servant "djinns" had not been fantasy, but realism.

Myth and folklore represent "elementals" variously as devas, sylvans, dwarfs, trolls, fauns, brownies, undines, djinns, nixies, goblins, etc. The places to study them, Blavatsky wrote in *Isis Unveiled*, were the "neglected alcoves of libraries" where "works of despised hermeticists and theurgists" had been gathering dust for centuries.

Elementals had always been understood to be capable of metamorphosis into "omnifarious forms and shapes." At one moment they might "act the parts of demons, another while of angels or gods, and another while of the souls of the departed." The fifth century Neoplatonist Proclus had spoken of them as having an "elastic, ethereal, semi-corporeal essence." For the medieval Sufi mystic Ibn al' Arabi they were shape-shifting spirits both luminous and earthy, which, depending on the will of God, presented themselves to humans in sublime or terrifying guises.

Blavatsky wrote in *Isis Unveiled* of elementals having "neither immortal spirits nor tangible bodies. They are a combination of sublimated matter and a rudimentary mind.... The most solid of their bodies is ordinarily just immaterial enough to escape perception by our physical eyesight, but not so unsubstantial as not to be recognized by the inner, or clairvoyant vision." (It was understood in the British Isles that people who perceived fairies possessed "second sight" or the "third eye.") So if the Loch Ness Monster, say—or a UFO-related "alien"—were an elemental, it would be real enough for those *capable* of seeing it, at least at the moment they saw it, but it might assume the next moment some different form, or none. In any case, sending camera-equipped divers into Loch Ness looking for the monster would likely be a waste of time.

Blavatsky's experience of elementals dated from her early childhood in Ekaterinoslav, Russia, where she had claimed intimacy with green-haired nymphs known as *russalkas* that haunted willow trees along river banks. She claimed to have once summoned them as a four year-old to tickle to death a serf-boy who annoyed her. The boy was next seen weeks later when fishermen discovered his drowned body.

A Minneapolis friend of the author of the present essay, Jerry Downes, a poet who worked as a hospital orderly, became acquainted with an Haitian living in Minnesota and once accompanied this man on a return to his home island. In the back country, the Haitian introduced Jerry to a voodoo doctor. Before they parted the voodoo man asked Jerry if he would like to have a spirit to do his bidding.

At the time Jerry's superior at work was a woman making unreasonable demands on her staff. He said he would like to see this woman frightened badly, but not hurt. The voodoo man retired to a back room of his hut, performed certain mumbo-jumbo, and returned with a glass bottle containing, he said, a water spirit. Back in Minneapolis Jerry followed the protocol specified by the Haitian for launching the spirit on its task.

That day a powerful windstorm arose in the quarter of the city where the targeted woman lived. She was gazing at the storm through a floor-to-ceiling plate glass window in her apartment when a blast of wind shattered the window, sending dagger-like glass shards flying into the apartment. They stabbed into the wall behind the woman, outlining her figure perfectly—but none struck her.

Terrified upon learning what had happened, Jerry wished to have nothing more to do with the spirit. On the banks of the Mississippi River that flows through Minneapolis he followed the voodoo doctor's instructions for releasing the water spirit back into Nature, but had for some time an uncomfortable sense of its lingering presence.

Olcott in *People from the Other World* (1875) mirrored the views of both the monks and Blavatsky in representing the psychological state of spiritualist mediums as a form of slavery. "Their own will is set aside, and their actions, their speech, and their very consciousness, are directed to that of another."

There were resemblances between the passive receptivity of mediums, and that of patients in mesmeric (hypnotic) healing widely practiced in nineteenth century America; and mesmerists were sometimes surprised when their subjects spoke of being in communication with spirits of departed persons. Blavatsky thought, however, that what they were experiencing might actually be something very different, and usually was. The passivity of mesmeric subjects, and the mediums and "sitters" at séances, left them open to potentially dangerous interactions with elementals and "earth-walking" spirits (to be discussed below).

In *Isis Unveiled*, Blavatsky spoke of spiritualism's fanatical enthusiasts as having "magnified its qualities and remained blind to its imperfections." However, she acknowledged that the source of their fanaticism was the "genuineness and possibility of their phenomena." Whatever else might be said of spiritualists, they were religious empiricists who "give us facts that we may investigate, not assertions that we must believe without proof." A spiritualist had firsthand experience of beings in an invisible world that—if one knew how to manage them—were "capable of making a god of him on earth."

Blavatsky did not take her ability to produce marvels with the assistance of elementals all that seriously. Olcott thought she had probably wasted a good deal of time and energy in such productions, but her purpose in doing so had been to awaken in others consciousness of dimensions of being generally blocked by common life. (The Church Father Origen remarked that had Jesus not worked the miracles, people would never have been convinced he was the prophesied Messiah, and the Church would never have come to exist.) Olcott admitted that "the great range of marvels of educated will-potency which [Blavatsky] showed me, made it easy for me to understand the Oriental theories of spiritual science."

Spiritualists recognized two kinds of mediums, "physical" and "mental." They were responsible for "phenomena" of different kinds, and mediums who could produce the one kind usually could not produce the other.

The specialty of "mental" mediums was, in Blavatsky's words, "subjective, intellectual phenomena." In trance states of varying intensities during séances, mental mediums received messages presumed to originate with departed spirits. The messages might be conveyed orally, with the medium adopting the voice of the departed person in ventriloquism, or in automatic writing in which the spirit wielded the pen hand of the medium. When messages reflected faithfully the voice, intelligence, interests and style of a deceased person—even his or her handwriting—they could be very convincing.

Nothing guaranteed, though, that these messages actually came from the Other Side. Blavatsky thought they usually didn't, because spirits once released from the physical body by death into what her Tibetan mentors called Devchan (a state of being, not a location) usually had no more interest in the affairs of the living. Communication with them might be possible, if the bond of love had been strong—but as the result of intense desire among the living for such communication, not of spirits' ongoing concern with the life left behind. (Eighteenth century spiritualist Emanuel Swedenborg's understanding of the situation differed somewhat from Blavatsky's. His angels—all departed humans in one stage of posthumous development or another—were the media of divine influence flowing into the human world. However, his angels, like Blavatsky's spirits, were oblivious to earthly existence they had left behind, and unaware of the influence they exerted in it. They were surprised to hear of this influence from Swedenborg during his out-of-body visits in the spirit-world.

For Victorian-era scientists and intellectuals, denying the supernatural had been virtually *de rigeur.* The fellows of the Society for Psychical Research, founded in England in 1882 for the scientific study of depth-psychological phenomena, were sometimes accused of rigging experiments so as to prove the reality of the supernatural. In fact, though, Brian Ingles remarks in a foreword to Alan Gauld's *Mediumship and Survival* (1982), many of the SPR fellows were intent on proving that phenomena that had been regarded as supernatural in the past were, in fact, the issue of depth psychology. Interest in the *question* of "survival" remained acute among Victorian-era members of the SPR, though, and Ingles remarks on the curiosity that paranormal researchers of more recent times, whose interests resemble so closely those of the Victorians, are generally uninterested in that question.

There were some very intelligent people at the turn of the twentieth century convinced that, assisted by mental mediums, they were communing with departed spirits. One was Frederic Myers, a founder of the Society for Psychical Research, and author of the monumental summary of SPR studies, *Human Personality and its Survival of Bodily Death* (1903). His study of spiritualism had begun in 1873, the same year he entered into a Platonic love relationship with Annie Marshall, wife of a psychologically-disturbed cousin of his. Myers and Annie had attended séances together, and soon after her suicide in 1876, he began receiving through various mediums intimations of her survival. However, the most compelling evidence that Annie was messaging him came during 150 sittings a few years before his own death in 1901 with medium Rosina Thompson. Myers had included that evidence both in a document printed privately for several associates, and in the manuscript for *Human Survival*. Historians Alan Gauld and Deborah Blum have concluded, however, that Myers' wife Eveleen, offended by the idea of her husband's prolonged amour with a ghost, had excised Myers' best evidence for afterlife from the manuscript of *Human Survival* before it was published. Even so, Jeffrey Kripal has written, the published text includes "thousands upon thousands" of hints about the source of Myers' belief.

The alternative to assuming that that a talented medium could access the "other side" was to suppose that he or she might possess an "omniscient telepathy" that could provide detailed knowledge of people living or deceased. This was an alternative often brought to bear on the clairvoyance of American medium Andrew Jackson Davis, the "Poughkeepsie Seer." Hardinge Britten in *Modern American Spiritualism* spoke of the "vast amount of logic" spent on the idea that the learned disquisitions pouring from this barely educated fellow, which might seem to be originating on the Other Side were "only the reflex of minds still upon earth." A "super ESP" might give a medium like Davis access to what Blavatsky and others referred to as the "shell" of a deceased person: a subtle-material composite of worldly experience that survives for a longer or shorter period after physical death, before fading away. The medium William Britten spoke in *Ghostland* (1897) of this remnant of physical existence, presumably the subtle-material stuff of ghosts, as "a sort of vague, shadowy existence which at length melts away and becomes dissipated in space."

Another "supernormal" possibility was that a telepathic medium at a séance might be tapping into the memories of "sitters" for what they knew of deceased persons. (One séance attendee, as an experiment, had been meditating earnestly on a fictional character he had imagined, when a medium informed him that the character was communicating from the Great Beyond.)

Also, there might be a fine line between mediumship and simple dreaming. Figures out of popular culture like Abraham Lincoln and Ben Franklin had a way of showing up at séances spouting bromides which suggested that intelligence on the Other Side was subtracted rather than augmented. Hardinge Britten noted wryly that long residence in the spirit-world seemed to entail a "deterioration in grammar and orthography."

Conceivably the reach of a mental medium might be "supernormal" at some moments, "supernatural" at others. The psychological source in either case would be what Myers called the "Subliminal Self" that bore general resemblance to the Jungian Unconscious. Hardinge Britten thought that while some of Andrew Jackson Davis's revelations might well have been "supernormal," there remained "a large amount of original matter which can only be accounted for by admitting the hypothesis of spiritual perception in realms of super-sensuous existence, and inspiration from a world of supra-mundane knowledge."

The fruits of mental mediumship, whether "supernatural" or "supernormal," were at any rate intra- or inter-subjective, and as such did not offend the conventional modern dichotomies of mind and matter, subjective and objective.

The same could not be said of phenomena at the séances of physical mediums which combined the resources of the "Subliminal Self" with astonishing physical manifestations: mysterious "spirit-rappings," levitating furniture, guitars or people that flew about the séance rooms, accordions that appeared to play themselves, and materializations not only of grapes or books, but, as discussed elsewhere in "Materializations" in this volume, complete human figures.

How were materializations and the other phenomena produced by physical mediums to be understood?

Olcott's views had not yet undergone Blavatskian influence when he wrote in *People from the Other World*, copyrighted in 1874 (the same year he met Blavatsky at the séances in Vermont) that materializations proved "the resurrected spirit can reclothe itself with an evanescent material form by the power of its will over the sublimated earth-essences...." In Vermont, Blavatsky had tried unsuccessfully to dissuade him from this conviction, and to convince him that materializations they witnessed were not the embodiments of spirits, but merely "doubles" that the medium William Eddy spun out of his psychosomatic person. The sources of materializations might, for that matter, be other persons at a séance.

Among the materializations Olcott and Blavatsky witnessed in Vermont was one of an African magician in native getup. He was a person Blavatsky had once met in her travels, and she told Olcott that it had been her recollection of the magician that had prompted the manifestation. Olcott found this impossible to believe at the time, but later confessed, "I had not gone deep enough into the question of the plastic nature of the human double to see the force of her hints, while of the Eastern theory of Maya I did not know the least iota."

Spirits of deceased persons that communicated through mental mediums could demonstrate intelligence of the kind they had possessed in life, but as Blavatsky pointed out materialized figures were notoriously dull. "There are mediums whose organisms have called out sometimes hundreds of these would-be 'human' forms," she wrote, "and yet we do not recall... one expressing anything but the most commonplace ideas." If materialized figures were, in fact, deceased persons making curtain calls in the physical world, why shouldn't they communicate as "persons of their... respective education, intelligence, and social rank would in life," rather than falling invariably into "one monotonous tone of commonplace and, but too often, platitude?" It seemed necessary to conclude that intelligent spirits do not materialize, and "the spirits that do... have not intelligence."

Blavatsky admitted several exceptions. In order "to accomplish some great object in view, and so benefit humanity," a deceased person might be re-embodied, but the exigency would have to be very great "to draw a pure, disembodied spirit from its radiant home into the foul atmosphere from which it escaped upon leaving its physical body." Examples of such exceptions were the avatars of Vishnu, the angels that appeared before Abraham, apparitions of Elias and Moses, and the resurrected Jesus' appearances before Mary Magdalene and the Apostles.

The second exception were persons so depraved in their lifetime as to be entirely "unfitted for the lofty career of the pure, disembodied being" who, after death, could be "irresistibly attracted to the earth where they lived a temporary and finite life amid elements congenial to their gross natures, prowling around and sucking vitality from living persons susceptible to their influence." In world cultures, these spirits had been known variously as earth-walkers, ghouls, demons, incubi or succubi. They had possessed medieval nuns, monks and witches who came to bad ends on the rack, or on the stake amid purifying fires. Asian Indians had feared these "brothers of the shadow" and employed "all kinds of music, incense, and perfumes" to keep them at bay.

Asians usually regarded with horror phenomena produced by physical mediums "as misfortunes, the work of evil spirits, often of earth-bound souls of near-relatives and intimate friends, and their greatest desire is to abate them as unqualified nuisances." In the West during the nineteenth century, families might be delighted to discover one of their members had mediumistic powers, but in the East where it was assumed only "pariahs and other degraded castes" patronized mediums and sorcerers, such a discovery would be regarded as a calamity. Educated Asians, Olcott wrote, "discourage these necromantic dabblings as soul-debaucheries, and affirm that they work incalculable evil both upon the dead and the living."

Blavatsky regarded the passivity of the mediums and sitters at séances as an invitation to these dark spirits to "clothe themselves in the effluvia of the medium and those present [appropriating] their magnetic sweat [?] and other fluids."

English Catholic priest Montague Summers in his *The History of Witchcraft and Demonology* (1926) argued that attentive study of the records of the early modern witchcraft trials, coupled with knowledge of materializations at séances, cast doubt on cavalier modern dismissal of witches' claims to have had sexual intercourse with demons. The *Compendium Maleficarum* (Milan, 1608) had spoken of novice witches being assigned a *Magistellus,* or familiar, capable of manifesting for sexual purposes as male or female, satyr or buck-goat.

Summers had been acquainted personally with a circle of people in an English provincial town bored with the usual round of dances, concerts, and dinner parties, who began experimenting with table-turning, Ouija boards, and crystal gazing. Conceived originally as entertainments, these practices became obsessive. Meetings that had been monthly or weekly became nightly. Mixed with spirits' expressions of undying love, and reassurances concerning the afterlife, were urgings to murder, suicide, and debauchery. The faces of enthusiasts became pasty and drawn, eyes dull and glazed. Friendships and normal social intercourse lapsed. Some in the circle began sensing danger in the situation, and "outside circumstances" finally forced the interruption of their practices, but those who had been most seriously involved found ridding themselves of the "[spirit] controls to which they had so blindly and so utterly submitted" extremely difficult.

In Blavatsky's view, if "brothers of the shadow" were not the parties responsible for the grotesqueries at the physical séances, elementals were. The monotheistic religions' prohibitions of idolatry expressed an awareness of both the existence and potency of elementals. Canon Mahe, an early nineteenth century French scholar of antiquities whom American anthropologist W.Y. Evans-Wentz quotes in *The Fairy-Faith of Celtic Countries* (1911), observed that the critically important element in the "idol-worship" of primitive societies was not the idol per se, but rather the will and emotion invested in it during ritual practices which attracted and empowered spirits not necessarily benevolent or trustworthy. The Church Father Cyprian (third century) spoke in "On the Vanity of Idols" of spirits that "lurk under the statues and consecrated images" which "give efficiency to oracles," but "are always mixing falsehood with truth, for they are both deceived and they deceive." Idol-based religiosity was regarded as a diversion from the moral concerns of monotheism, an improper focus of human attention and effort.

There were, however, Platonizing philosophers during the Renaissance, nominally Christian, who did not agree with the orthodox position on elementals. Florentine priest-scholar Marsilio Ficino was enthusiastic about magical works attributed to Hermes Trismegistus when they reached Italy in the fifteenth century. Trismegistus was supposed at the time to have been an Egyptian priest of immemorial antiquity, although it was later determined that writings attributed to him were the works of various Neo-Platonists in the early centuries AD. Frances Yates in *Giordano Bruno and the Hermetic Tradition* quotes Ficino's admiration of "Egyptian" formulae for the animation of statues:

> They [Egyptian priests] mingled a virtue drawn from material nature to the substance of the statues...and after having evoked the souls of demons or angels, they

> introduced these into their idols by holy and divine rites, so that the idols had the power of doing good and evil. These terrestrial or man-made gods result from a composition of herbs, stones, aromatics which contain *in themselves* [italics mine] an occult virtue of divine efficacy. And if one tries to please them with numerous sacrifices, hymns, songs of praise and sweet concerts which recall the harmony of heaven, this is in order that the celestial element which has been introduced into the idol by the repeated practice of the celestial rites may joyously support its long dwelling amongst men.

In the next century the heretical monk Giordano Bruno, who was also interested in the magical treatises, wrote in *Heroic Furors* that Egyptian statues had been "full of life, full of intelligence and spirit, capable of many important functions. These statues foresee the future, cause infirmities, and produce remedies, joy, or sorrow."

Many people witnessed Blavatsky's ability to produce wonders with the assistance of elementals. When she and Olcott went to India after leaving New York, she had been, for extended periods a guest of A.P. Sinnett and his wife at their summer house in Simla, a village in the Himalayan foothills of northern India. Sinnett was managing editor of an English newspaper, a sensible Brit who enjoyed his roast beef and sherry. Spiritualism had been in the news, but Sinnett had been only mildly curious about it before meeting Blavatsky.

Blavatsky also made the acquaintance of A.O. Hume, a British government official stationed at Simla. Neither Sinnett nor Hume was the kind of fellow likely to be easily conned by a charlatan, but both men, like Olcott, were convinced of the authenticity of the wonders Blavatsky produced.

English administrators and their families in India gravitated to Simla in the summer to escape the searing heat of major cities to the South. A group of them that included Blavatsky had been on their way to a picnic destination one day when they met a district judge, Syed Mahmood, whom they invited to join their party. He did. His presence left the party one teacup and saucer short, but at the picnic site Blavatsky put an elemental to work on the problem, and announced that the needed cup and saucer would be found amid the roots of a nearby tree. Access to the roots required a fair amount of digging in hard soil, but not only were the cup and saucer found where Blavatsky had said they would be, but their design matched the others brought to the picnic.

On another occasion in Simla, a dinner party, Blavatsky asked Mrs. Hume if there were something she would like to have that would be difficult to find, but "not wanted for any mere worldly motive." Mrs. Hume recalled a brooch her mother had given her that she had lost. She would like to have it back, she said.

Blavatsky asked her to imagine the lost brooch vividly in detail, and to draw a rough sketch of it. Mrs. Hume did these things. Blavatsky then wrapped a coin in her own possession in two cigarette papers, and pocketed it in her dress. Later in the evening she announced that the papers had disappeared, and that the brooch would be found in the garden in a "star-shaped bed of flowers." The guests went into the garden. Hunting among the leaves of the flower bed Blavatsky had mentioned, they found Mrs. Hume's brooch wrapped in two cigarette papers.

Olcott remarked that the incident illustrated "an important law" where materializations were concerned. The first step in creating "anything objective out of the diffused matter of space" was "to think of the desired object—its form, pattern, colour, material, weight, and other characteristics. The picture of it must be sharp and distinct as to every detail; the next step was to put the trained will in action, employ one's knowledge of the laws of matter and the process of its conglomeration, and compel the elemental spirits to form and fashion what one wishes made."

When the Tibetan monks decided Sinnett and Hume might be assets in the development of the Theosophical Society in India, both men began receiving communications from the monastery that were conveyed to them, by mysterious means. (Letters from the monks Koot Hoomi and Morya to Sinnett were collected in 1923 as *The Mahatma Letters.*)

Blavatsky remarked in a letter to Dr. de Puruker that the Brothers scarcely ever wrote letters personally, but "precipitated" them telepathically sentence by sentence "along the etheric currents" to a *chela* (novice) in their order who did the actual writing. Once written, the messages would not come through the post, but simply materialize out of thin air, perhaps to be found found lying on a desk. Olcott wrote that when traveling he had "phenomenally received" letters from the monks that had simply dropped out of space "into a steamer on the high seas and in railway carriages."

Such communications from the monks did little to improve either Sinnett's or Hume's understanding of their production and delivery, or of any of the other marvels they had witnessed in Blavatsky's presence. Both men were admonished by Koot Hoomi that to comprehend these matters in terms of their own rationalistic *Weltanschauung*, and without subjecting themselves to years of the self-abnegating discipline of body and mind required of monks, would be impossible. Sinnett wrote in *The Occult World*, published in 1883 shortly after he met Blavatsky, "that one can never have any exact knowledge as to how far her own powers may have been employed, or how far she may have been 'helped' [by the Brothers] or whether she has not been quite uninfluential in the production of the result."

Walter Carrithers, in a 1947 defense of Blavatsky, remarked that for a half a century the popular press had "almost unanimously boycotted all facts in favor of" her. H.L. Mencken's comment in "Hooey from the Orient" was typical: Her reputation rested, he said, on the "illimitable credulity of her followers."

Richard Hodgson's apparently authoritative report on Blavatsky on behalf of the Society for Psychic Research, published in 1885 in the Society's *Proceedings,* had probably contributed significantly to the common view of her. He represented her as an imposter, forger, Russian spy and instigator of frauds. By the time the SPR report came out, A.O. Hume had lost interest in Blavatsky and the Theosophical Society project. Even so, he was outraged by Hodgson's allegations that the Tibetan "Brothers" existed only in Blavatsky's imagination, and that she had been the author of communications supposedly sent by them: "The proofs I have had [of the Brothers' existence and influence] have been purely subjective and therefore useless to anyone but myself—unless you indeed consider it proof of their existence that I here at Simla received letters from one of them, my immediate teacher [the monk Koot Hoomi] dropped upon my table, I living alone in my house and Madame Blavatsky, Col. Olcott, and all their *chelas* [novices] being thousands of miles distant."

Hodgson's careless use of evidence became obvious enough in time to embarrass the Society for Psychical Research. Sir William Barrett, a onetime president of the Society, declared Hodgson's report a "blot on the *Proceedings*"; and Theodore Besterman, the Society's "Research Officer" wrote off Hodgson in 1931 as a "plain and uninspired individual" and declared that the Society had disclaimed responsibility for Hodgson's "facts, reports, or reasonings."

The view of Blavatsky as a charlatan and wooly-minded esotericist survived, nonetheless. Walter A. Carrithers' pamphlet, "The Truth about Madame Blavatsky" was been occasioned by the 1946 publication of a Blavatsky biography, *Priestess of the Occult,* by Gertrude M. Williams. Carrithers criticized Williams for embracing uncritically what had long been the standard view of Blavatsky that associated her not only with the "fraud and trickery *deluxe*," but "scandals, shadows of lovers dead and gone, bigamous marriages."

Joseph Howard Tyson in the preface to his *Madame Blavatsky Revisited* (2006) admits to having been under the influence of views of Blavatsky like Williams' when he first turned his attention to her while writing a book on famous nineteenth century visitors to Philadelphia. His intention had been to give Blavatsky a "flippant three page treatment" before his studies made him realize her "humor, intelligence, and good faith," and the three pages he had planned morphed into a sympathetic book-length study.

MODERNITY AND METAPHYSICS

The workaday illusion that the human world and one's immediate concerns in it exist independently of Nature is virtually unavoidable. One can't be very well be thinking simultaneously about how to acquire dinner, and the significance of one's digestive system in the cosmic scheme of things. That said, the extinction or frailty of cosmic perspectives offsetting quotidian consciousness in modern Western societies— the "anti-metaphysical orthodoxy" someone has called it—is perhaps unique historically.

It is nearly impossible to imagine anyone in our part of the world today expressing the unbridled enthusiasm for the Creation in this effusion of Emanuel Swedenborg's from *The Soul, or Rational Psychology* (1749): "All things are full of Deity, and we admire in each and every thing the order which is attributed to Nature and its perpetual preservation, not by itself, which would be absurd, but by some higher Being from whom it has subsistence. We see blended together a multitude of phenomena going to prove a regulating Providence."

Compare, for example, Michel Foucault's angst-filled description in *The Order of Things* of the "strange empirico-transcendental doublet" in modern knowledge: The mind cannot pretend to grasp "the order which is attributed to Nature" by a "higher Being." The mind, vis-à-vis its objects, can only "inhabit, as though by a mute occupation, something that eludes it." Paradoxically, "the *not-known* perpetually summons thought toward *self-knowledge*." The modern *cogito*, more torturous than Descartes', becomes, "What must I be, I who think and who am my thought, in order to be what I do not think, in order for my thought to be what I am not?" Things "turn in on themselves." They have their own "internal space," their "hidden veins."

I left college in the 1960s a "secular humanist" convinced, in the words of American philosopher Josiah Royce (an enthusiasm of mine back then), that "human knowledge is an island in the vast ocean of mystery, and that numberless questions which it deeply concerns humanity to answer will never be answered so long as we are in our present limited state, bound to one planet, and left for our experience to our senses, our emotions, and our moral activities."

Ideas that were in the air—a jumble in retrospect—fed my "secular humanism": Freud's 1927 *The Future of An Illusion* that represented religion as a collection of "illusions… insusceptible of proof"; Wallace Stevens' remark in *Notes Toward a Supreme Fiction* that what "sends us back to the quick of this invention"—a Cosmic Mind—is the "celestial ennui of apartments"; Kenneth Rexroth's comment in a mid-century essay on Martin Buber, that the sources of the Old Testament God were "metaphysical greed" and "ontological confabulation." (The universe "is not orderly in the same way as the mind of man. Only as a concept is Nature a unity.") Etc.

But my "secular humanism" had less to do, I think, with any specific author or ideas, than with my admiration for a teacher who was a Kantian. Kant had written in the *Prolegomena to Any Future Metaphysics* (1783) that people who wax metaphysical are just projecting categories of human understanding useful in experience onto metaphysical reality which they *cannot* experience. Attacking Swedenborg in *Dreams of a Spirit-Seer Illustrated by the Dreams of Metaphysics* (1766) Kant scoffed at speculations concerning "hidden properties of things"—*telos*, final cause. Philosophy must dispense with "this phantom of knowledge."

Ethical concerns had ostensibly rescued God and the Creation for Kant (he wrote in *The Critique of Practical Reason* of having to destroy knowledge to save faith) and it may never have occurred to him that confining knowledge to the *Ding für uns* might obscure the primitive awareness that knowledge exists *in a world.* This had occurred, however, to his German contemporary, philosopher and man of letters Friedrich Jacobi, who saw implicit in Kant's idealism a substitution of the knowing self for God and Nature. Kant's epistemology, by focusing attention on subjectivity, encouraged obliviousness of the Creation.

Ideas can work their way into sensibility with strange effects. Kant's epistemology, if it had on the one hand encouraged modesty about the scope of human intelligence, had also fostered monster egos in some of his Romantic disciples. Josiah Royce observed in *The Spirit of Modern Philosophy* (1896) that if the world is "indeed the world as self-consciousness builds it, the true self [may be seen as] the self that men of genius, poets, constructive artists, know; hence the real world is such as to satisfy the demands of the man of genius, the artist." In the philosophy of the young Friedrich Schlegel, "best do they comprehend truth…who have experienced the most moods. The truly philosophical attitude towards life and reality is therefore a sort of courageous fickleness."

A corollary of regarding the human world as a "self-generated and autonomous realm of meaningful experience" (as sociologist Harvie Ferguson puts it in his *Modernity and Subjectivity: Body, Soul, Spirit*) is the notion of selfhood as an absolutely free choice independent of natural limits. Ergo, to accord the body with a choice of "sexual orientation," its surgical modification is not out of the question; the cooling of male sexual desire with age rather than being a virtual inevitability written into physiology becomes a misfortune remediable with pharmaceutical assistance; death appears to be an anomaly rather than an inevitability, and we erect memorials to those who die "tragically," e.g. in the 9/11 disaster.

"Ought we not remind ourselves, we who believe ourselves bound to a finitude that belongs only to us, and which opens up the truth of the world to us by means of our cognition," Foucault writes, "ought we not to remind ourselves that we are bound to the back of a tiger?" Foucault is talking about formal thought here, but his remark has a wider applicability in modern culture.

The sciences have obviously made heavy contributions to the modern "anti-metaphysical orthodoxy." But scientists in the seventeenth century had commonly regarded the laws of Nature they were demonstrating as better explanations of how the Divine Mind operated in the world than the old Aristotelian metaphysics. For Baruch Spinoza, in the "Preface" to the *Tractatus Theologica-Politicus*, the place to seek the divine was not in miraculous interruptions of natural order, but its regularities. Swedenborg (1688-1772) was a particularly interesting late example of this mentality, and I will dwell on him for a moment.

Swedenborg is remembered most commonly as the spiritualist he became later in life, but he was a polymath who earlier had studied mathematics, physics, chemistry, astronomy, geology, and anatomy—always with an eye to their metaphysical implications. In the *Economy of the Animal Kingdom* he speaks of his ambition "by continued abstractions and elevations of thought," to proceed "from the posterior to the prior sphere; or from the world of effects, which is the visible, to the world of causes and principles, which is the invisible." Everywhere in the universe he saw resemblance and continuity, a "mutual adaptation of inner and outer, higher and lower, grosser and more subtle spheres or bodies" and "a reception, communication, and transference of motions and affections from one to the other," as Frank Sewell writes in the preface to his nineteenth century translation of Swedenborg's *The Soul, or Rational Psychology.*

For Swedenborg, influence of every kind radiated continuously from the Divine Mind to the "inmost and most interior heavens" populated by various ranks of angels, then to the realms of lower spirits, and finally to the material world. Therefore, whatever existed, whatever happened, had an ultimate divine source. Swedenborg's doctrine of "correspondences" expressed this monism. "You would swear," he remarks in *Animal Kingdom,* "that the physical world is merely symbolic of the spiritual world, and so much so that if you express in physical terms…any natural truth whatever, and merely convert those terms into the corresponding spiritual terms then…will come forth a spiritual truth or a theological dogma."

Correspondence-hunting of another kind abounds in *Arcana Caelestia,* his multi-volume work of Biblical exegesis. Nothing, in *Genesis* was to be taken literally, he wrote, but "the smallest particulars down to the least iota, signify and enfold within them spiritual and heavenly things." Believing with church father Origen that literal readings of Biblical images and stories were pointless, and that interpretations should express the spiritual insights of the interpreter, he informs his reader what these "spiritual and heavenly things" were.

A guide to Swedenborgian correspondences, many Biblical, went through several editions in the nineteenth century: The apple tree corresponds to the joy derived from spirituality; apes, to those who pervert understanding of the Holy Word—i.e. fundamentalists; bread, to spiritual sustenance; fierce animals to the passions; a candlestick to intelligence; linen breeches to conjugal love (?). One of his correspondences echoing various passages in Scripture analogizes God's radiant influence throughout Creation with the sun's influence on Earth. (The poet William Blake, who was influenced by Swedenborg, wrote in "A Vision of the Last Judgment," "When the sun rises, do you not see a round disc of fire somewhat like a guinea? O no, no, I see an innumerable company of the heavenly host crying 'Holy, Holy, Holy is the Lord God Almighty.'" Whether Blake actually saw bands of angels as the sun rose or not, the image expresses the faith-based experience of the sun as opposed to the gold-coin sun of realism.)

Swedenborg thought that the "Book of Nature" could be read in the same way as the Bible, the one as rich in "correspondences" as the other. Whatever correspondence-seeking owed to what he had seen firsthand in his work in the sciences, it was more evidently a play of the imagination which would have served to sustain an awareness of first and last things amid the distractions and fragmentariness of experience.

Swedenborgian theosophy was an example of the type of thinking, or imagining, which had originated in the Middle Ages known as "natural theology." Its fundamental premise, as described by Michel de Montaigne in *Apology for Raimond de Sebonde*, was that there is "not any part or member of the world that disclaims or derogates from its Maker." In Swedenborg's eighteenth century, scientists and learned people tended to be impatient with this kind of thing. Swedenborg observed that in the "physics, chemistry, mechanics, geometry, anatomy, psychology, philosophy, the history of nations, and the realm of literature, criticism, and language study" of his time, Nature was being treated simply a given, a source of raw material for the human mind to work up. He could see, and did not like, the consequences of this outlook for both intellect and sensibility. In *The Spiritual Diary* (composed mostly during 1747-8 when he was about sixty) one reads, "Whatever is taught by the sciences concerning the natural causes of phenomena—such as those things that are in the human body, concerning the senses and similar things, also whatever is deduced concerning a knowledge of the soul and the like, is full of false hypotheses in which not a single verity is laid open to the sight [because] thoughts are not allowed to extend beyond grossest Nature; therefore spiritual and celestial things are considered as nothing."

When Swedenborg's "spirit-seeing" began later in life, he encountered angels shocked to learn from him of humans who did "not yet know that the life of man is never man's, but that all life is infused by God-Messiah. Indeed the…fallacies are so great that men can scarcely suppose otherwise than that the eye sees of itself, and that the interior mind sensates of itself, and that man's understanding understands of itself." A person working in modern knowledge embraced the delusion that "everything is his own, and that he both thinks and acts from himself." Foucault's tiger to whose back we are bound had become the caged pussy cat on our compact little island of human intelligibility. (One thinks of the fictional old astronomer in Samuel Johnson's *Rasselas* who, after spending most of his life studying the heavens, had concluded he was personally in charge of the weather and the equinoxes: "The sun has listened to my dictates, and passed from tropic to tropic at my direction." As death approached, he worried over what might become of the world when he was no longer around to oversee its operations.)

In trance states induced by restraint of breathing Swedenborg claimed that his spiritual double paid out-of-body visits to the spirit world. There, he had learned firsthand that the spiritual body of a person after death was simply a duplicate of his or her physical person. Basically nothing had changed. During one of these excursions Swedenborg encountered a recently deceased acquaintance of his, a fellow "quite learned in earthly things" who had never believed in life after death. Now that he was dead, nothing in him having changed, he thought he was still alive, a post-mortem confusion not too unusual, judging from Hans Holzer's twentieth century books on haunting ghosts. (Medium Sybil Leek was once working with Holzer when she made contact with a female spirit who wanted to know where her body was. Leek told her she really had no further use for a body and should get on with her life in the hereafter. "No, I want my body," the spirit replied. "Where is it?")

The publication in 2013 of a weighty six hundred page collection of academic essays misnamed the *Oxford Handbook of Natural Theology*—hand-held its weight strains the wrists—testifies to a recent revival of interest in natural theology among scholars of religion. This revival scarcely qualifies as an intellectual revolution, though, and it will be a rhetorical convenience in what follows to refer to natural theology in the past tense.

Though sometimes represented as independent of revelation, natural theology presupposed Creator and Creation. Natural theologians studied what could be known of the Divine Mind by reading the "Book of Nature" as opposed to Scripture. Thomas Aquinas's *Summa Theologica*, which fused Christian theology with Aristotle, was the medieval masterwork in the genre.

A natural theologian might consider the various traditional formal arguments for the existence of God, e.g., the "cosmological argument" concerning the origins of the universe. The "argument from design" contemplated harmonious relationships of parts to wholes in ecosystems, and the orchestration of natural phenomena to serve creaturely needs: "The earth itself exists that it may be inhabited by animate beings, the mineral kingdom that it may produce the vegetable, the vegetable that it may nourish the animal, the lower species of animals that they may serve the higher," Swedenborg wrote in *The Soul, or Rational Psychology.*

William Paley in his 1802 *Natural Theology,* a university text in England during the first half of the nineteenth century, observes that "the proboscis with which the bee is furnished determines him to seek for honey; but what would that signify if flowers supplied none?" He speaks of the "variety of mountain and valley, forest and fertile plain, promontory and shallow estuary" so "well-suited to [humanity's] capacities and enterprise," and dwells at length on the intricate design of the eye, and its modifications in creatures suitable in their various environments. "The operation of causes without design may produce a wen, a wart, a mole, a pimple, but never an eye."

The anonymous author of *Arguments Natural, Moral and Religious for the Immortality of the Soul* (1805) remarks that since every natural desire has an appropriate gratification, the universal desire for life after death must have one, too. "Never before the present age of reason and philosophy" had it been supposed that the desire for life after death was "implanted in the breast to delude and disappoint."

Coupled with observation, such teleological play of the imagination, though démodé, is not difficult to kindle. Only ponder the humble yet elegant banana, attractively packaged and preserved in its yellow skin which Nature provides in sizes convenient for single servings; or apple seeds that, rather than being distributed irritatingly throughout the fruit reside at the inedible core like a message of hope; or the protective shells of nuts, inviolate to moisture long enough when buried to guarantee squirrels a food source through the winter.

In natural theological musings, the purposive workings of the Divine Mind are likened to those of the human mind. The character Philo in David Hume's eighteenth century "Dialogue on Natural Religion" complains about this, since human ideas "reach no further than our experience," and "we have no experience of divine attributes and operations." Philo grants that the universe probably did arise "from something like design," but to say more than that on the subject would require "the utmost license of fancy." But Neo-Thomist Etienne Gilson asks in *God and Philosophy*, 1941, why we should assume that a projection of our own designing, purposive mentality onto Nature is erroneous since our mentality *is itself in Nature*. Why suppose that it exists to mislead understanding rather than guide it?

For anyone not predisposed to skepticism there is a good deal in Nature to suggest design. Alfred North Whitehead in *Modes of Thought* (1938) notes, as Plato and Aristotle had, the "large-scale preservation of identities amid minor changes"—people, squirrels, seeds, bananas, apple trees, stones. Swedenborg in *The Soul, or Rational Psychology* remarked that that there "is no entity and no substance in the universe without form; that it is anything, and that it is such as it is, is owing wholly to form." The existence and perpetuation of distinct forms, and the relations among them, suggests intelligent design.

Kant and Darwin had both observed that when one studies the relationships of parts to wholes in living beings, one inevitably thinks in terms of design and purpose. As far as they were concerned, though, that was just the way the human mind works, not a revelation of metaphysical reality, although Darwin apparently had his metaphysical moments. The Duke of Argyll once remarked to him that he found it impossible to contemplate certain "wonderful contrivances for certain purposes in Nature" without envisioning them as expressions of Mind. Darwin responded with a haunted look before saying, "Well, that often comes over me with overwhelming force, but at other times"—he shook his head vaguely—"it goes away."

Supposing that Nature evinces the workings of a cosmic Mind does no doubt tend, as Hume said, to "license" imagination. One thinks 0f those sermons in which pastors descry the hand of the Almighty at work in some local event—or the sort of person given to whimsical reflections on bananas and apple seeds. Even in the Middle Ages, natural theology wasn't every thinker's cup of tea, and later Scripture-based Protestant religion could do without it. A commonplace of twentieth century religious historiography was that Reformation theologians had washed their hands of natural theology, although Michael Sudduth challenges this notion with a flurry of quotations from reformers' writings in *The Reformed Objection to Natural Theology* (2009). But in the twentieth century Karl Barth voiced a heartfelt "Nein!" to natural theology's investing God with all-too-human feelings and longings.

Philip Clayton, a professor theology at Claremont School of Theology, describes in one of the *Oxford Handbook* essays, "Scientific Critiques of Natural Theology," a symposium convened at Cal Tech to explore the question, "Does science make belief in God obsolete?" Attendees were mainly scientists of agnostic or atheist persuasion. When Clayton and other speakers presented "nuanced" natural theological arguments representing religious claims as plausible, or compatible with *science*, audience boredom was palpable. Only those speakers who focused on how current scientific research might suggest the operation of Mind in Nature sparked interest.

But there is really no way to get from science to natural theology—or metaphysics of any kind—without taking seriously questions scientists, qua scientists, have no occasion to ask, and for which there are no empirical answers. Clayton describes many of the currently fashionable arguments against theism advanced by scientist-atheists like Richard Dawkins as "disappointing, even embarrassing, to those who know anything of the philosophical literature." Alternatives to the idea of cosmic design popular among scientists have been principles like "blind force," "chance," and "sudden variation." Gilson saw these as revealing only a preference for "a complete absence of intelligibility to… nonscientific intelligibility"; and what might seem unintelligible if *only* scientific explanations are allowed will not necessarily seem that way otherwise. However, if one clings to the idea that only scientific explanations are acceptable, even the hypothesis of an aboriginal "Big Bang"—for which there *is* a scientific basis, and which the Catholic Church has assimilated to the dogma of Creation—may not seem a particularly solemn or mysterious event. The flippancy of the term "Big Bang" suggests accident rather than design, maybe even a practical joke. When *Sky and Telescope* magazine asked its readers in 1978 to propose other names for the hypothesized universe-generating explosion, among the entries was, "What Happens If I Press This Button?"

In *The Mysterious Universe* (a popular book of the 1930s) Sir James Jeans mentions the speculation first advanced in the eighteenth century that the solar system originated when a wandering star approached the sun closely enough to raise a great tidal wave on its surface. Fragments of the sun that split away cooled to form planets. What bothered Gilson was what Jeans, after describing this speculation, went on to say that, unlikely as it might seem that life would have emerged on planet Earth, "into such a universe we have stumbled, if not exactly by mistake, at least as the result of what may properly be described as an accident." This was "the surprising manner in which, so far as science can at present inform us, we came into being."

That would certainly be surprising, Gilson agreed, but Jeans' remark was an egregious example of the scientific preference for "a complete absence of intelligibility to… nonscientific intelligibility," and as a speculation about how life forms emerged on earth less plausible, a priori, than supposing the operation of a purposeful Mind.

Gilson criticized also evolutionary biologist Julian Huxley's philosophically naïve treatment of Darwin's empirically-derived conception of the "struggle for existence" *as if it were a metaphysical principle.* Evolution certainly does involve what can be characterized as struggle, but Huxley had given Struggle for Existence the status of a Greek god. As such, it was a close cousin to those other scientific divinities, Chance and Sudden Variation. The trouble with all such deities for the monotheist Gilson was their limited reach. How was it that the species embroiled in the Struggle for Existence came to exist, struggle, and evolve in the first place? What would seem to have a greater claim to legitimacy as a metaphysical principle than the Struggle for Existence is a conatus in Nature to preserve and perpetuate species, whatever may be required, including struggle and metamorphosis. The eighteenth century taxonomist Linnaeus had said something of the sort when he represented the "war of all against all" in biological life as the means by which God maintained balance in Nature—an overview of the situation not only more mysterious and awe-inspiring than Huxley's Struggle for Existence, but more plausible, because more inclusive.

The question may be asked, also, whether restricting the concept of evolution to the empirical investigation of living forms on earth is to underestimate its scope. Some years ago a friend sent me an old book he'd come across somewhere in a used bookstore, with a note: "This is very strange." The book, published in 1884, was *Esoteric Buddhism* by A.P. Sinnett. It *is* very strange, and repeated readings have not made it seem less so.

Sinnett was the managing editor of a prominent English newspaper in India when he first met Madame Blavatsky, the founder of the Theosophical Society. She and the American co-founder of the Society, Henry Steele Olcott, had gone to India from New York intent on organizing Indian branches. Earlier, Blavatsky had studied with Tibetan Buddhist monks dwelling high up in the Himalayas. Her ties with them had continued, and through her mediation Sinnett entered into a correspondence with a Buddhist adept, Koot Hoomi, who agreed to impart to him the outlines of "esoteric Buddhism's" understanding of the cosmos—with the caveat that only persons who had undergone the strenuous initiatory discipline of the Mahatmas could possibly appreciate its verity.

Darwinian evolution, Koot Hoomi explained, was "simply an independent discovery of a portion—unhappily but a small portion" of a principle operative not only on earth, but throughout a chain of seven worlds of which Earth was a member. In this chain, best imaged as a circle, Earth, Mars and Mercury were perceptible to humans. The other four worlds were of a materiality too subtle for people—at least most people!—to observe. Evolution was a principle at work throughout these worlds which became capable of sustaining life repeatedly, before losing the capacity to do so, then regaining it once more. Humans and other life forms evolved continuously during seven cyclings of the chain through millions of years.

WHAT IT'S LIKE ON THE OTHER SIDE

I.

Emanuel Swedenborg (1688-1772) had been a physical scientist, and an administrator with the board that oversaw the Swedish mining industry, before he began communicating with the spirits of deceased persons. In his most famous work, *Heaven and Hell*, he wrote of having conversed with spirits "person to person, sometimes with one, sometimes with several in a group, without seeing anything about their form to distinguish them from man." Among his otherworldly contacts were highly evolved angels, all of whom had been humans at one time, and who remained "wholly men in form, having faces, eyes, ears, bodies, arms, hands, and feet." They "see and hear one another, and talk together, and in a word lack nothing whatever that belongs to men except that they are not clothed in material bodies." Certain of these angels were distressed to learn from him that the church of his day tended to represent them as "formless minds" or "ethereal breaths."

Swedenborg's experiences with spirits began when he was in his fifties. Earlier, his twentieth century biographer Signe Toksvig remarks, there had been nothing in his writing to suggest more than a "decent Deistic rationalism" of the kind common among seventeenth and eighteenth century scientists. Swedenborg's own account of the matter was that the "eyes of the spirit" had been opened in him. (Vision of this kind is the subject of the second part of this essay.)

English popular writer Isaac Taylor wrote in *Physical Theory of Another Life* (1837) that the danger to religion in his time was not "vain and presumptuous intrusions into its mysteries," but "cold withdrawal of all attention and curiosity" from its "high themes." That being the case, there was "seasonableness in the endeavor to engage attention upon tranquil but vivifying anticipation of another life."

Scarcely anyone today is likely to have heard of Taylor (1787-1865), but a lengthy 1841 piece on him in the *North American Review* stated that "hardly any author has exerted a wider influence" than this "eclectic philosopher and theologian." The entry on Taylor in the English *Dictionary of National Biography* of 1903 speaks of him having been regarded by some in his day as "the greatest lay theologian since Coleridge."

Taylor could not, like Swedenborg, claim to have paid visits to the other side. His approach to the afterlife in *Physical Theory of Another Life* was speculative rather than reportorial. Natural theologians since the Middle Ages had supplemented revealed truth of Scripture with contemplation of the "Book of Nature" for what it might reveal about the Divine Mind, and that was Taylor's approach in contemplating the afterlife.

In the natural state of the human being, body and "mind" were combined. (He sometimes uses the term "mind" as others might "soul" or "spirit".) In the afterlife, "mind" would be separated from body—the *physical* body. He refers early in his book to St. Paul's mention in *I Corinthians 15* of the "spiritual body" (*soma pneumatikon*) of the resurrected Jesus who appeared in the disguise of a gardener before Mary Magdalene, shared a meal with the disciples, and invited doubting Thomas to touch his wounds. Paul did not elaborate on the nature of the "spiritual body." For all Taylor knew, it might be just a transitional state between a physical existence and "sheer incorporeity." In any event, the resurrected Jesus had demonstrated the survival after death of a sort of body not entirely unlike the physical body. What characteristics might it be supposed to have?

It would undoubtedly excel the corporeal body in freedom and powers. Taylor was not given to disturbing the elegant flow of his prose with references to influences, and there is no suggestion that he was aware of Swedenborg. (The impression one gets reading *Physical Theory of Another Life* is that he had never learned anything from anyone.) But his speculations about the spiritual body often resemble what Swedenborg claimed to be matters of fact for the "eyes of the spirit." (Edwin Paxton Hood in *Swedenborg,* 1854, noted the similarities between the two writers, without pursuing them in his text.)

As mentioned above, Taylor uses the term "mind" as others might "soul" or "spirit." In physical life, mind and physical body are combined. "The body is to the mind the means of a mode of existence... which in its incorporeal state it could never have known." The awareness of time in the embodied "mind" is a consequence of its experience of day and night, sleep and waking, youth and age, hunger and satiety, the beating of the pulse, the progression of seasons, and the motions of heavenly bodies. Change and motion measure time for earthlings, and since these are properties of matter, the experience of time is also an experience of space.

Taylor's ruminations on the human space-time experience recall Swedenborg's having once attempted to explain time to a puzzled angel. "I was obliged to tell him... how the sun appears to be carried around our earth, and to produce years and days, and how years are divided into four seasons." This was hard for the angel living beyond space-time to understand. His experience consisted simply of a succession of mental and affective states—swift for those who were happy, of varying duration for those experiencing hope, and hellishly prolonged for those in despair. The succession of psychological states in a "spiritual body" resembled what a person asleep and dreaming experiences during temporary abstraction from the "regular motions of the material world."

Spatial metaphors are unavoidable in talking about the "other side," but of course it is not a place, so there are no distances to be crossed in it. The only experience of angels analogous to the human experience of space, Swedenborg said, was proximity to spirits with whom they were simpatico, and remoteness from others, either state achievable instantaneously simply by willing it, with none of the inconveniences of travel.

Apropos, Taylor speculated that with the physical body's drag eliminated, "locomotion by simple volition" ought to be possible for the spiritual body; and "is there not," he wrote, "a latent or half-latent instinct in the mind which speaks of a future liberty of ranging at will through space?" (One thinks of those dreams of flying so many people have.)

That Swedenborg's angels would have difficulty comprehending our experience of time and space might seem surprising, since they had all once been natural human beings. However, memory loss is commonly associated with the transition from one ontological state to another. Reincarnated persons cannot usually remember previous lives; people abducted by fairies into Fairyland, or by aliens into hovering UFOs, are told they will not remember what happened to them; and people can know that they have dreamed, without being able to recall their dreams' contents.

For Taylor, the angelic incomprehension of time and space Swedenborg described would have illustrated a truth he saw in play throughout Creation: For any species, reality is an expression of its constitution *in situ*. An insect with a lifespan of a day or two might be "running through a century of joyous sensations." (William Blake: "How do you know but ev'ry Bird that cuts the airy way/Is an immense world of delight clos'd by your senses five?") We know there are species whose powers of vision, hearing, and smell exceed ours. The microscope and telescope testify to the limitations of our sensory equipment. Those limitations are felicitous, of course, in preventing debilitating information overload; and the limitations of memory have similar value. "By the medium of corporeity," Taylor wrote, "the mind is defined and its power rendered applicable to definite purposes." For better or worse, sensory life, memory, character, emotion, and mentality in humans are all expressions of our peculiar embodiment. (In an unintentionally funny passage, Taylor writes, "The [readily disturbed] human mind now may be compared to a lake among the mountains exposed to gusts and eddies from every ravine that opens upon its margin; and troubled, too, by gurgling streams from beneath.")

In his third chapter, "Probable Prerogatives of Spiritual Corporeity as Compared with Animal Organization," Taylor speculates that for the spiritual body divorced from the physical body, and the distractions of the senses, there ought to be a marked gain in intellectual acuity, and a liberation from "illusions, humiliations, and false judgments" that disturb mental life as we know it. Abstract truths (e.g. those of mathematics or metaphysics) which embodied persons pursue laboriously, and often erroneously, ought to be graspable intuitively; and thought on *any* subject might have something of the indubitable certainty of mathematics.

The expansion of powers in the spiritual body Taylor envisioned was for Swedenborg matter of fact. Angels could comprehend in an instant what humans could not in an hour, and express succinctly what for embodied humans would require numerous pages of writing

Taylor imagined, also, that the sensory life of the spiritual body, no longer dependent on gross sensory organs, would be intensified. Swedenborg's spirits had revealed to him, as did the spirits who later communicated with Victorian mediums, that on the other side spirits freed of the physical body were treated to brilliantly illuminated, colorful panoramas of gardens, "groves of trees, rivers, mansions, houses, stunning things... all glistening as though they were made of gold, silver, and precious stones." In the *Spiritual Diary* Swedenborg wrote of spirits present with him so exhilarated by the performances of this-worldly street musicians "they scarcely knew but that they were in heaven." There were marriages in heaven, too, he said, and sexual sensitivity that was out of this world.

Natural bodies are, in Taylor's metaphor, castles rather than open tents. Corporeity involves seclusion and individuality of minds, so that for communication to be possible there must be elaborate systems of signs and symbols ("external notices of thought"). Subtle as these may be, they often fail to express "the heights and depths, and refinements of human passions and affections." One could imagine there would be among spiritual bodies, on the other hand, a "direct and plenary communication" of thoughts and feelings. "The veil of personal consciousness might, at pleasure, be drawn aside, and the entire intellectual being could spread itself out to view." Whatever a spirit thought or wanted would be conveyed immediately to other spirits "as if formed to their sight." That was exactly the case, Swedenborg said. There was no "veil" to be drawn aside in the afterlife. A person could not conceal feelings or thoughts which were out in the open for all to see, and were determinative of a person's eventual assignment to some specific realm of Heaven or Hell.

The number of species in Nature differently constituted from us, and therefore experiencing the world in ways we do not, suggested to Taylor the probable existence of ranks of beings invisible to us ordinarily "elaborate in structures and replete with life, agitated by momentous interests, and perhaps by frivolous interests."

This, too, had been not merely speculation, but observed fact, for Swedenborg—and for some other people historically. The sublunary region (always a scene of anomalies, including the UFOs of recent times) has often been regarded as a province of such entities. Thomas Lance in *The Spirits of the Dead and the Spirits of the Air* (1845) wrote of them: "The vast aerial circle, then, is peopled with spirits, or, I would rather say corporeal beings of a substance infinitely more attenuated than ours, and invisible: not essentially invisible, but relatively so to us. Our organs of sight may not be so constructed as to be capable of perceiving them, or they may be somehow disconnected with those peculiar vibrations of the aether which render objects visible to us. However that may be, when the impediments are removed, they are seen." Among these entities were not only ministering angels, but "dreadful inhabitants of the air... constantly intent on our destruction."

Not everyone sees an angel, said the sixteenth century physician and alchemist Paracelsus, but those who *do* should confirm their reality for everyone else.

The manner of such seeing is the subject of the part of this essay to follow.

II.

What are known as "near-death" experiences may occur during surgeries, or in the aftermath of serious automobile accidents. The sensorium closes down. In ostensible separations of mind or soul from body, people claim to view from aerial perspectives emergency crews or physicians working over their bodies, and before regaining the use of their ordinary sensory faculties, they may also believe they are visiting brilliantly illuminated otherworldly landscapes populated by ancestors and angels.

Dr. Kenneth Ring, a psychologist, writes of such seeing-without-eyes associated with near-death experiences in *Mindsight* (2008), a book he co-authored with Sharon Cooper. The properties of "mindsight," for those who have experienced it, are often peculiar. One near-death experiencer claimed to have enjoyed panoptic vision; it was as if he had eyes in the back and sides of his head. Another reported peculiar microscopic vision. A third thought her out-of-body perceptual life was synesthetic, combining tactile with visual impressions.

Curiously, congenitally blind people have experienced "mindsight" in near-death episodes, and never before having seen anything have not understood at first *what* they were experiencing. A skeptical view of "mindsight" is that it's just dreaming induced perhaps by shock or anesthesia, but as Ring and Cooper point out the congenitally blind never dream *scenes*—only sounds, smells and tactile sensations. There is evidently a kind of vision "that comes into play when, *whether one is blind or not* [italics mine]... when an individual is thrust into a state of consciousness in which one's sensory system is no longer functional."

If these experiences are what they seem to be, regarding them as adumbrations of postmortem existence is plausible. It is as if being near death were *close enough.* Zen Buddhist scholar D.T. Suzuki in his study of Swedenborg wrote of "a spiritual realm separate from that of the five senses; and when we enter a certain psychological state we apparently communicate with that realm." If a Buddhist, or Emanuel Swedenborg, could access this realm through ascetic practices, it might also be entered spontaneously and involuntarily by people in near-death experiences. (Swedenborg once mentioned in this connection the experiences of people suffocating or drowning.)

Ring and Cooper admit, grudgingly, the resemblance between "mindsight" and a type of out-of-body experience occultists and mystics associate with liberation of the "etheric body" or "astral body" from the physical body. (To refer to it as the "spiritual body" would be appropriate.) However, Ring and Cooper shy away from these comparisons: "From a scientific point of view [esoteric] thinking is not useful as an explanatory vehicle…[since] it rests on various *ad hoc* assumptions and concepts that make it immune from any testable…consequences." *Ad hoc* assumptions and concepts, may not be "testable," but they do have *some* experiential basis, after all; and as terminology "mindsight" is scarcely less esoteric than the "astral body."

Ring and Cooper mention the criticism of mindsight voiced by Keith Augustine, "Executive Director and Scholarly Paper Editor" for "Internet Infidels." Augustine in "Hallucinatory Near-Death Experiences" (online) psychologizes such phenomena, noting the resemblance of mindsight to other "altered states of consciousness…temporary departures from the normal (alert) waking state" that occur, for example, in hypnosis or meditation. He doubts that the experiences Ring and Cooper describe, compelling as they may have been for those who had them, demonstrate the separability of spirit from body. Nor can they be trusted to deliver trustworthy reports of "objective existence." He refers to cases in which people in near-death states have claimed to witness from aerial perspectives events that did not actually occur.

Confirmations by doctors, nurses, or emergency crew personnel of what near-death experiencers claim to have observed from elevated perspectives while "out-of-body" are naturally of interest, though commonly difficult to acquire. Locating such personnel can be difficult, and their memories of the incidents in question may be imperfect. However, there have been enough cases in which the factuality of what people claim to have observed in the near-death condition has been confirmed to convince Ring and Cooper of mindsight's reality.

Scientists interested in mindsight, but wanting more proof of it, have designed experiments Anthony Peake describes in *The Out-of-Body Experience* (2011). In near-death states during surgery people have claimed to hover in spirit over operating tables and perceive things invisible from floor level, e.g. accumulations of dust atop light fixtures. With that in mind, researchers have placed high up in hospital cardiac care units and emergency rooms objects a near-death experiencer might be expected to see. While the experiments continued, there were patients who claimed they attained the aerial perspectives associated with near-death experiences, but none reported seeing the objects they would have had the experiments succeeded. At the time Peake wrote the experiments had not been numerous, but the conclusion they suggested was that people in near-death states do not actually experience veridical out-of-body perception.

A remark concerning paranormal experiences of Jungian psychologist Aniela Jaffe may be pertinent, though: "If we lie in wait for them…[try to] measure, to photograph, to make statistics," we are usually foiled. It is to be observed, also, that while "mindsight" is not simply dreaming, it involves the same resources of the psyche that are in play in dreaming; and dreaming, that *may* convey uncanny knowledge of matters present or future, cannot be counted on to do so.

The prerequisite for the communion with spirits and angels Swedenborg enjoyed was that a person be "withdrawn from the sight of the body, and the sight of his spirit... opened"—i.e., "mindsight." His biographer Signe Toksvig writes in *Emanuel Swedenborg: Scientist and Mystic* (1948) of "a suspension of bodily sensations during which a man could receive angelic wisdom," whether in the forms of apparitions, automatic writing, or clairaudience—all of which Swedenborg had experienced.

The prerequisite for a "suspension of bodily sensations" was "abandonment of the lust of the will," the appetitive ego. A technique of Swedenborg's for opening the "sight of the spirit" was restraint of breath and an associated deceleration of pulse-rate that induced trance states. This practice is found also in yoga disciplines. Swedenborg writes in *Spiritual Diary* of his respiration being "so formed by the Lord that I could respire inwardly for a considerable time without the aid of external air... in order that I may be with spirits and speak with them." He had practiced breath control in youth while praying, and noticed that it occurred spontaneously during intense contemplation. Toksvig saw Swedenborg's attraction to breath-control as one expression of an intense will to "be rid of his ego."

Trance states were not necessarily required, though, for the "sight of the spirit" to open in Swedenborg. He might be walking in a city street with friends when he would become aware of his spirit acquaintances' presence. Then he would have to shift his attention back and forth between the two realities, a separate mode of apprehension being appropriate to each.

Immanuel Kant, self-described as having no "inclination to the marvelous, or a weakness tending to credulity," made fun of Swedenborg in *Dreams of a Spirit-Seer Illustrated by Dreams of Metaphysics* (1766). Scoffing at Swedenborg's "spirit-seeing" was of a piece with Kant's disavowal in that work of his own earlier metaphysical interests which had included reflections in *Universal Natural History and Theory of the Heavens* (1755) on "various classes of intelligent beings" associated with various planets.

There were, however, ambiguities in Kant's response to Swedenborg's "spirit-seeing" that survived for years. He had gone out of his way to confirm reports of Swedenborg's clairvoyance, and was especially impressed by one instance of it. Swedenborg, attending a dinner party in Gothenburg, had envisioned a fire raging in distant Stockholm. Pale and alarmed, he informed the other guests that the fire was threatening his house. Later that evening he expressed his relief that the fire had been contained short of the house, and messengers from Stockholm who arrived in Gothenburg some days later confirmed the accuracy of Swedenborg's visions.

Kant once attempted to initiate a correspondence with Swedenborg that never materialized; and Gregory R. Johnson, a translator of Swedenborg's works, thinks Kant may well have been thinking of Swedenborg when he wrote in *Anthropology in Pragmatic Perspective* (1798) of people in whom a kind of mental derangement enables them to take "self-created ideas as perceptions of external objects"—i.e., to experience visions. Such a state of mind, bypassing the limitations of the senses, might allow for an experience of noumenal realities.

VARIATIONS ON A THEME OF OTTO RANK'S

> Rank[3] was aware that mortality is central to the human condition, that the fear of mortality and the wish for immortality are governing principles in the life of each individual, and that we play out our individual bids for immortality through creation, procreation, and identification. The wish for immortality, argued Rank, is ultimately responsible for the development of culture and civilization as well. —Esther Menaker, in *Separation, Will, and Creativity: The Wisdom of Otto Rank.*

> "The more laden he is with years, the more readily he speaks of his death as a distant, quite unlikely event." —E.M. Cioran, in *The Trouble with Being Born*

The fear "central to the human condition," as Otto Rank describes it in his often brilliant *Art and Artist: Creative Urge and Personality Development* (1932), has nothing to do with specific threats—it's just innate awareness of human limitedness: "Life fear is given along with the life process itself."

But he contemplates an equally primitive, offsetting "eternizing" instinct which "all our anthropology, sociology, biology—yes, and psychology" fail to acknowledge. To speak of this instinct as a "wish for immortality," as Menaker does in the passage quoted above is perhaps a bit misleading, since Rank sees it operating in psychological phenomena with no obvious connection to the idea of life everlasting: e.g., in the human attractions to permanence rather than change, artificial environments over natural ones, and form as opposed to randomness.

3 Otto Rank (1884-1939) was a disciple of Freud who extended psychoanalytic theory into the study of the arts and culture more generally.

In *Art and Artist* Rank is concerned primarily with this instinct as it plays in the arts. Referring to anthropologists of his time who had studied primitive body ornamentation and shaping, Rank italicizes the remark of E. von Sydow that these practices imposed "*form on the natural material of bone, flesh, and blood, as an assertion of its own independence* [from Nature]." Symbols of the tribe or totem-group ornamenting the natural body assimilated it to a permanent group identity.

The modern tattoo has generally a personal rather than a collective significance, of course, but its appeal, too, is its permanence. "A tattoo," actress Angelina Jolie says, "is something permanent when you've made a self-discovery, or something you've come to a conclusion about." Tom Leddy remarks in an online essay, "Kant's Aesthetics: Tattoos, Architecture and Gender-Bending" that students who relish tattooing today "tend to connect the practice with their quest for self-knowledge and self-creation." The tattoo is an enduring record in the flesh of what one has learned or become.

Other simple expressions of the "eternizing" will are to be found in the abstract, repetitive visual patterns of craft ornamentation—rug-weaving, fretwork, mosaic design—"abbreviations of the infinite," Rank calls them. The more primitive the art, the stronger the impulse to abstraction will be, and the firmer art's connection with "collective ideologies." There are illustrations of such abstraction in the stiff, simple, hieratic Biblical characters and saints in Gothic church sculpture and frescoes. Later naturalistic Renaissance painting which not only represented religious figures as flesh and blood individuals in natural poses, but emphasized the stylistic peculiarities of the individual artist, reveal the waning of a "collective immortality ideology" and also a tendency of art to supplant religion, at least for its creators. However, the Renaissance artist's achievement of what Rank calls an "individual immortality of deliberate self-perpetuation" expressed the eternizing will as surely as the art it replaced.

Art, even severely realistic art, is never simply a copy of Nature. Even when the artist is intent on verisimilitude, the governing impulse is domination of process and flux. Rank, like Freud, saw a certain resemblance between the neurotic who withdraws from experience to avoid its perils, and the artist who retreats in order to dominate experience. There is a psychological removal from process in either case, the difference being that the artist is willful and productive, the neurotic neither. (Rank thought that Freud, in equating creation in the arts with sexual repression, had failed to acknowledge that an artist seeking an "individual immortality of deliberate self-perpetuation" may espouse a sexual repression that is monkish and voluntary.)

The uncanny "eternizing" effect of art held John Keats' attention as he contemplated those figures on the Grecian urn:

> Fair youth, beneath the trees, thou canst not leave
> Thy song, nor ever can those trees be bare;
> Bold Lover, never, never canst thou kiss,
> Though winning near the goal —yet, do not grieve;
> She cannot fade, though thou hast not thy bliss,
> Forever wilt thou love, and she be fair!

My first reading of "Ode on a Grecian Urn" reminded me of a teenage experience of mine identical in substance with Keats', if not in content.

I was a freshman in high school when the managing editor of my Ohio hometown's daily newspaper hired me to write local sports. My first assignment was to cover a baseball game. Aged thirteen, and none too sure that I could write publishable newspaper copy, I labored long and hard over my article on the game that had ended when a long fly ball scored the winning run from third base. As I finished my last draft I experienced a sudden sharp intuition of how strange it was that language had preserved the game-ending fly ball and could hypothetically evoke the memory of it forever.

Between 1859 and 1863, still photography was still a novelty when Oliver Wendell Holmes published three essays about it in *The Atlantic Monthly.*

Stuart Ewen in *The Politics of Style in Contemporary Culture* (1988) writes that what Holmes found most remarkable about photography was that "the momentary glance, the ineffable memory, the detailed and textured surface, could now be lifted from its particular place and time, separated from the powerful grasp of the material environment, yet still remain real, visible, and permanent." In other words, photography spoke to the "eternizing" instinct.

The fine arts had always done that, but a drawing, a painting, or a sculpture was a relatively slow, laborious, production requiring special aptitude. "Taking a picture," on the other hand, was quick and easy, and after later simplifications of the medium, and the emergence of the "Kodak," nearly anyone could do it. Holmes was prophetic in foreseeing a time when everything under the sun would be photographed, and, Ewen writes, "the image would become more important than the object itself...would, in fact, make the object disposable....Form is henceforth divorced from matter."

I am not sure what exactly Ewen meant by form "henceforth divorced from matter," but something of the sort seems to obtain for those of our contemporaries who go about the world with cellphone cameras snap-shooting everything in sight. At a show of Cezanne paintings in Atlanta where I live, there was a fellow who, rather than looking at the paintings, was going from one to another taking pictures of them, as if fearing their escape.

In that exhibition there were a number of pictures of perishable comestibles, favorite subjects of still-life artists: fruits, vegetables, a loaf of bread, a cheese, a freshly killed pheasant, etc. Still-lifes, which "eternize" things that routinely enter our mouths and make their ways more or less cheerfully through our digestive tracts, are vivid illustrations of Rank's point about the relation of art to experience.

So is the painted nude. I once asked painter friend why he painted nudes. "I like looking at naked women," he replied, and no doubt he did; but since he not only looked but *painted* there was obviously more to it than that. Picasso, judging from his numerous, sometimes salacious, drawings of artists and models in studio scenes, obviously found the male painter's act of reducing a winsome frock-less lass to a small, static, oily image on a canvas as curious a phenomenon as Keats' bold lover perpetually near the goal but never winning. The psychological effect of painting a nude is as uncanny as painting edibles or immortalizing a game-winning fly ball.

Back when Internet-surfing was a novelty, I once paused over the Earth and Moon Viewer's vivid photograph of Earth afloat in velvety black space: a toy marble, blue swirled with white, escaped from a child's game. I called my wife to have a look. "Makes you feel pretty insignificant, doesn't it?" said she over my shoulder.

Actually, no. Like any picture, this one, by miniaturizing and framing its subject, mastered it. I *knew* I was a perishable bundle of protoplasm on that jolly marble, but I didn't *feel* that any more than I feel the world is round and space is infinite. Sitting there in front of my computer screen with my nice cup of green tea I was the lord of all I surveyed, a permanent fixture in the universe.

An astonishing failure of imagination, but how common!

The painter DeKooning once said while contemplating the night sky with a friend, "The universe gives me the creeps." A variation, this, on Blaise Pascal's *pensee* that infinite space terrified him. Neither man said, though, how often these fits affected him, or how long they lasted. These are significant omissions, if you ask me, because when DeKooning was busy rendering permanent on canvases his vision of women as tormented bundles of desire, frustration, and conflict, there would have been things on his mind other than the creepy night sky; and Pascal, a busy man of the world, must have had many *pensees* to block his awareness of infinite space.

Is that not, in fact, the effect of most *pensees*? We may not be immortal, but we feel as if we were.

Goethe once remarked that he believed in the immortality of the soul because he could not imagine the end of personal consciousness. Who can? The trouble here, Freud said in "Reflections upon War and Death" is that trying to imagine the extinction of consciousness *requires* consciousness. "Every one of us is convinced in the Unconscious about his own immortality," he wrote. Young men's heroics in war celebrated later with medals and encomia as "selfless devotion to abstract general ideals" were better explained by the inability of young men to imagine their personal demise. (That is probably the best explanation, too, of how many young people behave behind the wheels of automobiles, and their willingness to play American football.)

The first time it occurred to me *I* might die, I was four or five years old. I was standing on the back porch of my parents' home in Ohio. A very large moving truck had just flattened my pet rabbit. There came swimming up out of the mazy, purling stream of childish consciousness the thought that my fate might eventually resemble the rabbit's. A second thought came swiftly on the heels of the first: *That's impossible.*

Freud and Rank would have understood.

Now that I am over seventy years old, it is clear to me—fitfully—that I am not going to get out of this thing alive, but I am very easily distracted from what I know. I have my projects. It is as if sun, moon, and stars can't wait to see how they will turn out. This may just be a rabbit-y creature singing in the dark, but that is not how it seems. The meticulous folderol of having a will drawn up in a lawyer's office recently was more like a pleasant social occasion than a reminder that the bell is going to toll also for me. I gave the lawyer a copy of a novel I had published, and we chatted about it.

One might expect obituaries in the morning paper to stir the *memento mori* in someone my age, but they're just entertainment over breakfast coffee, if I notice them at all, rather than pondering the latest scores in the National League, before rushing off to the word processor to launch my daily quest of literary immortality.

Rank saw the passion for "immortalization" at work everywhere in culture and civilization: collective ideologies and symbols, libraries and museums, embalming, monuments, historiography. Looking at the world from a Rankian perspective, one can see the will to transcend time and process in architecture and urban design, family and school reunions, antique collecting, diaries, revivals of 50s or 70s popular music, Elvis imitators, and genealogy studies. That the fixities of Biblical fundamentalism should appeal as strongly as they do to simple minds is not surprising; and the glory of Catholicism, the Minnesota farmer-father of a friend of mine used to tell his son, was that it *never changed.*

In American small towns after the Civil War "village improvement associations" intent on correcting the ramshackle add-on and sprawl typical of earlier continental real estate development abounded. Richard Francaviglia in his *Main Street Revisited* (1996) writes of streetscapes in American towns having taken on by the 1880s "a very stylized and highly standardized appearance. Designs inspired by the European folk-village or the postcard-pretty New England town in its prime would govern both new construction and the remodeling of older buildings. (In 1910, Jarvis Hunt proposed a facelift for downtown Wheaton, Illinois that would have made it a dead ringer for a Tudor village. Such a downtown was actually built, and survives to this day, in the Atlanta suburb of Avondale Estates.)

The associations' appropriation of that old-timey European word "village" was indicative of a will not only to surmount time and change, but to represent the place one lived as not just a hodgepodge of buildings and bodies, but a *community*. Solidarity with one's fellows, real or imagined, is one of the sturdiest bulwarks against the awareness of mortality. Who was it said that immortal life was never being alone?

Considered vis-à-vis the perennial instability of American social arrangements the picturesque downtowns developed by the village improvement associations, with their suggestions of historical continuity and communal coherence and civility, must often have been more invocatory than representative. Nineteenth-century landscape architect Frederick Law Olmsted recalled, late in life, a "simple, unsophisticated, respectable" village of his American boyhood that probably would have acquired by then, he imagined, a soldier's monument, a fountain, a park and "parklet," and a reading room for the literary periodicals, and become so altogether quaint-looking as to be "no longer a village at all."

If urban design is a means of transcending flux and mutability, so is language.

Working one summer between college terms as a reporter for the daily newspaper in my hometown, I was aware how frequently the term "community" cropped out in its pages, and how doubtful the reference of the term to anything in the town's actual life often was. Each day's edition included a "Community Calendar." There were articles on "community meetings," and "community celebrations," reports on baseball games at "Community Field." Community-this, community-that.

To think of our town as a "community" may have encouraged contributions to what was then known as the "Community Chest" (later the United Fund), but what people in my hometown did was, for the most part, what Americans did, and do, anywhere else: they went to work, paid their bills, had hobbies and private circles of friends, sent their kids to school, sat in front of screens and speakers, and ignored politics and religion. If some emergency requiring cooperative effort arose, they would pitch in—maybe even relish the novelty of it—but that was not generally what life required of them, and to speak of us as a "community" seemed more commonly the expression of a wish than a reality. Rousseau, in *The Social Contract*, spoke of a similarly dubious use of language in which people treated "city" and "town" as synonyms. But "city" was cognate with citizenship and civility. "Town" wasn't. ("Houses make a town, but citizens a city.") Similarly, a "community" isn't just an agglomeration of houses and bodies in space, but people doing things together.

At my desk in the newsroom one day I had just run across some reference to "the community" in copy I was reading when it occurred to me that maybe the newspaper *was* the community. Newsboys rolled the community into a tight little projectile they winged onto your porch every afternoon. A local commonplace was that there was "never anything in the paper," but when this nothing did not arrive in a timely fashion there were subscribers who became very agitated.

~

That in 1880 Ohio had thirty-seven colleges, many in small towns situated in what had been frontier territory not long before, struck the president of Columbia University at the time as remarkable, considering there were only three million Ohioans. England with a population of twenty-three million was getting by with four degree-granting institutions.

There were good practical reasons why Ohio towns would have wanted to host colleges. It was not always clear at the time which of these towns were going to survive. Having a college would encourage population growth and capital investment; local business owners could appreciate the value of having a captive population of young consumers in town during the school year; and the religious denomination that often supported college building financially were vying for membership in newly populated regions. Essential, though, to the realization of these practical benefits was the faith of more enlightened Americans in the redeeming personal and social influences of formal education.

The poet Wordsworth told Ralph Waldo Emerson during the latter's visit to England in 1833 that he thought Americans much too inclined to substitute "tuition"—formal education—for "moral culture," "social ties," and "education of circumstances." (American man of letters Paul Goodman was saying roughly the same thing more than a century later when he argued that what American youth needed wasn't more education, but better experience.) What Emerson failed to comprehend, though, was that in America "tuition," along with organized religion, seemed the only likely sources of "moral culture," continental "circumstances" not generally being very useful in that respect. Public support for tax-supported public education in the nineteenth century had swelled in response to barbarism on the frontier, and the appearance of gangs of immigrant "street Arabs" roaming Eastern cities. "The school room was where these young hoodlums belonged.…They needed to be civilized and americanized," Henry Perkinson wrote in a charmingly ironic little study of the American school, *The Imperfect Panacea: American Faith in Education, 1865-1965.* During the century Perkinson studies, formal education in America had been represented at one time or another as the key to solving virtually any social problem that arose, whether street gangs, racial injustice, poverty, class inequality, or bad manners.

Whether formal education could actually yield such benefits was questionable. In the 1830s, Josiah Holbrook, a principal figure in the nineteenth century American School Society, remarked sensibly enough that it would be "of little consequence to have our country studded with colleges and churches of the most costly and splendid architecture...except as they produce intelligence, virtue, and religion." But just as the idea of creating a pristine New England-style town center in a raw Western settlement might have maximum psychological value as compensation for the actual life there—so, too, structures of brick and mortar devoted to the cultivation of "intelligence, virtue and religion" might seem especially desirable in socio-economic circumstances with least actual use for these excellences.

Paul Goodman used to get to his feet at public meetings convened to discuss new school construction in New York, and propose modestly that if pupils were to spend less time in classrooms, and more in city streets studying what went on in cafeterias, movie theaters, stores, museums, and factories, there would be less need for new classrooms. Moreover, street education would have the advantage of diverting attention from the abstraction of subject matter as "curriculum" to uses—a consummation devoutly to be wished, he thought. After Goodman spoke there would be polite silences. Then discussion about building new schools would resume. Goodman felt himself confronted by a mass superstition with a solid architectural foundation.

Georges Bataille thought that the European cathedrals with their attached schools—permanent structures in space—had probably been as critical to the maintenance of medieval orthodoxy as the instruction provided in them.

There is a resemblance between the power of architecture and urban design to render ideologies—or hallucinations—permanent, and primitive cultures' distillation of their understanding of life in rituals, myths, and plastic representations passed unchanged from one generation to the next. The fundamental human impulse in art, and "culture and civilization" more generally, Rank thought, was to eliminate the "arbitrary and apparently haphazard character from human experience," an impulse perhaps never stronger than in societies characterized by fragmentation and change.

Serpent Mound in southwestern Ohio, Adams County, is a quarter-mile long coiled earthwork snake, one of numerous snake or serpent effigies in the United States prehistoric Indians crafted of mounded earth or stone. There were Indian burial sites near Serpent Mound at one time, and evidence of rituals having been performed at this sacred site.

Speculations about what Serpent Mound may have meant for the Indians have not been wanting. What appear to be the open jaws of the Serpent are evidently about to devour a second, small, detached oval mound. An egg? Or the sun? Serpent Mound is aligned with the setting sun at the summer solstice, and somewhat less clearly with the rising sun at the winter solstice, so maybe it was a primitive calendar like Stonehenge? (A nineteenth century pastor, Reverend Landon West of Pleasant Hill, Ohio, saw the oval object near the snake's mouth as the Forbidden Fruit. He envisioned Serpent Mound as God's reminder that the Garden of Eden had been situated in aptly-named Adams County.)

Whatever exactly Serpent Mound may have meant for the Indians, they clearly thought if it as connecting them with what Rank refers to as a second permanent reality with cosmic implications "next above, parallel with, or inside the first"—a reality beyond mutability and quotidian life of the kind found everywhere in "culture and civilization. The thread running through art forms primitive or sophisticated, ancient or modern, with or without religious associations or any expressed connection with the idea of immortal life, is a will to surmount transient Nature, to invest human experience with a transcendent value that, taken at face value, it scarcely deserves.

Considered in this light, Serpent Mound resembles in its own way the vision of the cosmos commonly entertained by learned people during the medieval and early Renaissance periods, with God, the angels, and the *primum mobile* at its outer reaches above the eternal stars, and the planets below rotating in concentric circles around the unmoving Earth superintended by its overlord, Man. Whatever basis this conception of the universe had in observation, it was most obviously the fruit humanity's seemingly innate sense its own (and Earth's) transcendent significance.

E. M. W. Tillyard notes without comment in *The Elizabethan World Picture* the curiosity that while most educated English in the later sixteenth century would have been quite aware of the sun-centered astronomy of Copernicus, the old imaginative view of the cosmos continued to influence period literature. One interpretation of this would be that the Elizabethans were just stubbornly refusing to give up a congenial fantasy.

A second, more likely one, would be that the Elizabethans were more capable than people generally are today of distinguishing between an empirical view of Nature, and the kind of metaphysical imagining supported by religious faith that an Unmoved Mover has generated and governs multiplicity. Faith and metaphysics liberate the imagination to envision permanences behind natural flux not apparent to the naked eye. It would not necessarily have seemed contradictory to an Elizabethan to embrace the Copernican revolution in astronomy, on the one hand, while continuing to subscribe to the medieval view of Creator and Creation on the other. Rank thought that to complain that there was nothing "realistic" or "scientific" about the old medieval microcosmic-macrocosmic universe, the "great chain of Being," etc. was to miss the point. The "macrocosmization" of the earth and humanity, rather than being an inferior version of what modern astronomy tells us, was superior to it as the expression of an "idealism *a priori* anchored beyond all [physical] reality."

That said, Rank's interest as a scientist was in these anthropomorphic visions as "internal phantom experiences" providing therapeutic relief from "life itself," and the "fear that is inseparable from real life and experience." Their psychological value was the same as that of other "eternizing" experiences contemplated in the present essay. "Everything that is consoling in life…therapeutic in the broad sense—can only be illusional," he wrote. The arts, like the religions with which they have been so often associated, or which they have supplanted, look beyond the "real" to the "unreal." Transcendence has "never been real and can never be made real."

One wonders, though. Whence this seemingly universal experience-defying predisposition to form and permanence that finds expression in so many and various ways? Why do we want to fixate things by taking pictures, or making pictures, of them? Why transform living, perishable things into still-lifes? Why is it so difficult to maintain a steady awareness of our mortality? Considering the manifold expressions of the "eternizing" instinct, and the magnification of human significance they yield—and recalling the ancient wisdom that God or the gods only speak to humanity from behind the veils of imaginal forms—to envision these "internal phantom experiences" as intimations of immortality is tempting. Especially if one is over seventy years old.

THE RATS AND I

I am able to devote my best hours most days to thinking and writing. This privilege that has made me something of a glutton where these pursuits are concerned—sometimes a glutton for punishment. Because I do not like the postpartum lethargy that tends to set in following completion of a project, I will start something new immediately rather than sensibly turning my attention elsewhere for a time. This hastiness is likely to yield counter-productive anxiety, irritability, and poor sleep.

That was my situation a while back after finishing a long piece of writing in which I had made casual reference to the phenomenon Carl Jung called "synchronicity." (He describes it in *Synchronicity: an Acausal Connecting Principle,* 1952, as "the simultaneous occurrence of a certain psychic state with one or more external events which appear as meaningful parallels to the momentary subjective state.") In a synchronic experience, there is there is no cause-and-effect relationship between the "psychic state" and the external event or events, at least none of any obvious kind, but their simultaneity will seem significant, even purposive.

A simple example: A while back I was studying the flap over spiritualism in mid-nineteenth century America that began with two young Fox sisters in upstate New York hearing mysterious knockings about their family's rural home. They discovered that a spirit, the source of the knockings, would answer yes or no to questions by knocking once or twice. If they ran through the letters of the alphabet audibly in sequence, the presence could also construct words and sentences by rapping choices.

The study at the back of my house has an exterior door. I was there reading about the F0xes when I heard a series of loud, insistent-seeming knocks at the door. Visitors to the house rarely come to that door, but what I heard resembled so nearly someone knocking that I called, "Who's there?" No reply. I got to my feet and opened the door. There was no one on the porch, but I saw out of the corner of my eye a bird just taken flight. There are woodpeckers in the neighborhood. The knocker had probably been one of them, although it would be unusual for them to attack a solid wood exterior doors while hunting for insects and grubs.

The simultaneity of my reading about spirit-knocking, and the knocking at the door, stirred a recollection that birds in myth and folklore, creatures of the sky, sometimes link the human world and the supernatural.

Just a thought.

Virtuoso guitarist and composer Jorge Morel, who emigrated as a young performer from Latin America to New York in the 1960s, recalls in *The Magnificent Guitar of Jorge Morel*, by John McLellan and Deyan Bratic, a performance date in 1967 or 1968 at Nashville where Chet Atkins, a popular guitarist and RCA-Victor records executive, was based.

Atkins had recorded Morel's arrangement of a piece for guitar, and Morel would have liked to have met him, but had not arranged to do so. Arrived in Nashville, Morel signed in at his hotel and went to a coffee shop where he met a man who remarked that he looked like actor Dean Martin. Was *he* an actor?

Morel identified himself as a musician, a guitarist.

"Would you like to meet Chet Atkins?" the man asked.

Yes, Morel would.

"We are going to RCA Victor to see Chet Atkins," the man said.

The stranger seemed trustworthy, so Morel followed him to the Nashville offices of RCA where employees greeted the man familiarly. Atkins, it turned out, was not present at the time, but the meeting with the stranger encouraged Morel after returning to New York to send Atkins a copy of an album he had recorded for a company less prestigious than RCA-Victor. Atkins not only admired Morel's playing, but arranged a recording contract for him with RCA which led in turn, to Morel's tour of the United States and Canada with Columbia Artists, and significant progress in his career, and Morel and Atkins became personal friends.

Morel never learned the identity of the stranger he met in the coffee shop.

Where either of the two incidents I have mentioned is concerned, the interpretative alternative to synchronicity, "mere coincidence," would seem plausible. Sometimes, though, that interpretation of such curious "synchronicities" is less appealing.

During a distressing year in my youth (I was nineteen or twenty) I experienced a series of wildly improbable chance meetings that, read symbolically, had the effect of counsel where my personal situation was concerned. One such meeting might have seemed accidental. The series was astonishing.

I was taking some classes at Ohio State University during that period. One afternoon I trying to locate the office of a professor from whom I was taking a class. I was going along a hallway when I passed a girl I had once dated briefly in my hometown elsewhere in Ohio. An art student, she was in that unlikely location working on a sculpture of some sort. Having exchanged greetings and a few remarks with her, I continued on my way, and rounded a corner just as a man who had taught a course I had taken several years earlier at *another* university in Ohio emerged from an office door. His startled look probably matched mine. I could not explain the symbolic overtones of these unlikely meetings where my personal situation was concerned without devoting many pages to the task, but they were obvious to me.

Uncanny encounters like these abounded during that period. It was as if someone were trying to tell me something. Jung thought synchronic events, like "big dreams," could often impart wisdom bearing on the correction of psychological imbalances. "Inwardly and outwardly," Robert Aziz writes in his *C.G Jung's Psychology of Religion and Synchronicity,* "Nature works through the compensatory pattern of events to further the movement of the individual toward wholeness."

It was as a result of personal experiences of synchronicity that the phenomenon had long interested me, but I had never undertaken to study it systematically—if such a thing as possible! Having just finished a work of writing, rather than allowing my mind to rest for a spell, I turned my attention to the subject. This was a mistake, and I dreamed one night of observing from behind an isolating window a busload of jolly singing people equipped with a large supply of beer about to depart on a joyride to Africa (???). I also had several "impossible task" dreams in which I would be trying to accomplish something simple (finding an address, tying a shoelace) but could never get it right. The message was clear: relax.

Never say die, I persisted stubbornly in my study of synchronicity.

Days were becoming shorter, nights chillier, in Atlanta where I live. Summer, with a better sense of its limitations than I had of mine, was turning into fall. One night my wife left a few pears to ripen on a kitchen counter. We awoke the next morning to find them gnawed impressively.

The American South is a buggy place. Palmetto beetles that turn up in our house sometimes in warm weather will nibble on fruit, given the opportunity, but the damage to the pears seemed greater than anything a beetle could have produced. I didn't think too much about the matter, and didn't connect it with the fact that the following morning we found a large section of our kitchen floor coated with cooking oil. My wife skated across it in flip-flops. A plastic bottle of the oil on a kitchen counter was nearly empty. It had sprung a leak and dripped onto the floor. That was odd enough, but the oil's being spread over so wide an area was even stranger.

I noticed something else: The bar of hand soap in the tray by the kitchen sink had disappeared.

I mentioned these curiosities to a neighbor.

"Rats will gnaw on plastic bottles," he remarked. "They'll also eat soap if nothing else is around."

"An entire bar?"

He shrugged and grinned. "Big rat."

Rats? We'd been in the house thirty years and never had rats or mice.

"They're around," he said. "They may have just found your address. They usually leave droppings and urine puddles to guide their friends to the goodies. You might look for them."

In a corner of our kitchen I found on the floor the droppings and urine my neighbor had mentioned; and reexamining the empty oil bottle I saw puncture marks in it that could well have been made by small sharp teeth. So the rat or rats had bitten into the bottle, then tracked oil across the floor?

A plastic bottle of liquid detergent in the laundry room was leaking, too, and the electrical cord on the crockpot had been chewed, exposing copper wire. I entertained an Alfred Hitchcock-ian fantasy: an invasion of furry, sharp-toothed creatures intent on reducing our house to rubble.

My studies in synchronicity came to an abrupt end.

As I sat down at my computer to seek online advice about dealing with rat infestations, there was a flutter of small wings near my ear, and a dull-gold ladybug landed on the mouse pad. Ladybugs seeking winter quarters sometimes appear in the house when the weather is changing. The rats were probably doing the same.

An online article informed me that rats will not only eat soap, but use it in constructing nests. So a pregnant mother rat preparing for her brood was soaping a nest in the crawl space under our house?

The best alternatives for exterminating rats, according to the article, were the classic steel spring-traps, and glue traps: black plastic pads coated with super-glue. Glue traps were more dependable than the spring traps. A rat steps into the glue and can't escape. Driving toward Home Depot for glue traps, I was aware of a surreptitious feeling of gratitude to the invaders for interrupting my studies.

I was up for some down-and-dirty rat-catching.

Back home, I coated a piece of cardboard with honey and peanut butter, placed it on the floor in a corner of the kitchen near the droppings I had found, and surrounded it with glue traps.

The article I had read warned about refuse piles in and around houses where rodents may nest. There was one under a porch of our house I had been ignoring for thirty years, the work of a previous owner. I must do something about it.

I donned old jeans and ran an extension cord into the dark, dank crawl space to bring light there. Garden hoe in hand, a committed Mr. Clean, I began pulling apart the refuse pile and lugged the junk out of the crawl space.

Rats do not tunnel, I had learned, but they will travel into basements through tunnels other critters have dug. Swatting a summer's accumulation of spider webs out ahead of me, I made my way over and under heating ducts looking for holes in the red Georgia clay floor, and found two side by side just inside a foundation wall large enough to admit the enemy—probably the work of the chipmunks that inhabit our side yard. I filled the holes with expanding plastic foam.

My return to the house following an afternoon in the grubby depths was leaving purgatory for heaven. My god, the elegance of the interior! Painted walls! Draperies! Chrome-plated faucets! Four-legged chairs! What would they think of next?

The cold beer descending my gullet was a religious experience.

My wife looking at my dubious jeans coated with red clay and spider webs looked pretty good to me.

"You're an unholy mess," she said.

I let that pass.

Doffing my work clothes I stepped into the lovely caressing warm shower water. It was a shame I had squandered so much of my life thinking and writing when I could have been so happy as an exterminator.

At two-thirty the next morning, a terrified squealing from the kitchen awoke my wife and me. She got out of bed to investigate.

"The poor little thing's pulled the trap out into the center of the floor. It's desperate," she said when she returned to bed. "Can't you do something?"

"Not now," I replied, and went back to sleep.

The squealing, intermittent through the night, was fainter and less frequent by the time I was out of bed in the morning. Rat and trap were still in the center of the kitchen floor where my wife had seen them. The rat started at my appearance, but seemed pretty well exhausted by attempts to escape overnight. It was not very large, and had cute little ears.

The instructions provided with the glue traps had omitted to say what a person did with a rat caught in one. I could see how addressing that subject might have tended to discourage sales. I could shovel up trap and rat, and toss them into the back yard, but that would probably mean a long, slow, agonizing death for the rat, which had suffered enough already.

Steeling myself for the performance of a more humane alternative, I took a plumbing wrench from my tool chest and clobbered the rat on the head. The rat writhed and squeaked feebly. Once was not enough. Neither was twice. The third strike produced a brief lull, then a little shudder as the nervous system closed down.

I didn't feel very well the rest of that day. I certainly didn't feel like studying synchronicity. We probably had more than one rat on the premises, but I'd had my fill of glue traps. I went back to Home Depot for spring traps: instant, impersonal killers.

In a long checkout line directly in front of me were an adolescent boy and his mother. The boy wore a Detroit Tiger t-shirt and baseball cap. I remarked, smiling, that the shirt seemed out of place locally. "I don't like the [Atlanta] Braves," he said. His voice was changing—high one moment, low the next. His mother explained they had just relocated to Atlanta from Ann Arbor.

A parade blocked my usual route from Home Depot to my neighborhood, forcing me to go a roundabout way I never had taken before.

I placed the baited spring traps along a wall in the crawl space beneath the kitchen and over the next few days caught three more rats. There was no evidence of more being present after that.

Cleaning the trips of dried bait and traces of blood in preparation for storage, I was aware that my appetite for studying synchronicity had revived. It occurred to me that the arrival of the rats, forcing my abandonment of that study for a time, might itself be conceived as synchronicity—an illustration of how "Nature works through the compensatory pattern of events to further the movement of the individual toward wholeness." Stubbornly refusing rest, I had been ignoring the advice I was getting from dreams. So a diversion of a more dramatic kind had been necessary? Well, it was a thought. That would not mean, of course, that my state of mind *caused* the rats to appear. They had their own designs. There is in synchronic experiences a coordination of apparently unrelated events and purposes.

As I thought about the matter, I was aware that theme of transformation had pervaded my experiences associated with the rats' invasion. Summer was turning into fall. The rats entering our house, like the ladybug that had dropped onto my mousepad, were undoubtedly seeking winter quarters. Dealing with the rats forced me to abandon not only my mental labors, but the comfortable interior of my home for a descent into the unsavory crawl space with its trash heap, earthen floor, and spider webs. The boy in the checkout line at Home Depot on the brink of manhood had a voice that cracked, and he and his mother had just relocated from Michigan to Atlanta. A parade forced me to drive home from Home Depot in a new way. These experiences in combination had enabled my recovery of psychological equilibrium.

Was I reading symbolic significance in "mere coincidences"? Was it simply because I had been studying synchronicity that I was thinking about my dealings with the rats in synchronic terms? Or was my reading about synchronicity itself a contribution to a synchronic experience, a preparation for understanding it?

The most vivid and convincing synchronic experiences, the ones least likely to seem coincidence, tend to arise in association with intense, problematic psychological states, but all that I had been experiencing when the rats appeared was mild intellectual fatigue. On the other hand, C.D. Broad remarked in a 1949 article in *Philosophy*, if synchronicity ("paranormal causation") is a reality, it must be operating continuously "in the background of our normal lives," unnoticed usually because our attention is elsewhere. Jung had obviously thought so. Ira Progoff, one of his disciples described how the psychiatrist while conversing with patients in his garden summerhouse, would be constantly noting peripheral events: the movement of waves in a lake visible from the gazebo, the appearance of certain insects, wind in the trees, etc. While there was no *causal* relation between the events in the natural surroundings, and the analytic work in progress, Jung regarded the situation in its totality as resembling a work of literature or art whose elements acquire significance by their relation to one another.

The *I Ching*, the Chinese book of wisdom, interested Jung. A person seeking its advice about some state of affairs tosses three coins. The toss yields heads and/or tails in some one of sixty-four possible combinations, each represented by a hexagram associated, in turn, with a text. One then contemplates the text for what it may suggest about the situation in question. Between the concerns of the person who tossed the coin, the result of the toss, and the text, there are no causal relations, and yet the text may seem to have uncanny pertinence to the matter in question.

Austrian physicist Paul Kammerer (1880-1926) was particularly interested in one specific type of synchronic manifestation: seriality, the uncanny recurrence within a narrow time frame of identical or similar data such as names, words, numbers, or whatever. Kammerer spent hours seated in public places watching people pass by and noting repetitions in types of hats, coats, shoes, briefcases, etc. that were more frequent than one would expect, presupposing randomness. It was as if some magnetism in Nature drew like and like together acausally. He wrote of the matter in *Das Gesetz der Serie* (The Law of the Series).

One day, I was pushing a grocery cart along a wide aisle in a bustling suburban Atlanta farmer's market, intent on finding a sack of apples. Out ahead of me there were twenty or twenty-five other shoppers when, for some reason, I thought of Kammerer and seriality. The moment I did, I noticed that three-quarters of the people out ahead of me wore black clothes. I glanced over my shoulder at a similar number of shoppers. None wore black.

If, as Broad suggested, "paranormal causation" operates continuously in the background of our normal lives, it is not surprising that it is usually unnoticed, the prerequisite for observing it being a suspension of the mind's natural purposiveness. People busy with some equivalent of looking for a bag of apples miss a lot. Whether sitting on a park bench watching people go by, and looking for acausal seriality would be a valuable use of one's time might be questioned, but the mind of a person doing that might be less idle than one would suppose. I intended to stop writing right here, but cannot resist adding this note: Having stepped away from my word processor after writing the previous paragraph, I picked up a section of the local newspaper open to the daily horoscopes lying on our dining room table. I never read the horoscopes, but that day I glanced at the entry for my birthdate which read, "The things that interest a different species are outside of your usual observation. When you try to understand the world through them, your own world expands."

A further addendum: It was maybe a year after my encounter with the rats that it crossed my mind one morning that it had been some time since I had had—or at least noticed—an experience with "synchronic" implications. It would be amusing to have another. Just a fleeing thought, I didn't dwell on it.

That afternoon, I was in a neighborhood post office buying stamps from one of two clerks working at a long counter. The second clerk was chatting with a young woman about her newborn son. What was his name?

"Tucker," the young woman said.

"That's very unusual," the clerk said.

"It was a favor to my grandfather. He loved the Tucker automobile. He was always talking about it."

"Tucker? Never heard of it," the clerk said.

"It was a luxury car in the early twentieth century."

I turned to the young mother. "My father in Ohio owned one of those cars."

She was wide-eyed. "He *did*? There were only something like four hundred of them made!"

"It had big swooping fenders and a lot of chrome in the front. The Tucker stood idle in our driveway all through World War II. He couldn't get parts for it."

"Small world," said the clerk.

"There's something else I should mention," I said, "Tucker my middle name."

The young woman stared at me.

She and I continued our conversation in the post office foyer "Do you have a picture of your father's Tucker?" she asked.

"I think there's one in an old family photo album."

"I'd love to see it."

"I'll see if I can find it."

She gave me her name and address. I did not tell her my first name.

I found the picture of the old Tucker with me, James Tucker, three years old, posed leaning back against the bumper. I cut it from the album and mailed it to her, with a note to which I signed my name, and she sent he a thank-you note, with her new son's full name in the return address on the upper left corner of the envelope: "Tucker James Miller."

II

CHRISTMAS AS THE MEANING OF LIFE

My Ohio ancestors were farming people mainly, and rural jubilation accompanied my birth as first son. Grandmother said when Dad heard over the phone I was born out at the hospital, he embraced Grandad, and the two danced around in circles. An old Welsh custom, another hand for work in the fields having appeared from nowhere—for all I know.

Dad was a commercial artist.

Once upon a time, a farmer and his wife bred most of the company they would enjoy. Children were both help, and social security in old age. But machinery had reduced the utilitarian significance of large farm families by the time I was born; and, my family's future was to be in towns or cities where children were not actually "our most important resources," though people might continue to think so.

My parents had probably never really asked themselves what they hoped to gain in return for the trouble and expense of raising my brothers and me. The law of the land had always been, be fruitful and multiply. Theirs was not to reason why. Having children and raising them was what people *did*. If they had not done that, how would they have kept busy? How many of us got into the world through this trap door?

There were no reports of jubilation comparable to what accompanied my birth when my brothers arrived in the world. Had my parents begun to suspect their continuing fruitfulness and multiplication was kneejerk antiquarianism? Had they a dim intuition that children might be something like early American furniture?

My sixteen year-old daughter reads the foregoing and says, "Dad, that's silly."

"Silly yourself!"

People who live in small towns are not necessarily much aware of the countryside, proximity notwithstanding. When I was a child, my family used to "go out for a ride" in the country. I was surprised at times to see it there. Intimations of the Berkeleian enigma: Was the country there when I was not?

The fact that my father commuted into the mysterious city of Columbus to work in advertising seemed, in a way, to put us at even a further remove from our rural past than living in town did, and it subtly undermined the reality of the town. The town had always seemed to me a chrysalis, or stupor, from which I was awaking. It never once crossed my mind that I would live there as an adult.

The rural past and surroundings asserted themselves most definitely at year's end when in elementary school we sang, "Over the river and through the woods/To Grandmother's house we go." I was amazed, the first time we sang that: Something in school had reminded me of my own experience!

Christmas afternoons, my family went over the river and through the woods to Uncle Bill's house for textbook festivities: decorated tree, gift exchange, aunt-uncle, turkey and trimmings—the works. Old acquaintances should not be forgot, and we old acquaintances laughed pretty hard at everything. But the truth was, the town and country factions of our family were a bit strange to each other. Not surprising, this, considering that, come Christmas, we might not have seen much of each other since the Christmas before. It was odd, greeting a relative once a year and handing him yet another three-pack of Fruit of the Loom.

The distance between us was only seven miles in space, but different practical lives had generated differences in style and temperament epitomized for me in the tableau vivant recreated annually at Bill's hearth: my father the ad-man (dapper, humorous, hard-smoking) seated beside Bill the farmer (gentle, droopy-lidded, never far from slumber, it seemed. Hard physical labor seemed responsible for Bill's placid Yule fatigue.)

One Christmas Eve, my father declared, "Christmas is a time for family."

It allowed for the possibility that the rest of the year might not be; and, in fact, he consorted with the extended family mainly when the sugar plum fairies were up and about.

I once overheard two country-dwelling female relatives muttering about his spotty sociability. These were women seriously devoted to "visiting." Visiting went way back. It consisted of driving to a relative's home and spending eight or ten hours there chatting and eating things. I suspect the last thing my commuting father wanted to do weekends was get out there on the highway and log some more miles in visiting. Couldn't these rural relatives understand that?

No, the law of the land was, a person not working the land *visited.* The fact that my father in advertising was working Faerie Land did not alter the formula.

I do not think our female relatives had ever expressed openly their opposition to Dad's weekend reclusiveness, because side by side with *Thou shalt visit* in the law of the land was, *If you don't like what someone else is doing you can keep your mouth shut.* People's differences, the unique properties of monads, were protected somewhere in the *Constitution.* What had we monads come into the Garden of the World for, if not to enjoy the liberty Nature intended? Nature intended also that women should not say things about what farmers did. Dad was a man, i.e. a farmer, and page after page in the law of the land pertained to women bossy to farmers.

Minneapolis, the late 1960s: My wife and I were graduate students.

My parents could not see why, now that I had a college degree, I was in Minnesota "studying Renaissance letters." It sounded, Dad said, like opening other people's mail. There was nothing in either the Old or the New Testaments about our being put on earth to read letters.

Everyone thought I would make a lot of money, so why wasn't I getting down to business? Why an apartment by a truck-garage where in frigid January ice-glazed semi-cabs awakened reluctantly from sleep at six AM? Why the tacky furniture?

More importantly, where were the grandchildren? Muted but chronic concern with the state of our sexual apparatuses surfaced in letters from home. Had we seen a doctor? "Put down your books now and then and run around the block," Dad advised.

We could have used some children about then—sent them out to feed the chickens. Taken them visiting.

If we could not afford children, we were not in a much better position to keep up Yuletide appearances, standards for which are pretty high in this country. But I remember a Saturday night in December when, fearful of offending the ancestral spirits, or whomever, we sat on the floor of our apartment surrounded by small gifts, a quantity of Christmas wrap, mailing paper, and tape. A bottle of red wine stood in the middle of this assortment.

Nieces and nephews were beginning to pile up. "Who *are* all these people?" my wife said, staring at the list. "Why are we sending presents to people we've never seen?" If I had known then what I now know, I would have said, "Yes, and we will not know them any better a quarter century from now when they send us wedding invitations."

~

"I would have liked to have had a sister or a brother," my daughter says.

"There would have been competition for the goodies," I point out, "and what would another child have been *for*?"

"Well, what are *you* for?"

"Wish I knew! Hows about yourself?"

She chuckles, shrugs her shoulders.

"See, we're all in this together."

"What if I have a kid some day?"

"Well, it's happened before, it could happen again."

"What'll I call it?"

I propose "Gratuity."

My wife in the next room croons, "Call me Inconceivable…."

"Now that we have dealt with the only child question, I think we should press on to the state of the Super-Ego," I say. "I have been writing about that."

"Prepare for a lecture," my wife says.

"I have written a compendium on teaching a child nothing. I think you could learn from it."

My daughter laughs. "What's a compendium?"

I hand her mine, as illustration.

THE STATE OF THE SUPER-EGO

What are the young to be told? The longing of the gratuitous young to believe that what their elders tell them (however preposterous) comes straight from the Logos dovetails marvelously with the longing of most adults to say something authoritative to children. These two desires in combination will probably suffice to refrigerate the leftovers of a culture almost indefinitely.

The adult failure to set down firm, archaic guidelines for conduct is almost certainly a cause of psychological problems in the antiquarian young, and we must perhaps expect that if children are not swiftly and firmly archaized, they will turn out badly.

Parents who have no idea, really, what the Super-Ego wants of them may take the Catholic way out and send their children to the nuns who will know even if no one else does. And there is also the this-I-know-because-the-Bible-tells-me-so approach of fundamentalists.

An alternative worthy of consideration, I believe, is that the parents take the child aside and reason with him or her concerning what it is to be born with a lot of archetypal baggage (dated assumptions about authority figures, etc.) and then raised amid languages laden with archaisms. It can be explained that the parents suffered from this same dubious inheritance when they were little bastards.

"You will realize eventually," the parents can say, "that you inhabit a retro-organism with expectations bound to be disappointed by your parents' lack of system. As you take up your position on the shooting range of adolescence, you will no doubt feel inclined to potshot at us as authority symbols, and you should feel free to do this—what else are we for? But remember, you will only be punching holes in dummies."

Where the urge for commands, limits, regulations, etc. are concerned, the child can be encouraged in atomism, but told that if it cannot restrain itself, it might work off the instincts for order harmlessly enough in the worship of some ahistorical, authoritarian coach or teacher. He or she should be warned, however, that this practice has been known to cause blindness.

Christmas, 1985: We were driving from our home in Atlanta toward Mother's in Ohio when my wife mentioned having received a letter from a cousin in Toledo she had not seen in a quarter-century. One of the cousin's daughters my wife recalled having once seen in a crib circa 1960 was getting married. The betrothed couple, avid skiers, were staging their wedding in Boulder. We were invited.

"Do we send a present?" I inquired.

"A twenty-five dollar check."

"Why?"

"We just do."

I thought about it. "Should we be setting a precedent here? I mean, think of how many of these unknown relatives are out there."

"We send the check."

I recalled a Christmas afternoon at Uncle Bill's in the country years ago when, after the gift exchange and turkey dinner, the advertising man and the farmer sat in armchairs on either side of a crackling fire, as if posing for a greeting card illustration. The conclusion of the gift exchange had pretty well exhausted the interest of the holiday visit, as far as I was concerned. My brothers and I, and our older rural female cousins had fallen apart for lack of reason not to, and people had drifted off into different parts of the big farm house.

I looked out the "picture window" in the living room. The afternoon stared back at me across a corn-shock littered gray sea frozen in mid-chop. In the distance, enkitchened women cleaning up were banging around pots and pans. The refrigerator door opened and shut, opened and shut, like some simple, annoying task in a dream accompanying fitful sleep one keeps trying to get right but never can, a task like falling asleep itself.

Dad broke the silence by engaging Bill in a bit of "farm talk." I was surprised, as always, to realize he could do that, but the two men soon fell silent again there by the fire. They looked like two figures in a wax museum, as the antique mantel clock went tock-tock-tock, and bonged gently the quarter hours with irritating regularly.

Perhaps, I thought, one of my cousins could be induced to show me hers. I would be inclined to reciprocate, I felt, but the discrepancy in ages was simply too great. How do you march up to a girl eight inches taller than you and say, *Would you mind dropping your pants?* There was also some question in my mind, too, as to what one did next. That she might know, being older and more experienced, was an intriguing thought.

Uncle Bill started snoring. Dad was asleep, too, I noticed. The clock chimed, and then Dad was snoring. It was counterpoint by Spike Jones.

At the time of our 1985 trip north for Christmas, a divorced brother of mine was living in Marion, Ohio, with his divorced girlfriend. My wife, daughter, and I attended a petty-bourgeois brunch at their house. My brother and I, living in different parts of the continent as we do, seldom see one another, and since we have little in common, we haven't much to talk about.

I once mistook his daughter, my niece whom I had not seen in a long time, for his new girlfriend.

At a brunch, I met not only his actual girlfriend and her

grown children, but *her* girlfriend whose children were also present. I got my niece right this time, but the rest of it was just too complicated. Waiting for the woman wearing a Christmas tree-shaped apron with colored electric lights blinking up and down the green length of her to pile a slab of Butterball Turkey on my plate, I was thinking, *What if we had turned up at the wrong address and been mistaken by some other family for its long-lost in-laws?*

I got into the spirit of the occasion, making what I thought were several valuable contributions to a discussion of interstate traffic around major American cities.

A baby seated in a high-chair barfed smashed sweet potatoes and gazed at us with startled blue eyes above a slobbery orange kisser.

A toast was proposed at the entrance to the adjoining room. I missed what it was all about, but raised my glass with the others.

Then a woman screamed, and someone knocked over a chair: A toilet had backed up. A shag carpet was threatened. Classic menfolk leapt to their feet, I among them. We thrashed about in the construction of a makeshift bath towel dam to stem the tide until the arrival of mop and bucket.

Worn down by this labor, and the food and drink, I sat at the hearth with my brother for televised pro basketball: a "crucial game," the announcer said. One city was again battling another city. Neither was ours and the troops were all mercenaries.

Lulled by the fire's warmth, my brother soon fell asleep. I did not know I had, until my daughter mentioned it later as we were driving away. "So I dozed off, eh?"

"Out like a light," my daughter said. "You know what Johnny did?"

"Johnny?"

"Your nephew," my wife said, "the little guy with the red hair who kept asking if they could go home now."

"Oh yeah, I liked him."

"Johnny said there was something he wanted to show me," my daughter said. "He took me by the hand and led me upstairs to a bedroom and dropped his pants."

That rang a bell.

During that same visit back home, I was shocked to learn from a cousin that Uncle Bill had once considered selling his farm and moving to Georgia in the 1950s, cattle-raising having evidently been a lucrative business there at the time. His deceptively placid Yule countenance had concealed a willingness to pull up stakes and go to a place as godforsaken as the rural South? Law of the land or no law of the land, Aunt Louise had resisted this farmer's proposition with all the force in her slender frame and "for once" (as my cousin put it) had prevailed. Energized perhaps by this victory of continuity over drift, Louise went on to her triumphant researches in the genealogy of my father's side of our family which yielded diagrams which proved conclusively that the generations were connected like the hipbone to the thighbone.

REVIEWING AMERICA, LAND OF FAERIES[4*]

This work may be the ultimate test of a reader's capacity to suspend disbelief. If one can tolerate being told—repeatedly through more than thirteen hundred pages—that he is surrounded by faeries (i.e. elves), he will be treated a vision of American life as broad as it is infantile.

If we are to believe Ossian, faeries have infiltrated virtually every aspect of American life. Apparently, however, they no longer manifest themselves in the old ways as "little people" or strange animals—with a few exceptions such as UFO pilots, television personalities, Big Foot, and the phantom panthers of Central Ohio. Ossian's faeries exert their influence through what the British folk of antiquity knew as *glamour*: enchantments of the senses that compel people to see and hear things that are not.

To my own way of thinking, Ossian's "faeries" are metaphors through which he would illuminate the make-believe that, undeniably, permeates and shapes our concrete experience. At times, indeed, Ossian seems to be using the term in this sense. But he is basically a faerie fundamentalist, even though he sugarcoats this pill in various ways. Here is typical Ossian:

> *Social action has always been a province of the faeries. Regardless of the merits of a cause, or its conceivable effectiveness, a conflict between The Cause and The Status Quo can evoke a fellow-feeling valuable for its own sake—because it is so difficult to come by otherwise. Social action resembles, in that respect, football, war, and the love of parakeets.*

---

4 *An essay review of AMERICA, LAND OF FAERIES. By Morgan Ossian. Atlantis Press, 1984, 1313 pages. No price listed. The fact that this book does not exist in no way invalidates the criticisms voiced here.

And here is Ossian on the mass media: "Erstwhile Life is presently valuable mainly as a source of visual and auditory hallucinations." That is why

> *certain Christian groups, understanding* agape *to be mainly on television have rushed miniature, translucent color pastors onto the tube with faerie messages not incompatible with the humanity displays on* Barney Miller *and* Mary Tyler Moore *reruns.*

Glamour, we are given to believe, is crucial today to any coherent view of self-in-society as well as to any sense of commitment or membership. For Ossian, the element of make-believe in culture, large always, is so conspicuous in America today, and stands in such loose relationship to actuality, that the very idea of a social body is "pure Disney."

I think Ossian's exposition of this view would go down easier, its extremity notwithstanding, if he were not so committed to a faerie realism that leads him into almost intolerably puerile remarks. For example, in his "Preface" he describes being punished by the faeries for shedding light on their machinations in the field of automobile travel. While at work on his chapter on Henry Ford ("There's a Faerie in Your Future") during the summer of 1984, he went walking one afternoon in an Ohio field, where he was struck a glancing blow by a car that missed a curve. The car was, in fact, a Ford. Ossian's pen hand, his left, was sprained. His conclusion about this episode: "Faeries prefer to work in secret."

This episode from the author's life is an excellent example of how his mind works. He never misses an opportunity to back away from the face value of an experience into musings on its faerie-transcendental implications. As a result, although the book is full of particulars and illustrations, its atmosphere is somehow foggy. Many of Ossian's contentions are simply beyond empirical validation and criticism. Either you believe with him, on a basis of shared intuition, or you do not.

He is absolutely relentless in pursuing his faerie monomania into the obscurest crannies of our common experience. In his chapter of popular music, Ossian writes, "What is the crossed-eyed Barbra [Streisand] looking at while singing of those lucky people, the people-needers, if not the faeries?" There is even a lengthy subchapter on the faeries' influence in the literary quarterlies which are "excellent examples of how faeries slip glamour into American experience." Writers for these magazines are, in his view, "the luckiest people in the world, since they are evidently people who need people rather than food or housing." These writers assure their editors ("themselves lucky") of a steady supply of mail.

> *The editors, on the pretext of placing before a nonexistent audience quality literary efforts doomed otherwise to the closet, may harmlessly indulge sociological prurience and do-gooder instincts, and thus experience countless faerie delights. They may even be able, on occasion, to service airmail lusts.*

No less absurd is his stating, at the beginning of a preposterously long historical survey of minor spirits (chapter three), that since faeries and faerie-like entities have appeared throughout the world at all times, one must suppose, *a priori* ("even if there were no *a posteriori* evidence—and there's a bundle") that faeries throng the American continent.

One of the difficulties here, I think, is that Ossian is not as fazed by psychological explanations of apparitional phenomena as one might hope. For example, he states his agreement with Jung that an "autonomous unconscious complex" (a psychic content repressed or otherwise not integrated with consciousness) may press into the sensory life as a ghost, faerie, or whatever. "Yes," says the accommodating, eclectic Ossian, "such are precisely the psychological conditions that favor faerie manifestations."

Ossian believes that the faerie illusions of *glamour* of the kind we experience may be so crucial to the functioning psyche that they possess human consciousness. They make what is desirable, though impossible, *seem* possible. Since what is desirable but impossible differs in various human situations, Ossian's faeries come with a dash of Hegelian mercury. They are able to change from one form to another in response to historical exigencies: We get the faeries that we need and want.

If one has accepted his argument up to this point, it follows as day from night that the faeries who appeal to modern, urban Americans would not be the same ones once attractive to the rural folk of the British Isles. The traditional British faeries which interest Ossian are chiefly those seductive, parasitic ones who, to improve their own stock, stole human children from cribs and left behind changelings, extracted the vital "foison" from human agricultural production for their own uses, ran off with nursing mothers whose milk might benefit faerie infants, and used music and flirtation to allure exceptionally beautiful or talented human beings into unsatisfactory marriages. These faeries improved their own lots at the expense of the tightly woven rural communities on which they preyed, seducing people by tapping into repressed longings for escape, caprice, aesthetic pleasure, and infidelity. Mortals drawn into Faerie Land to partake of the sustenance there were seldom satisfied again at a human table, intercourse with faeries being not only delightful, but dangerous.

Our American faeries are not, Ossian argues, the faeries of earlier times, nor is faerie *glamour* what it once was. Modern, urban Americans are born escapees. They know almost from the cradle that "all relationships have been ruined," and dwell in environments in which communal responsibilities are "minimal, obscure, or ambiguous." Caprice is, for them, a birthright.

As a result, Ossian believes, "what is unconscious or repressed for The Americans[5]* is not the urge to escape social limits and relationships—but rather, the urge to escape *into* them." Faeries attack always at the point of least resistance. Precisely because America provides such substandard housing for communal passions, today's faeries come forward brandishing illusions of relationship, common cause, and duty.

> *The modern faeries do not lure people into an exciting, treacherous world outside the village gates, but through make-believe village gates into make-believe villages. The places to go hunting faeries in America are not the wildwood and the heath, but the ballpark, the classroom, and the pet cemetery.*

Even though the thrust of faerie activity so described is opposite to what it was in days gone by, the element of menace in faerie activity remains, Ossian tells us, because the glamorous social surrogates purveyed by the contemporary faeries "leave critters high and dry." They deprive The Americans of "a capacity for the excruciating but life-giving Dionysian apperception of collective acommunalism [sic]."

Whatever that means.

Among the oddities of this work is Ossian's quirky sense of the pertinent, although one must admit that as a faerie hunter he leaves few mushrooms unturned. There is, for example, a chapter on E.T., "that loving, companionable little sprite, successor to Lassie, who came out of the friendly skies of United to befriend children like you and me here on the Other Side."

---

5 *Ossian has an irritating habit of referring to "The Americans" as if he were de Tocqueville back in his study after travels abroad. According to the dust jacket, Ossian is from Ohio.

(Space exploration, for Ossian, is "the quest for faerie brothers and sisters.")

There is a chapter on shopping malls which Ossian insists on calling "faerie castles." There is another on the faerie aspects of metal detectors ("Searching for The Grail'), and one on Martin Buber claiming that the modern faeries are "into I-Thous." A separate chapter focuses on the cola wars, and another on the uniformed weekend soldiers who recreate historical American battles. ("In rural scenery, grown men divided into faerie armies enjoy an updated, adult version of Red Rover.") Also deserving mention is the somehow impassioned subchapter devoted to Frederick Jackson Turner's hypothesis of the frontier origins of American history and culture—not exactly a *fin de siecle* hot potato. In it, Ossian argues, contra Turner, that a unique American experience did not originate in the interaction between European civilization and The Americans on the moving frontier—but between The Americans and the faeries.

The chapter titled, "The House of Broth"—one of his most extended illustrations—deals with a Minneapolis massage parlor whose newspaper ads state in bold type: WE KNOW WHAT YOU WANT. Down in the fine print, what you want turns out to be soup, skating parties, and Socratic dialogue.

The chapter opens with a summary of the conclusions Ossian reached after conducting a national survey of massage- and conversation-parlor employees. Ossian regards the owner-operator of The House of Broth, Laureen Too, as a "non-existential heroine." During the Seventies, she operated a modestly profitable business in Minneapolis known as Hand-Me-Downs. But her real success began in 1978 when, acting on an intuition, she began bibbing her customers and spooning hot chicken soup into them. The provision of games of checkers and Monopoly, and square dancing, ensued. Having doubled her profits in a year, she developed the volleyball courts on the second floor.

Then in 1981, having renamed the business The House of Broth, Too acquired Candy and Ellie, unemployed graduates of a Big Ten doctoral program in a mill town, and began experimenting with Socratic dialogue. She had hired Candy and Ellie more out of pity than anything else, not knowing at first what use she might make of them. "Shoot, their profs made money off 'em, then dumped 'em in the streets without jobs," Too told Ossian. "I just thought us whores had to take up the moral slack."

Even so, two Ph.Ds. in The Broth made Too uncomfortable until she discovered "how many guys are turned on by a smart chick grappling with their ideas."

For Ossian, The House of Broth serves as an example not only of how sociable *glamour* triumphs over solipsistic reality, but of how the ideas of sexuality and relatedness tend to "faerie-fusion" in the American imagination. Ossian's meditations on this phenomenon, together with his arresting conception of Horniness, originated in his 1972 reading of Philip Slater's *The Pursuit of Loneliness.*

Responding to social criticism of the Fifties that portrayed Americans as compulsive conformists, Slater remarked that it would be truer to say Americans *aspire* to conformity, since it is not really all that easy to come by. Slater's observation produced an *O altitudo!* in Ossian, from which blossomed his concept of Horniness—in his own estimate his "most important contribution to American thought."

When he defines Horniness as "blocked relational passion," he does not disavow the term's slang use, and one suspects he does not want to. ("The horny Sodomites and Gomorrahans were people who needed people. They were certainly among the luckiest people in the world.")

Horniness, and a related concept, "The Solipsistic Relationship," are introduced together in chapter sixteen, "The Horny Renaissance." Stylistically, that chapter seems to me a turning point in the book. From there on, Ossian's language becomes more and more amazing, and the boundary between brilliance and madness progressively more difficult to discern.

We are told that the Renaissance ("an age of social fragmentation and rampant Hamletization—one of the hornier periods in *Weltgeschicht*e") was in many ways like modern America. ("Has any age other than our own held out so many provocations to the composition of *The Faerie Queene*?) His comparisons between the "horny American fashions" of both mainstream and counter-culture, and similar creations in the wardrobes of the Elizabethans, are engagingly bizarre. Ossian believes that while flamboyant dress is commonly regarded as the outward evidence of inner panache and self-possession, it actually serves to "get a rise out of people as a relationship-surrogate.... In the event of social breakdown, dress rises to the occasion by grabbing the eye and groin in such a way that people could *swear* they are in relationships."

The Solipsistic Relationship is a one-sided experience in which an apparent object-relatedness conceals an actual void. Among his examples are hula-hooping, listening to "The Prairie Home Companion" on the radio, and honking your horn because you *do* love Jesus or Willie Nelson. The "personal relationship with God" easily slips into this category, as do relationships with gerbils and cockatoos. Roller-blading to the accompaniment of headphone music, and eating things, are other examples, with Ossian making the claim impossible to substantiate that, "as the depth and variety of relationships have declined, The Americans have found a greater and greater consolation in mastication." ("Television commercials have assisted in this development by depicting tube-fairies in climactic relationships with hot pizza slices, golden brown chicken breasts, and burger buns packed with a loose cole slaw. These relationships clearly rival in intensity that between St. Theresa and God....That cigarettes are faerie-friends goes without saying.")

Across chapters twenty-four through thirty, in which the careers of Alexander Graham Bell and Thomas Edison are the main victims, Ossian discusses the solipsistic relationships struck up by the "classical American gizmo-inventors with their gizmos," and the subsequent complicity of The Americans who "took the gizmos to their bosoms." In these chapters, Ossian pulls out all the stops. The diction that has been gathering weight for over seven hundred pages now drops crushingly on the past century of American technical ingenuity. For Ossian, it was through the inventors' ingenuity that the faeries administered the *coup de grace* to American sensibility, absolving it completely of connectedness to material reality and allowing for the development of a technology-based "parallel world."

Both for the inventors themselves, and for the horny consumers of the inventions, the chief value of the new gizmos, Ossian says, has been "to enlarge the variety and quantity of relational surrogates." If Horniness led the inventors to seek glamorous love-objects in their gizmos, it also led the consuming public to "embrace the gizmos as fetishes." ("What could be more inviting than the telephone for people with nothing to say to each other?") The effect of "all the gizmos going at once" has been "to bring Faerie Land ever nearer."

Ossian thinks it noteworthy that modern communications devices were first promoted by the faeries during the last quarter of the nineteenth century and the early twentieth century, which was also the heyday of spiritualism in America. By the time the Civil War was over, "Americans had concluded that if communication were to occur, it would have to involve either the gizmos or the dead." Ossian believes the mediums did yeoman duty "in soothing American Horniness while the modern media were in development. (The translucent colors of modern television remind him of those on the Other Side described in certain mediumistic transmissions of the last century.)

If the modern gizmos have supplied innumerable Solipsistic Relationships and helped to relieve Horniness, they have also rescued Americans from the feeling they were not getting enough "experience." Henry Ford once remarked that, as a youth in rural Michigan, he never felt he got enough, and nothing could be worse. He looked to the automobile, along with the movies and radio (I quote Ossian) "to stifle the proliferation of rubes."

Ossian acknowledges a paradox in Americans having so often felt that their experiences were too limited, since every American "has as a birthright a supply of experiences." The problem, he thinks, is not so much a shortage of experiences, as "deficiencies of relationship and significance in the ones people do have." These deficiencies have a long history. The reason the American Transcendentalists had such small patience with forms of transcendence devoid of sensuous content, Ossian thinks, is that "their sensuous experience seemed inadequate. The crucial thing for them was not to get *beyond* the world, but to get *into* it in a vital way." The Imagists assumed the same disposition later: "They insisted significance in a poem should be fused into concrete images. Such poetry would prove that one had had compelling sensuous experiences. Being abnormal, or miraculous, those should be the stuff of poetry."

If the character of the experiences, and not the number, is the root of the difficulty, then the automobile is not the solution Ford hoped it would be. Nonetheless, responsive to the faeries as Americans are, they regard sitting still as experience-deprived, and driving about on the national's highways as experiential. For Ossian, the fact that this feeling survives the actual experience of driving is "best accounted for by the distastefulness of the alternative."

Ossian notes, without comment, Loren Coleman's observation in *Mysterious America* that automobiles have a way of coming to obeisant standstills upon encountering Big Foot, a phantom panther, or a UFO. Respect expressed where respect is due.

How, in all this, the brilliance is to be separated from the lunacy, is anyone's guess. As my readers will have gathered, Ossian is guilty of astonishing juxtapositions and lapses in logic. He seems, in fact, to aspire to the intellectual level of the peasants of antiquity, eschewing historical and sociological research of the usual sober, plodding, inconclusive variety in favor of intuitive fireworks. His distaste for documentation is apparent not only in his refusal to document, but in his definition of the footnote as "one unsound opinion corroborated by another."

Still, his style is engagingly vivid, and his specific insights into American life, always surprising, are at times telling. If only there did not hover over everything the dreadful faerie philosophy! Only once in *America, Land of Faeries*, in the concluding chapter, does Ossian confess to any uncertainty about that philosophy. There, he describes how, as he approached the end of his project, he lay sleepless in bed one morning before dawn. Musing on the possibility that his thousand pages might be simple nonsense, dazed with doubts and sleeplessness, he rose and donned his green slippers with the curled toes. Naked otherwise, seated on the toilet, he stared dully at the university below. Opening his morning paper, he read how the Southern Baptists were in that summer of 1984 debating whether sin had originated with women, and whether, if it had, that would be sufficient to prevent their ordination. His mind, trained by long application to its task, filed away this item in the "Faerie Controversy drawer."

Then he turned the page and read an item concerning "Mr. Leakey and his horny archaeological crew at Lake Victoria in Africa who were searching for archaic subhuman life as faerie relational surrogates. They had come upon a cache of almost perfectly preserved ape skeletons, proving beyond a doubt that some old apes did not have tails." Ossian writes, "in a twinkling, my faith in my vision was reaffirmed, for I knew then that I had attained in my studies that kind of certainty that would allow me to deduce from a few simple principles the whole of contemporary social reality."

I would be surprised, though, if many of his readers agree with him. Eccentric and meaningless as the presences around us are, they are obvious.

APOCALYPSE!

Judging from recent science fiction, video games, films and "dystopian" literature, enthusiasm for the end of the world is running pretty high. A Wikipedia article lists some favorite nightmares in popular entertainment: nuclear warfare, pandemics, extraterrestrial attack, dysgenics, divine judgment, devastating climate change, and resource depletion.

Then there are those pesky zombies. An Atlanta neighbor of mine driving home from work did a double-take recently at the sight of a troop of them lumbering over a hill toward him—cast members of a film being shot locally.

Atlanta Journal-Constitution columnist Jay Bookman writes of the zombie shtick: "It touches a deep metaphorical chord to watch 'normal' people fending off assaults from bizarre, mindless, people-like creatures who can't think or feel like we do, but can kill us, nonetheless." Bookman sees a psychological connection between zombies, and the preoccupation of the "America is going to hell lobby" with immigrant invasions from south of the border, gays who marry, and self-styled domestic terrorists.

Watching the world as we know it demolished on a screen isn't quite the same as experiencing the real thing. Theatrical Doomsday isn't psychotic fantasy, either, but where such entertainment is concerned Freud's observations on such fantasy are interesting to contemplate. For him, psychotic fantasies had their basis in a failure of "libidinal cathexis"—emotional withdrawal. ("Libidinal cathexes" are found in marriage, friendship, humanitarian sympathies, and aesthetic response. For people lacking them, the world has effectively ceased to exist. Hence, apocalyptic fantasies.)

The case of Daniel Schreber, a German judge, intrigued Freud. Schreber had published an autobiographical account of his personal psychotic episodes, during one of which he heard a voice announce that a world disaster would occur in 212 years. He was informed later by one of his voices that this calamity had already occurred, and he was the last man standing. The doctors, nurses, and patients around him were hallucinations. (A megalomaniacal sense of specialness often attends such visions, Freud noted.)

Freud's evaluation of Schreber's mentality in *Psychoanalytic Notes on an Autobiographical Account of a Case of Paranoia (Dementia Paranoides)* was that the man had "withdrawn from the people in his environment, and from the external world generally, the libidinal cathexes which he had formerly directed on to them. Thus everything has become indifferent and irrelevant to him." Schreber's apocalyptic nightmare was a metaphor of his subjective state.

However, as Jonathan Lear observes in his study of Freud, *Love and Its Place in Nature* (1990), failures of "libidinal cathexis" are not necessarily simply the result of peculiar psychological development in an individual. Libidinal cathexes presuppose a "world lovable by beings like us"— a "good enough world"— a society responsive in various ways to the human predisposition to relationship. "If the world is too chaotic, too unresponsive, too unloving, then it is unlovable"; and as Freud's studies of the troubled relation between self and society in the modern West suggested, the existence of a "good enough world" was not to be presupposed. A Freudian reading of the apocalyptic visions that abound in our popular culture would be that they are an expression of collective emotional withdrawal, a general failure of libidinal cathexis.

WON'T YOU COME HOME, BILL BAILEY?

I drove along Interstate 20 in Atlanta in my Honda. The dark mass of Atlanta-Fulton County Stadium loomed on the left, the illuminated golden dome of the Georgia State Capitol on the right. I steered the car through a road improvement maze up the exit ramp onto Capitol Avenue, and stopped for a red light by the Capitol.

The passenger-side door of the car opened. A black man stepped into the car, sat down, and closed the door. His entrance was so casual, and the silence afterward so prolonged, I thought at first he had mistaken my car for some other. A fruity smell had come into the car with him.

"Gotta sawed-off shotgun," he said. "Do what I say, or I'll blow your brains out."

"All right."

"When that light change, you drive right on."

"OK."

"Where you going?"

"My wife's waiting for me over there," I said, pointing off toward the university buildings.

"You ain't got no wife!" he barked. The point of the remark was intimidation. There was an oblique reference to Atlanta's large, predominately white, intown gay population.

"I *do* have a wife," I said—it seemed well to insist on that—"and she's waiting for me over there."

"You ain't got no wife. Keep driving, faggot. I need a hit. Get me money, or I'll blow you away!" He wiggled something in his jacket pocket.

Well, this might be *it.* I had always wondered what *it* was going to be like. Looked as if it might be wall-to-wall reinforced concrete.

"Whatcha got on you?"

"I don't know."

He glanced out the back window to check traffic. "Pull over and stop." I did. He wiggled the thing in his jacket pocket. "Sawed-off shotgun," he said. "Blow you away."

I took the wallet from my pants pocket and held it open for him to see: a one dollar bill, a practical joke. I recalled those stories of people getting shot in holdups *because* they had nothing to give.

"That it?"

"Yeah."

"Gotta bank machine card?"

I hesitated. "I don't know." What I really meant was, I was not sure I knew how to use the one I had.

"Do you, or don't you? Don't mess with me, faggot white boy!"

"I have a Mastercard," I said.

"Where's it work?"

"Little Five Points, I think." I never used the card to get cash.

"OK, let's go. No monkey-business, hear what I'm sayin'? I don't want you punching no funny numbers in that machine."

I got back on I-20 headed east. "Should I take the Boulevard exit?"

"No, man, Moreland."

Boulevard would take us to Little Five Points about as directly as Moreland, but not as quickly, probably, and he was in a hurry for that hit.

I drove down I-20 trying to keep the car in its lane, my nervous system under control, and an eye on him. I should be planning something, I thought, but the circumstances were not conducive to the development of schemes.

To gain access to my account at a bank machine, I would need a password, I knew. What was mine? I had a vision of what might happen if I couldn't come up with money once we reached the bank machine. "This is going to sound like a double-cross," I said, "but I don't think I can get money with my card."

There was a several-second delay while he processed this remark.

"What you mean, you can't get money? You want to get yourself killed, honky?"

I tried to explain my difficulty as succinctly as possible.

"Cut the shit, man, get me the damned money!"

I was getting angry myself. "Look, I'm trying to help. What I'm telling you is, going to Little Five Points will be a waste of time."

My dander quieted him. "Where you get cash?"

"I don't, my wife gets it downtown."

"We reached the Moreland exit, and I drove off the freeway.

"Hey, what you doin'? I tell you to turn?"

"You said Moreland, this is Moreland."

He looked around as if not quite sure where he was.

We went up the curved exit ramp onto Moreland. I braked for a red light. "Look," I said, "I know how to get you cash. You know that Kroger store on Moreland?" I pointed south.

"Yeah."

"I can write a check for you there."

"Gotta check on you?"

I usually carried several. I removed my wallet from my pants pocket again, and opened it. Nothing. "I'm not far from my house," I said. "I could get a check there." Should I have said that?

"Where you live?"

"Grant Park."

"Let's go."

Did I really want to do this? Well, I was doing it. I drove south on Moreland to Ormewood, made a right turn, and headed over toward the Park.

"I think there's a fifty dollar limit for cash at Kroger's," I said. "Will that be enough?"

"Yeah."

Really? I might not get out of this alive, but my Mastercard account would be intact.

"Where you live in the Park?"

"Jackson Street."

"Who home?"

"Nobody."

"Better not be... Don't you go for no gun, neither."

"I don't own one."

On Jackson, we passed the middle-aged black woman my neighbors had dubbed "Wonder Woman," a self-appointed vigilante who roamed our streets at night wearing blue Spandex tops. The heavy object that we speculated was a handgun swagged udder-like in the belt purse at her waist.

I pulled up in front of my bungalow and cut off the car motor.

"My old neighborhood," he said quietly. "Old lady and me lived right up the street there when we first marry."

"At Tyrone's rooming house?"

"Next door... You know Tyrone?"

"We swap produce from our gardens in the summer."

"Yeah, he always have that garden. Used to be a Mexican in the basement."

"Chico? He's still around. These days he lives in the shed out back with a German shepherd. What's your name? Next time I see Tyrone, I'll tell him…."

I laughed at my breach of holdup-victim etiquette. "Well, I guess I'm not supposed to ask that, am I?" I punched him on the shoulder lightly.

He shrank from my touch. "Gotta be a faggot if you live around here. Ain't nobody here but old folks, crazy niggers, and faggots."

"And writers," I said.

"Riders?"

As I got out of my car, Uncle Fester, the pop-eyed, double-chinned, bald Addams Family look-alike strode past, hands clasped behind his back, eyes to the pavement. He was wearing his all-weather black turtleneck sweater.

I went up the walk to the house, and onto the porch. I was searching for my door key when my companion realized—none too soon—it would not be a good thing for me to get into my house alone. He got out of the car and, limping slightly, hustled up onto the porch.

I turned the key in the lock and pushed the door inward.

Our cat lay stretched out full length on the loveseat in the foyer: Liz Taylor doing Cleopatra. Her eyes went from drowsy slits to green marbles at the sight of the stranger. She arched her back and hissed.

"May have to blow away the damn pussy," my companion said.

I laughed. In the light of the foyer, I saw a hint of a grin flicker at the edge of his mouth. He was a little taller than I. He had regular features and a short beard trimmed recently. His eyes were liquid—he was on something—but they were not unresponsive. There was something in his jacket pocket, all right, and he kept his hand on it.

"Might be some cash in the bedroom," I said, recalling the small wicker basket where my wife kept spending money sometimes.

I walked to the bedroom at the back of the house. He followed.

Two or three days' worth of socks and underwear festooned the back of a chair. The bed was unmade. A walk-in closet door off its hinges lay horizontally along a wall. A second door I intended to install in place of the other stood vertically against an adjacent wall.

"Excuse the condition of the room," I said, "we weren't expecting company."

Now, he not only knows where we live, I thought, but where the cash is. But what we saw as I raised the wicker basket lid was not likely to trigger fond memories later in a starved drughead.

"Have to write that check, I guess," I said cheerfully.

A small picture frame containing a snapshot of my wife and her sister stood beside the basket.

"That your wife?" he said.

"The one on the right."

"Pretty," he said—in a way that did *not* disturb me.

"Smart, too. A college professor."

"Thought profs made a lot of money?"

"Depends."

I walked out of the bedroom into the dining room. In the distance, John, our neighborhood drunk, was railing at something or nothing, having polished off his bottle and (as one of our neighbors described this nightly phenomenon) "turned into a pumpkin."

The checkbook lay on the mantel. I picked it up. Behind me there were sounds of feet struggling, and then the bedsprings went *scrunch.* My companion must have tripped over something and fallen onto the bed. I tore a check off the pad. "You all right in there?"

He came limping from the bedroom. "Damn house is falling apart."

A wide-brimmed straw hat with an absurd high crown I wore for its shade while revising manuscripts outdoors lay on the dining room table. My companion paused before it, then put it on his head and approached the small mirror mounted in the mantel to consider the effect.

"Like to have me one of these," he said.

"If you want it, it's yours."

His eyes filled with gratitude. It must have been a very long time, I thought, since anyone other than chemical demons gave him a gift.

He turned to me. "You know what's wrong with this whole thing?"

"What's that?"

"I'm trying to do my tough guy act, and I'm getting to like you."

"Well, say faggot white boy ten times," I suggested. Had I overstepped a line?

He shook his head back and forth helplessly. "Man, this is unreal."

"*Tell* me about it," I said, slipping into companionable black English. If I had had no clear plan in mind when I brought him home with me, it seemed now that I could not have done better. In his old neighborhood I was not an abstraction. I knew Tyrone and Chico. I had a wife. I did not have much money, obviously. Bringing him home allowed him to imagine we were of the same ilk. What he did not know would not hurt him: Only by living where I did, as I did, could I afford my regular writer's hit. I shot up with ink. Paper white I might be, but my soul was really quite black. I was already thinking about my next fix, likely to involve him. I considered offering him a beer.

He seemed less in a hurry for *his* fix now. I did not think he had only needed someone to talk to, but the talking had quieted him.

"Need money," he said, "but hate takin' it off a friend."

"What are friends for?"

"You want to go through with this?"

Absolutely, this was getting to be interesting.

We got back into the Honda, drove to Moreland Avenue, and turned south toward Kroger's.

The portion of Moreland Avenue we drove along was

a business strip serving a rainbow population of blacks, poor whites, gays, Asians, Latinos. There were fast food restaurants, liquor stores, used car and used furniture operations—and Value Village, the Amvets used-everything store.

A sign in front of a used car lot:

$20,000 BAD CREDIT? NO PROBLEM
BANKRUPT? NO PROBLEM

What unifies Moreland Avenue, apart from signs on telephone poles for Al's Low-Overhead Plumbing executed, apparently, by Al's own heavy hand, are monsoon-like broken glass rains which sweep over parking lots leaving them sparkling and crunchy.

"Now when we get there," he said, "I don't want you running up to no guard."

"We should buy a few things," I said. "They won't give us cash, otherwise."

We turned off Moreland into Kroger's parking lot.

"Pull right up to the door," he said.

"That's grocery pickup."

"Do what I say, white boy!" He was cranking up the tough guy act again. "Know what they gonna say in there," he muttered. "Here come the crazy nigger and the faggot white boy." He seemed concerned about his image. I wondered if he remembered he was wearing my hat.

I knew about black homophobia, but I'd never seen it close-up like this. For a guy cruising the streets for highs, doing god-only-knew-what with his sexuality, if any were left, what a magnet for projected emotion the gay! To rip off a gay devil downtown would be a job for Robin Hood—God's work almost.

We entered the store. As if to dissociate himself from me, he led the way. He scooped up three packs of cigarettes from a rack at the rear of the store, then turned around and started for the checkout. Bringing up the rear, I coughed.

"Gotta cold?"

"Sinus problems," I said.

"Getcha some this, clear it right up," he said sweetly, reaching to a shelf for a bottle of Pine-Sol all-purpose cleaner which he handed me.

I ran a check through a check-approval machine, and we stood in a checkout line behind a few customers.

"I'm going to be writing the check," I said. "Wouldn't it be better if I held the groceries?"

He handed me the cigarettes. "You make everybody feel this stupid?"

"Stupid? What's stupid?"

"Stupid stealing from a *friend.* I ain't robbing you, you giving me a gift."

Robbing someone at gunpoint seemed to be for him a bit like paying a prostitute to be nice.

"You think I gotta gun?" He wiggled the thing in his pocket.

A thickset little black woman in line looked back over her shoulder and up at us with huge brown eyes, dropped a six-pack of Cokes on the checkout conveyor belt, and sprinted for the door.

The checkout clerk looked after the woman, then turned to appraise with beady eyes my friend and me. She was one of those super-lean Appalachian white women who would look as if we were in a depression even if you tied her to a post—or one of her cousins—and force-fed her lard and honey.

"How y'all doin'?" she said, eyes darting back and forth between the faggot white boy and the crazy nigger.

"I'm alive," I said.

I got my man his money, and we left the store. It had been, by my standards, an expensive evening. I assumed that now he had the money, our dealings were concluded. But he opened my car door and seated himself. "Drop you off somewhere?" I inquired redundantly.

"Freeway," he said.

A fine place, the freeway, for him to drop *me* off. "Are you planning to steal my car?"

"Not now."

The freeway had figured in his original plan. In this instance, as before, he had responded slowly to altered circumstances.

"I'm going up past the Capitol," I said. "I can drop you off there."

"OK."

We got onto I-20 headed west. "You want some of this back?" he said, holding out the fifty dollar bill as if we could slice it down the middle.

"It's yours."

"Mumma would turn over in her grave, if she knew I was messin' round in the street like this.... I come from a good Christian family."

"Me too," I said. "So what are two nice guys like us doing on Moreland Avenue at midnight?"

"Everthin' fucked," he said. "No job, no money.... You gotta job?"

"Not exactly."

"I got two little ones. Old lady and 'em in the projects. I'm gonna take this money, and buy 'em food."

"Good idea."

"You wanna meet my wife?"

The prospect of a guided tour through the projects tempted curiosity strongly, but duty called. "I really have to pick up my wife."

"You can tell your friends tomorrow you run into a crazy nigger downtown."

"You're OK," I said. The other half of the book-title suggested itself: *I'm OK.*

"I want to pay you back for this loan when I can," he said.

"Well, you know where I live."

"Name William Bailey," he said. "If you don't hear from me, you call me at —- —- ——." He repeated the phone number twice, slowly, so I would be sure to get it. "You think I gotta gun?"

"I don't know."

He withdrew from his jacket pocket a rolled-up magazine.

"Good bluff."

"I couldn't shoot nobody.... You believe in Jesus?"

"I believe in Jesus," I testified.

So we were not only two addicts, and unemployed sons of good women, but brothers in Christ.

The semiphore by the Capitol was red—again. I brought the Honda to a halt. Bailey held out his hand, and what began as a white man's handshake melted into the more intimate black brother fingerlock. "Take it easy, man," he said.

"You too. Good luck."

He got out of the car and shut the door. I reached to the passenger-side door, set the lock, and took several deep breaths as I watched Bailey, still wearing my moonshiner's hat, disappearing into the shadows.

Christine, having put in calls to the Atlanta police, the sheriffs of three counties, the emergency rooms, and the Georgia Bureau of Investigation, was waiting for me in front of her classroom building, as usual.

I recounted my adventure on the way home.

"So you were robbed by the famous Bill Bailey?"

This had not occurred to me, but it was so. "Won't you come home, Bill Bailey?" I sang, "Won't you come home?"

LANCÔME OF PARIS HAS A GIFT FOR YOU

In the 1950s, a Western anthropologist couple parting from African Bushmen gave each woman in the tribe enough cowrie shells to make a necklace. There had been no cowrie shells among the Bushmen before that. When the couple returned to Africa a year later, they discovered the women had not kept the shells, but made gifts of them to others. The shells were now distributed in ones and twos all over the region.

Lewis Hyde tells this story in his *The Gift: Imagination and the Erotic Life of Property*, as an illustration of how in primitive "gift societies" goods pass freely from one member of a community to another, rather than being regarded as personal property. The tendency of a gift economy is to strengthen human ties, even as our own economy valorizing personal property tends to weaken them.

However, the appeal of the repressed and the tabooed being what it is, either form of economic life must often seem alluring to those involved in the other, and there exists in Western populations, I think, acute susceptibility before the imagery of gifts and favors.

Some years ago I was working part-time as a manufacturer's representative in Atlanta, work that took me frequently into department stores. In a capitalist society, a retail establishment might seem the last place a subliminal fascination with gifts and favors would find expression. But I became very aware of the many ways in which the "better" department stores represented themselves for their clientele as cornucopia of favors and freebies. The natural response to gifts and favors, or what are perceived as such, is an inclination to reciprocate, and for a shopper in a retail emporium that means, of course, a loosening of purse strings.

One needed to look no further than the décor of these stores for examples of supposititious generosity. Compared with the stripped-down, no-nonsense, cement-floor, exposed-rafter discount store or buyers' club, the department store's interior is a bower of sensuous bliss. Upon entering, a person who has just left the abstractions of the freeways, or the mean streets of a city, finds herself in a haven of finished wood, marble, chrome, neon, mirrors, foil, potted plants, polished glass, artful displays—an environment exotic in somewhat the same way Depression-era movie "palaces" were, and, like them, psychological relief from urban harshness.

In the stores I visited in my work there was an omnipresent, distant, soothing Muzak—maybe even, on occasion, a real life café pianist in tux and bow tie rendering pop classics with a Liberacean density of ornamentation. If there was a bakery shop, the scent of warm cinnamon tinged the atmosphere.

Elevators and escalators! The first place a child of my generation would likely have experienced either of these gravity-defying treats for the lumbar would have been in a department store.

In one store, a banner, "Lancôme of Paris Has a Gift for You," hung over a counter where cosmetics company reps worked on the faces of women, enticing them with free "makeovers" to purchase outrageously expensive creams and lotions. Perfume femmes, mysterious in black suits, stockings, and veils ambled about this spicy domain, atomizers poised to poof. An aristocratically slender fellow with a floppy British haircut would leap from behind a counter at the male shopper to say, "Polo, anyone?"—and hand the mildly startled passer-by a gift ounce of a Ralph Laurens aftershave by that name, intended obviously for neither sissies nor rednecks.

When a retail establishment holds a "sale," it is as if the clientele were being done favors. Cowrie shells on the house!

One might suppose that no one would fall for this ploy in an age of consumer sophistication, but the magic of the term "sale" seems inexhaustible. Its appeal is to emotion, not reason, and for people hard up for favors—and which of us is not, a little or a lot?—the idea of a sale can be very seductive. In truth, though, "sale prices" in the stores I frequented would usually have been described more accurately as regular prices the retailer had decided to advertise. (To give advertised sale prices a veneer of legitimacy, preposterously elevated and suspiciously irregular "regular prices" might appear on merchandise tags the week before the sale, or maybe between December 27 and January 15 when the ambiance of the department store interior is that of a royal tomb.)

The psychology of the sale bears a certain resemblance to that of gift-giving. Sales seem friendly. They seem all the more so if they attract large turnouts, providing opportunities for people-watching, hobnobbing, palaver, and flirting. Sales are often coordinated with holidays (the July 4th sale, the Day After Thanksgiving Sale, etc). This is practical, since people are more likely to shop when not working; but there is implicit in the holiday sale the suggestion that *to celebrate is to shop*; and the sale which mimics gift-giving stirs generous, sociable impulses, as do holidays.

Experienced sales associates described to me strange fits of purchasing they had witnessed sometimes on busy retail floors during sales, when people, as if they feared being left out, would begin buying things simply because others were. There would be a collective will to expenditure and extravagance reminiscent of primitive societies' orgiastic festivals. "It's like spearing smelt during a run," one associate told me; but he added that post-sale remorse in shoppers caught up in the madness probably accounted for the unusually large number of items returned a few days later.

An appliance store in Atlanta once held a "Midnight Madness Sale" on a Friday night from nine PM to one AM. The idea was to draw a crowd to the store on what was ordinarily a very slow night in retail. There was to be wine and cheese for all comers, and television and newspaper advertising for the event conflated the sale with the imagery of parties: bubbling champagne glasses, and pointy-hatted individuals in states of advanced hilarity tooting New Year's Eve-style noisemakers.

It was evident as the witching hour approached Friday night that the ballyhoo had not overcome people's disinclination to shop until they dropped at the end of a work week. Sales associates, spines turned to noodles by twelve-hour shifts, draped themselves over demonstrator washing machines and dryers to nibble listlessly on cheddar and crackers. It was all the floor manager could do to keep some of the guys out of the wine. But around about midnight, two mini-skirted young women with flamboyant hairdos and spike heels bolted through the front door and made their way clickety-clackety over the foyer's marble floor onto the showroom rug, startling the cheese-eaters. "Hey! Vo ist duh party?" Turned out they were Germans who'd just jetted into Atlanta, seen the sale commercials on the television in their hotel room, and taxied out to the store to get in on the whoopee.

***

Walking out of a store with merchandise, having only signed one's name to a slip of paper in a credit-card transaction, bears a certain resemblance to receiving a gift from a distant benefactor. No one *thinks* of a credit card purchase that way, of course, but what one thinks and what one feels are not necessarily identical, and seeking to benefit from this discrepancy, retail chains with their own credit card programs attempt to conflate credit card purchases with gifts. They do this by offering special favors to those who use their cards: advanced information about sales, extra discounts during "pre-sale" periods, telephone-ordering and layaway privileges. (One national chain's credit application form invited the applicant, to "reward yourself" with a card, as if borrowing money at an extravagant rate of interest were suitable recompense for *being* a self.) When sorcery like this works, as often it must, or it would not be practiced so widely, one must suppose a collective susceptibility before the imagery of gifts and favors powerful enough in some people to overwhelm reason

Any time a person acquires something from someone else by any means whatsoever, a relationship of a kind is established, and there is a sense of involvement in a common life. There must often be a fine line between buying something one cannot really afford with a credit-card, and the compulsive shoplifting familiar to department store employees in which people pilfer goods—even things quite useless to them—as antidote to loneliness.

Undemanding merchandise-return policies were one means by which Atlanta department stores worked their magic of generosity. People want to return merchandise they have purchased, or been given, for various reasons. If prevented from making returns because they haven't receipts of purchase, their chagrin will tend to spill over onto the stores where the purchases were made. To prevent this, some department stores at the time I frequented them were refunding the retail price for items returned without requiring proofs of purchase. This was a tremendous boon to career shoplifters whose main problem was not to abscond with goods, but how to realize anything like full retail value for them on the street. A generous return policy made it possible for thieves to return today what they, or a friend, had stolen yesterday, confident of payment in full.

I was particularly familiar with the household small electrics sections of department stores chock-full of gizmos that promised to save people time and labor. That there was consistency between the psychological appeal of these machines, and the role played by favors and gifts in the stores' marketing strategy, sometimes occurred to me.

There was, for example, a "tie carousel" to replace the old-fashioned, serviceable wooden or chrome rack in men's closets. One pressed a button on the battery-powered tie carousel, its small electric motor purred, and ties rotated to facilitate selection.

To replace Grandmother's pan of hot water and Epsom salts for tired feet, there was the "European Luxury Foot Spa Massager" with "powerful whirlpool functions and variable heat and massage options."

There was an "ultra power mixer" for the kitchen with attachments to grind grain, slice meat, strain fruits, and make pasta—supposing anyone had time and inclination to carry out these operations.

To dispel the monotony of chopping and dicing vegetables with a knife, there was the eye-opening "salad shooter" that hacked up vegetables noisily and spat them into a bowl.

Last but not least, there was the automatic, or "self-propelled," vacuum cleaner. For most reasonably able people vacuuming a carpet is not likely to seem exhausting labor, but the self-propelled vacuum's small transmission made it minimally easier to push than the conventional upright. (A *Consumer Reports* article observed of one such machine that it seemed such a modest improvement over manually operated models as to make questionble its substantially higher price.)

What this vacuum could actually do was undoubtedly less important than the illusion of magical assistance the idea of such a machine conjured. A sales associate proud of her ability to sell the self-propelled machines once described for me how she did it. First, she would let a customer push the floor model without the transmission engaged, in which case it was just an ordinary upright vacuum cleaner. Then, grinning widely, she would say, "OK, ready?", and having let the customer's expectation that he or she was about to experience a miracle build for few seconds, she would flip the switch engaging the transmission. Not everyone was charmed by the difference, but the "oh wow!" response she had induced in some people had less to do, she thought, with what they had actually experienced than *what she had led them to believe they were going to experience*. She had practiced a simple verbal magic that depended for its success on the customer's vulnerability before the idea of a mechanical blessing.

It is, of course, not only in department stores that the psychology of the gift is invoked in marketing. The pastime of two elderly petit-bourgeois widows, former neighbors of mine who spent most of their days together, was to order gadgets and gee-gaws from mail-order houses. Mail-order goods that come from afar bear a certain resemblance to gifts. Something to look forward to, they enliven the future.

The widows were partial to the kinds of merchandise featured in a catalogue they once showed me titled, "Things You Never Knew Existed, and Other Things You Cannot Do Without." Items promising assistance in life's tasks filled the pages of the catalogue: a battery-powered "electric posturizer" (a "micro electric feedback device" worn around the neck by people wishing to improve their posture that would sound a small alarm every time a person slumped); a "mind-machine" appearing to consist of a pair of dark glasses with an attached mini-cassette player, providing a "drug-free approach to ultimate relaxation." The widows had ordered from this catalogue the "bionic ear" that could "zoom in on a whisper at one hundred yards," promising further refinement of their already detailed surveillance of neighborhood life.

The items they ordered, like those sold in the housewares departments of department stores, appeared to be capable of lightening burdens or expanding natural powers. They seemed friendly. The widows' mail-order shopping illustrated the phenomenon Marxians describe as "reification" (thing-ification) when natural human sociability is rerouted into what are, in fact, relationships of money and commodities.

The widows, being nearly penniless, could not really afford the things they bought. They had availed themselves of revolving credit plans sponsored by the mail-order companies, and managed to make the required modest monthly payments out of their Social Security incomes. But the balances on their accounts kept mounting, and the daughter of one of the women told me that they would never be able to liquidate their debts

Fortunately, before payment of their debts had been required, both of the widows had died.

AGAPE, EROS, AND I

I.

Anders Nygren's *Agape and Eros* wasn't assigned reading in any college course I took, but every time I entered a university book store back in the late Fifties and early Sixties, there it would be on shelves of texts. The title sounded kind of sexy, and I finally got hold of a copy.

At the time, books offering sweeping historical perspectives that also spoke to some aspect of my personal experience had a tropismic attraction for me. *Agape and Eros* was definitely one of them, unlikely as it might have seemed that a densely-learned seven hundred page work by a Lutheran theologian at the University of Lund in Sweden would charm an Ohio small town youth whose religious background was as sketchy as mine.

Agape and Eros distinguishes between two forms of spirituality Nygren regarded as absolutely distinct: *Agape* (Christian love) is fellowship with God and man in ordinary life. Communal in orientation, it is self-sacrificing, humble, and generous toward both friends and enemies.

Eros spirituality, on the other hand, is individualistic and questing, often impatient of the common life, and esoteric in tendency. *Eros,* in its refined expressions (e.g. belle-lettres, philosophy, art) as in its rudimentary form—sexuality—is acquisitive and fundamentally self-centered. Among literary touchstones were the accounts of sexual desire alchemized as contemplation in Plato's *Symposium* and *Phaedrus*, and in later works of Platonizing Christians like St. Augustine and Marsilio Ficino. *Eros* is the presiding spirit in discussions of what constitutes human happiness in ancient Greek philosophy, and one finds it in the exultant crescendos and climaxes of classical music, the purple passages of great poetry, and the divine nudes of Renaissance painters.

For Nygren, *agape* and *eros* were alternative spiritualities not to be confused with one another or reconciled, although as his lengthy survey of the history of ideas reveals, they often had been. Catholic thinkers, like C.S. Lewis in *The Four Loves*, challenged Nygren's sharp dichotomy and its implicit "sack cloth and ashes" denial of any association between religion and pleasure. Pope Benedict XVI's first encyclical letter, "Deus Caritas Est," in 2006, while not referring specifically to Nygren, addresses the issue. Depending on circumstances, Benedict writes, "one or the other dimension" in human love may predominate, but to represent *agape* and *eros* as discrete rather than overlapping moments in the spirit is "a caricature, or at least an impoverished form, of love.")

When I read *Agape and Eros*, I did not know that Nygren's sharp dichotomy between the two forms of spirituality was a response to a specific situation in Swedish Lutheran theology early in the twentieth century. Certain liberal theologians in Sweden wanted to blend with theology insights from modern anthropology, psychology, and philosophy. Nygren and his colleague at the University of Lund, Gustav Aulen, believed conflating what belonged to reason and *eros,* with faith and *agape*, could only result in confusion among the faithful. Hence their sharp distinction between the one and the other.

Had I known about this issue when I read *Agape and Eros*, it would not have interested me. What appealed to me was Nygren's definition of *eros* as a tradition of thought and sensibility with a long history that was an alternative to Christian spirituality—Christianity being for me at the time the sort of vague, lukewarm atmospheric religiosity of my Ohio hometown, and the "church-related" Middle Western college I was attending. Nygren's purpose was clearly to represent *eros* spirituality as inferior to *agape*, but I was a blooming *eros* man with strong interest in the arts, not to mention girls. For me, Nygren's ranking of *agape* over *eros* was flawed, at least *in situ*, something

I have not really changed my mind about a half century later.

As far as I know, neither in *Agape and Eros,* nor in typical remarks of those who have criticized its thesis, has it been suggested that personal and/or collective circumstances might attract people to one form of spirituality rather than the other, and that a choice between *agape* and *eros* might be other than a free one. But the spirit, theologically correct or not, blows where it lists. Mircea Eliade often emphasized in his studies of the history of religions often made the point that *hierophanies* and *kratophanies* (revelations of the sacred and of divine power) are situational. A primitive Christian enclave in the Roman Empire, a close-knit rural village in Sweden or Norway, a convent or monastery, or an American Shaker or Amish community, would be inherently a congenial setting for *agape* spirituality. Conversely, a fragmented, open modern society which tends, to leave people to their own devices, for better or worse, is naturally hospitable to *eros* spirituality, whether manifest in the arts, scientific inquiry, scholarship in the humanities, or those forms of enlightenment through individual spiritual effort celebrated in the New Age religions.

The shadow cast by spirituality of the *eros* type is, of course, a nostalgia for "community," for which it provides no basis.

II.

Some years ago, my wife, daughter and I were traveling in the Midwest when we stopped for lunch in a small town Main Street restaurant in Wisconsin or Iowa. My daughter, an aficionado of second-hand shops, wanted to visit a Salvation Army store across the street from the restaurant before we returned to the road. We did, and while she and my wife were sorting through racks of second-hand clothing, I went to the shelves of used books.

My eyes were gliding along over mildewed paperback romances and decaying copies of *Future Shock* and *The Greening of America* when they braked at the spine of a slender hardback bearing the name of a fellow who had once been a colleague of mine on the faculty of an Indiana college. At the time, he had been in his late twenties, I was a little older. I knew that he had published fiction in the manner of C.S. Lewis and Tolkien (a type of writing I have always distrusted for its liberation of the imagination from existential limits) but I had not known of this book of his, a collection of sketches and short essays on religious themes.

He had left college teaching some years ago, as I had. According to the biography on the flyleaf, he had been for a time pastor to a small Lutheran congregation in Wisconsin. Leafing through the book I came upon a reference to the Hasidic legend of the Lamed Wufniks, and the remark, "I heard about this legend from my friend."

Indeed he had—*I* was the friend.

The Wufniks are thirty-six righteous poor men situated in various places around the globe who justify humanity before God. Except for them, God would annihilate the whole of mankind. The Wufniks are innocent both of their identity as our saviors, and of each other's existence. If one were to become aware of his special status, he would die instantly and be replaced by someone else, possibly in a distant land. Implicit in the legend was that since anyone might be a Wufnik, everyone must persevere in righteousness lest humanity fail God and perish.

During a social evening at my house some twenty years earlier I had read the legend aloud to my colleague from Jorge Luis Borges' *The Book of Imaginary Creatures*. My reading it disturbed him, as I was aware at the time. I sensed this had to do with his being an Evangelical Christian, and my being neither Christian nor Jew. I was of the *eros* persuasion; he was, ostensibly, an *agape* man. This difference that had made our relationship edgy from the start, although it bothered him more than me.

I cannot recall the chronology of his life with any accuracy, but I remember its elements. Son of a Lutheran pastor in the Midwest, he had suffered acute loneliness while attending a private religious academy as an adolescent. Later, he had attended a conservative Lutheran seminary and pursued medieval English studies. After teaching English for some years, he became a clergyman. Christianity and his literary interests seemed always to have been in some kind of balance or tension.

Like that other Lutheran, Nygren, my "friend" had seemed incapable of imagining socio-economic realities and influences powerful enough to challenge the viability of *agape*. For him, the differences between the world of the Biblical authors and the modern world were superficial rather than intrinsic. There was nothing new under the sun, nothing in human existence that might be of force to drive the life of the spirit out of the one mold into the other. That in certain existential circumstances, *eros* might trump *agape*, or that *eros* might be confused for *agape* (as Nygren believed had occurred often enough in the history of theology) were not possibilities that he had entertained, I think.

I, on the other hand, had studied under a disciple of the Neo-Hegelians Benedetto Croce and R.G. Collingwood. I had read enough in the pragmatists, the existentialists and Marx to have understood that "existence precedes essence." In all such thinking, the uniqueness of the historical moment limits and defines intellectual and spiritual possibility.

My intellectual background having been as different from my colleague's as it was, I don't think he ever had any idea where I was coming from. Innocence like his is common enough in the general population—notoriously among religious and political conservatives—but it was surprising in someone as educated as he, and it begged an *ad hominem*: He had spent most of his life in the cloistered, myth-y worlds of Midwestern rectories, religious schools, and English departments, places in which it was easier to ignore the existential demands on the spirit than in some others. As far as he was concerned, there was nothing in the contemporary world that might challenge the perennial wisdom of the Bible. What was critically important, now and ever shall be, was the individual's relationship with the Savior. He was no Pollyanna. There was ample room for evil in his worldview, as long as its source was the corrupted soul, rather than socio-economic dislocations and the contradictions of modern mass societies of which the Bible has, not surprisingly, nothing to say.

III.

I paid thirty-two cents for my "old friend's" book and took it home to Atlanta with me. When I sat down with it, I opened first to the mention of the Wufniks and me: "My friend said it was an old Hasidic legend. I believe it." (I.e., what was for him a figurative expression of the truth was, for me, just an antiquarian's toy.)

This remark comes in a short piece of reflective prose directly following a sketch describing an encounter between the pastor-author and a second person referred to at one point as "old friend." The latter, though never identified, seems younger and more callow. The meeting of the two occurs at Christmas time. The "old friend" is obviously unhappy.

"What's the matter?" asks the pastor.

In response the friend pours forth "words, memories, accusations." Just about everyone has done him wrong, it seems. "Reasons by the score whirl like blackbirds in the room, making you dizzy with their number." The "old friend" breaks down in tears at one point before regaining his composure to engage in what the pastor regards as some amateurish self-psychoanalysis.

The friend's complaints are never made specific, but what is noteworthy about them for the author is that they involve to external causes and other people's doing. ("People would rather suffer a hundred troubles other people cause than admit to one for which they bear responsibility.") The author listens patiently for a time to the friend's complaints before saying abruptly, "Why did you ask the Lord to leave your life?"

This turn startles the friend.

The pastor-author presses his attack. "When you dismissed the Christ, you denied the cause for Joy," he says, and he goes on from there to pelt his companion with spiritual counsel. The companion retreats into a stony silence. The pastor cannot tell if he is "winning the moment or losing it," but it's clear that he has lost it when the old friend gets to his feet, wishes the pastor a merry Christmas, and walks away from the conversation.

Speaking as if to the retreating friend's back—actually, of course, only to thin air as he writes of the experience later—the author remarks, "I hope you are not giving me a fine show of independence, that you have not chosen to be master of your soul and well-shed of the wimp religion." He declares himself prepared to wait a lifetime if necessary "to see the evidence of Christmas in your face"; and like the person who, thinks of the telling line he should have delivered during a conversation after it has ended, he announces that the old friend's problems derive from having in his soul "divided the One into the Many."

In his literary evocation of the encounter with the "old friend," the author seems very self-assured. However, the friend's breaking off the dialogue revealed strength of a kind, and had the author not been troubled by that, would he have been reflecting on the encounter and writing about it? And *was* the friend's attribution of his woes to external causes necessarily erroneous? Might not the contradictions and dislocations of modern life be as effective in "dividing the One into the Many" as the old friend's alienation from the Lord?

That the reference to the Wufniks and me (the "friend") comes directly after the sketch suggests that the "old friend" and I had probably coalesced in the author's imagination. The sketch was conceivably a fictionalized version of one of our conversations years ago—and a way for him to get in the last word. At the time of our acquaintance I had been seriously distressed by my work as a university teacher, my sense of the futility of the educational undertaking in the humanities *in situ* having become overwhelming. I wanted out, but for several years there had been practical difficulties in my getting out. Feeling trapped, I had sometimes recited for him a litany of woes resembling somewhat that of the "old friend" in the sketch. My emphasis, too, had fallen on the situational origins of my difficulties, and while I could not recall a scene between us as intense as the one the sketch describes, it was clear enough that he disapproved of how I construed my difficulties.

Our conflicting viewpoints ended in a standoff like the one in the sketch—a denouement more problematic for him than me since it isolated him in his faith.

A second sketch in the book resembled the first both in form and content. Here, too, the pastor-author writes in the first person as he addresses an absent "you" with whom he has experienced a failed I-Thou.

One summer night he is standing in a checkout line at a convenience store behind a frowzy, broad-beamed woman in shorts and flip-flops. Awaiting his turn, he contemplates her purchases on the conveyor belt: a Harlequin Romance and a copy of *People* magazine, Ayds tablets for reducing weight and potato chips for putting it on, vitamin pills for health and cigarettes for inducing lung cancer. He surmises reasonably enough that the woman is lonely and miserable. He believes we should all be happy, and will be, if righteous and sanctified. When the woman drops a quarter that lands near his feet, he kneels to retrieve it. As he straightens up, she extends her hand to receive the coin, and says "thanks" before he gives her the coin. *But he does not give it to her!* Evidently thinking that this poor soul could benefit from an infusion of pastoral warmth, he retains the quarter to hold her attention, and says, "Hello, how are you?"

The woman's face melts in response, and it seems for a moment she might burst into tears, but her mood turns swiftly to resentment at what strikes her—also the reader—as impertinent meddling. She grabs the pastor's wrist, claws the quarter from his palm, and makes a getaway. (The author fails to say how the checkout clerk responded to this quixotic behavior of his, and the longer one reflects on the omission, the more glaring it seems. *Security to aisle one! We have a weird man of the cloth trying to snatch coins, or coin snatch!*)

When the pastor retires for the night, the experience at the checkout troubles him so, he can't sleep, and in a disturbance of mind that resembled, I suspect, the one that had prompted him to write the other sketch, he leaves bed to compose a little piece titled, "To a Lady with Whom I've Been Intimate Whose Name I Do Not Know." In it, he acknowledges having made a fool of himself by invading the woman's privacy, but the reader is given to understand that this was holy foolery: "It is the Lord Jesus who asks, 'How are you?'" (In the other piece, he remarks similarly that it had been the Lord Jesus who unsettled the friend, "not me.") As in the other piece also, following his account of the contretemps comes elaborate spiritual advice for the now-absent suffering soul ("you"). But since the "you" in neither piece is likely ever to hear his written advice, the main beneficiary of it must be, of necessity, the writer.

Writing of these experiences, he reassures himself that his behavior, though fruitless in each case, has accorded with his faith. Each sketch describes a failure of *agape* followed by an attempt via the magic of the written word—a manifestation of *eros*—to cheer himself up by placing a spiritual misadventure in the context of faith. Father Mackenzie is darning his socks in the night.

A remark elsewhere in the book might have appeared appropriately in either of the two sketches: "I am convinced that we are not called upon to succeed in this ministry. Which is to say we are called upon to fail vigorously and joyfully." Scarcely surprising, if this is his vocation, that the myth of the Wufniks would appeal to him. The Wufniks are, as he states, "invisible to the world," and as a man of the faith so is he. There is, though, a significant difference. The just Wufniks are invisible not only to the world but to themselves, while the pastor seems all too conscious of what *he* is, and indeed the point of writing these sketches has been rather obviously to reassure himself of the importance of what he is, to justify his actions, regardless of their inconsequentiality.

It crossed my mind that the reason why writing had always been so important for him might have been that in it he could posit and defend without fear of existential contradiction the significance of the outlook and calling that had rendered him invisible. So he thinks of himself as being primarily an *agape* man, but his real commitment was to *eros*? Once when we were academic colleagues he was preparing a classroom lecture on Victorian devotees of "art for art's sake," people who had commonly substituted art for religion, or conflated the one with the other in what was clearly a triumph of *eros* over *agape*. He said to me, "Isn't it wonderful to come across people who think the same way you do?"

This struck me as odd at the time, coming from him, but it squared in a curious way with the sketches I had read: religion *as* art, as verbal magic. But that would be substituting the potency of language and images for communion, *agape* morphing into *eros*. In the great monotheistic traditions, religion is not a collection of potent images that reverberate in the minds of solitary figures, but the embodied life of moral communities.

In the absence of such life, the languages and imageries of those traditions may continue to resonate for the imagination, but in that event *agape* has indeed become *eros.* The romantic traditionalist can participate in the anomic life of modern secular societies—what alternative, does he or she have?—while enjoying in private moments the mood-altering magic of the languages and lore that survive from the religious past.

III

FRANCESCO ROBERTO, FROM HIS DIARIES

I.

Since my return from Naples to the palace at Whitehall, my guitar classes have not resumed, and I intended today to work on my passacaglia. I had only just begun when the note from the Duke of Buckingham arrived. He'd written some doggerel. I was to compose before sundown a little tune to accompany it.

If all the world were paper,
And all the sea were ink;
If all the trees were bread and cheese,
What would we have for drink?

If all the world were sand-o
What would we not lack-o?
And if, as they say, we had no clay,
How should we puff tobacco?

Buckingham's whims are underwritten by His Majesty Charles, so I did not feel I could ignore this request. I tossed off a little melody about as stupid as the lyric. What was he going to do with it? It seemed less likely to serve his philandering than the music I'd written for "On a Girdle" when he was chasing Lady Shrewsbury:

A narrow circle, and yet there
Dwelt all that's good and all that's fair;
Give me but what this girdle bound,
Take all the rest the sun goes around!

Et cetera. But when I delivered my little melody to him this afternoon I learned that the new song was, in fact, to serve a similar purpose. I was informed that my guitar and I were to participate tonight in a serenade of "La Belle Lily," the Queen's new maid of honor who has arrived from Paris to considerable éclat. She is fifteen or sixteen, tall and straight, delicate Roman nose, alabaster complexion, violet eyes, chestnut curls falling to her shoulders. Apparently she was raised at the French court during the exile of the English nobles. They say Louis XIV couldn't take his eyes off her.

I appeared with my guitar in the garden below Lily's window at dusk, as commanded. Buckingham apparently regarded his nonsense verses as the way into a girl's affections. He sang them, I plunked away on the guitar. Lily's Angora cat peered down at us disinterestedly from a windowsill. When the girl appeared, she did not seem more amused by "If all the world were paper" than the cat was, so Buckingham was reprising "On a Girdle" when an errant tomcat—a burly, puffy-cheeked old boy with a swagging gut—came loping down the garden path, spied Pussy in the window, and set up a caterwauling of his own. La Belle Lily giggled, and pulled a curtain across her window.

The disappointed Buckingham gazed upward with furrowed brow and gaping mouth.

Tom vented a short, irritated *meow* and lumbered off down the garden path. Buckingham followed after. My guitar and I brought up the rear.

I had just settled down to work on the passacaglia again today when the young man my patron Sir Samuel Tuke hired to make copies of my handwritten scores appeared at my door. The copies will be used in making engravings from which my collected compositions are to be printed. The copyist was having trouble interpreting some of my scrawls. As we were attending to them, I looked through what he'd copied already. There were a number of errors, a result of his carelessness, not my handwriting, so we dealt with those, too. All the while I was aware of time and life being squandered in the equivalent of funeral arrangements.

The morning was lost. Afternoons and composition do not agree with one another in my experience, so I sat at my fireplace and contemplated how I might convince Tuke that my youthful compositions should not be included in the collected works. I should never have mentioned them. When I did, Tuke seemed to feel it critical to my Eternal Fame that they be included in the collection along with my mature work. I think he envisioned a hoary pedant in some dusty archive pouring over my juvenilia centuries hence and detecting elements foreshadowing my mature production. (How much satisfaction would the Eternally Famous but dead composer find in such discernment?) At the time, rejoicing in Tuke's unsolicited offer of patronage, I was inclined to agree with anything he proposed. I told him that my youthful works—those that had survived—would be in various hands at Naples. He insisted that I go there at his expense and hunt them up. He arranged for my absence from the English court. Off I went.

Alas, a number of my youthful works *had* survived. Staying with my old friend Niballo, I played through them. They are quite worthless, an embarrassment if included in the collected works. I must convince Tuke of this.

My neighbor Madame Labouche's sense of my presence in our building is uncanny. I was tip-toeing past her apartment door en route to mine this afternoon when she popped out. The atmosphere of cinnamon that hovers always about her person emanates, I think, from her ratty, high-piled auburn periwig. She alluded again today to her Stuart ancestry, as she has a way of doing every time we converse. A host of *lumpen* nobles like her reside here in the backwater of the palace complex, I am told. I have no idea who most of them are. They blend seamlessly with the royal porters, scullions, gardeners, harness-makers, and musicians.

I try to stay out of Labouche's way, but once she has me in her clutches I often find her revelations concerning people at court engaging. How she comes by her information is a mystery, because she never seems to leave her rooms. I used to think she must be making up what she told me, but then I would hear others at court speaking of the same matters.

Today she asked if I knew that during my absence in Naples the inebriated Earl of Rochester had shattered King Charles's crystal sundial in the Privy Garden with a club. I hadn't. Charles was so distraught, she said, that he rushed off to Plymouth with Harry Saville and debarked in the royal yacht. There were reports a gale had blown them off course, and the King was drowned. These proved to be false when he turned up on the Isle of Wight.

It occurred to me that Labouche might know more about of Sir Samuel Tuke's background than I do. I asked her about him. She said she would make inquiries with her "sources."

Tuke knocked on my door today to inform me that we have been betrayed: One of the two engravers preparing the plates of my collected works has, without permission, contributed several of my pieces to an anthology being offered for sale by a commercial music publisher.

Why he was so upset escaped me. I pointed out that having a few of my pieces in an anthology might enhance the market for my collected works when they appear. This pacified him, and I hoped he would soon depart, but he had a second concern. Before I went to Naples we had agreed upon an order of the pieces to be included in the collected works. Further reflection since had convinced him that a more artful order was possible, and he described at length his rationale.

I could not see that one arrangement was more desirable than the other, but wanting to get to work on the passacaglia, I nodded my head in agreement with everything he said. This pleased him obviously. The moment seemed right to mention that I did not believe it would serve our interests to include my juvenilia in the collected works. I gave my reasons. I sensed that it was my having accepted his proposal concerning the order of the pieces that now secured his agreement to omit the youthful pieces.

I had opened my door to encourage his exit when he mentioned that he would like me to compose a letter of appreciation for his patronage that would appear in the front material of the collection— "I wish to acknowledge my appreciation for the patronage of Sir Samuel Tuke, without whose support and critical judgment the publication of this work would have been impossible"—that kind of thing.

Finally, he was gone. I placed my youthful compositions in the fireplace and nudged them with a poker repeatedly to assure all were thoroughly ashen and vaporized.

Madame Labouche was providing today a lavish account of the ball celebrating Duke of Monmouth's wedding last night, when I interrupted her to point out that as a member of the musical consort *I had been there*. This did not slow her down—and while performing I had as a matter of fact missed most of what was of interest.

According to Labouche, King Charles had hovered about "La Belle Lily" all night, while his mistress Barbara Villiers (pregnant by him, or *someone*) looked pale and unsavory by comparison. If Charles wasn't chatting up the girl, *Buckingham* was. Labouche speculated the two may intend to share the girl.

Apparently Villiers has taken Miss Lily under her wing and become her confidante and adviser.

Why, I asked, would the older woman befriend her competition?

"Oh, she's very wily, you know. How better fan the flames of love than trying to smother them?"

A confusing metaphor, but I took her meaning.

"She may fancy the girl herself," Labouche added. The English court seems intent on reviving pleasures forgotten since the fall of Rome.

Labouche has learned that Samuel Tuke was a major in Duke of York's regiment in his youth. Thereafter, he wrote an English version of a Spanish comedy received well when produced in London. He had promised more literary production to follow, but since he had apparently only written an article on the nurture of green Colchester oysters which the Royal Society published. This information, coupled with my knowledge that Tuke had recently become a guitar enthusiast and nominated himself as my patron, completed the portrait of a court dilettante. They are a multitude.

Since there is little or nothing these lords and ladies *have* to do, or wish earnestly to do, they distract themselves with various toys, like children. They take up one for a while, then drop it for something else. Those of the Roman Catholic persuasion pass the time of day imagining Protestant plots and conspiracies. When those don't materialize, they gamble at hazard or whist, or devise costumes for the next masquerade. (Currently there is great fascination at court with country dances like "Cuckolds all in a row" and "Gathering Peasecods.") For the younger court women, the avoidance of disfiguring childbirth is a sort of purpose in life. They discuss contraceptive procedures as openly as dinner menus. They are attentive to the nurture and training of lapdogs: "Now Cerberus that was *not nice*!"

The King, bored equally by politics and religion, is rapt in the presence of a beguiling décolleté or some ingenious new mechanical contrivance. I am told that lately he spends long nocturnal hours peering through the telescope at Greenwich, and then sleeps far into the afternoon.

Fireworks over the Thames last night—whiz, bang, boom, sparkle— spiders, horsetails, sunbursts— a heavy scent of gunpowder in the humid summer air.

The royal barges were on the river, and in the light of one aerial explosion I glimpsed Buckingham and Frances Lily on the deck of a boat. A third figure, I realized when he turned my way, was King Charles. I recalled Labouche's speculation that the two men might intend to share the girl.

I took a wherry upriver, and made my way on foot to Covent Garden. After days of periwigs, silk-swathed women, and perfumed lapdogs, rubbing elbows with sweaty humanity and inhaling the honest odor of garbage was a joy. I hopped over the carcass of a rotting hound, and exchanged a soulful look with brother rat crouching by a wall. Almost like being back in Napoli.

I had never before failed to locate Doll Sweet at The White Swan. Nob the taverner told me she's become an actress. Women in various states of undress now appear on the English boards, replacing the boys who played female roles formerly. Nob said Doll's elevation to the stage has not prevented her from continuing with her former line of work, though. He recommended that I wait, since she usually came in after her nightly performance. She did, and we had a pint together while she blathered about the new painted stage sceneries Davenant is creating.

In her room over the tavern, she showed me some newfangled condoms made from sheep's intestines.

I think the experience would have been more exhilarating had she not been describing throughout the plot of *The German Princess,* but 'twould do.

~

A new order from Buckingham today: My guitar and I were to appear at two-thirty this afternoon in La Belle Lily's private chambers.

Lily is the only attendant of the Queen except the King's mistress Villiers who enjoys a private apartment. Its main room features an Italian silk bed canopy, and settees with velvet cushions laced with gold thread. There is a large hour glass on the fireplace mantle. A tapestry on one wall depicts the divine huntress Diana looking on nonchalantly, arms akimbo, while her hounds chew on the bloody Actaeon metamorphosed as a stag.

When I arrived, Buckingham, Lily, and two of the Queen's ladies-in-waiting sat in a circle on an Oriental carpet. "Your arrival is timely, Francesco," Buckingham said. "We need another player for Hunt the Slipper. Put down your guitar and join us."

I have felt from childhood an aversion to all kinds of games. I told Buckingham, I did not know how to play Hunt the Slipper.

"Tosh, there's nothing to it, come join us," he insisted.

I joined the circle. Lily's long-haired cat, perceiving my lap as an excellent cushion, curled up on my thigh and began purring contentedly.

Lily smiled at me. "Minerva's a good judge of character."

"What *kind* of character attracts a cat, though," Buckingham put in.

"He's jealous," Lily said, "because he doesn't get along with Minerva."

"Nor with any cat. But dogs like me."

"Birds of a feather flock together," Lily replied.

Buckingham's assertion that there was *nothing to* Hunt the Slipper was correct. The seated players are "cobblers." The person standing is the customer who says, "Cobbler, cobbler, mend my shoe/ Get it done by half-past two." The customer hands a shoe to one of the cobblers, turns away, and counts to ten, while the cobblers pass the shoe behind their backs one to another. When the customer turns back around, he or she discovers the shoe is not ready, and says, "Then I must have it back." The cobblers say in unison, "To have it back you must find it." The customer then attempts to guess which one has the shoe, and if the guess is correct, the cobbler becomes a customer, the customer a cobbler.

Apparently Buckingham thought Lily would find this game amusing, but her reaction to Hunt the Slipper resembled her earlier response to "If all the world were paper/And all the sea were ink." So Buckingham ordered one of the women to fetch decks of playing cards. I now feared being implicated in a game of basset, or trente et quarante. I was told, instead, to remove myself to a chair in a corner and play my guitar while Buckingham and the girl built a card house. Gladly! I am always trying to find time from my duties at court in which to practice.

I played several preludes, a fantasia, a bouree, and the new chaconne to be included among the pieces I am dedicating to Louis XIV. As I finished the chaconne I glanced toward the construction site. Buckingham was on his knees, eyes narrowed, tongue protruding from the corner of his mouth as he added a card delicately to the top story of the structure.

Lily was staring with open-mouthed fascination at my guitar. Noticing this, Buckingham said, "Why haven't you and your guitar assisted in rearing our house, Francesco? Amphion made the stones of Thebes rise into place with his lyre."

Lily pointed at Minerva who lay on the carpet at my side, paws the air, belly exposed. "Like Amphion, Francesco has tamed the wild animal."

All the seats in the Banquet Hall, even those in the balcony, were filled for my concert last night.

Two years ago, when I first came to London from France, there was little interest in the guitar as a solo instrument. Now aspiring players and aficionados abound. I pass by open doors and hear lords and ladies flailing away at exercises I have provided. The pleasure I find in these scenes must be that of mothers watching their children mimic adult behavior.

The presence of La Belle Lily was in the front row at the concert was conspicuous because while others would be applauding and nodding approvingly to one another after one of my performances, she would be staring at me as if she'd just seen a ghost.

Labouche's gossip *du jour*: Young Lord Hamilton had made a gift of a miniature horse to La Belle Lily and taken her to a remote corner of St. James Park to instruct her in its management. "He's a dead man," Labouche said.

"You speak figuratively?" I remarked.

"He's a dead man."

Hamilton may not be dead, but he was not at court today. His whereabouts are evidently unknown.

The best of my guitar students, young Lord Arran, has excellent musical instincts, and large, slender, strong, wonderfully coordinated hands. He and I had concluded playing a duet this afternoon when I noticed Frances Lily standing in the open doorway to our chamber, Later, he and I were conversing in the hallway before parting when she approached and announced her desire to study guitar.

I mentioned my women's class in accompaniment. (Arran refers to the students as the Dumber Strummers).

This was not what Lily had in mind. "I want to play as *you* do," she said. Arran was standing behind her. His eyebrows went up and down in response to this declaration.

As guitar instructor at court, I am not paid by the head, and I have more than enough would-be guitarists to deal with as it is. But considering her standing with the King and Buckingham I could not deny her request outright. I would have to find ways to discourage her that were less direct.

I inquired about her previous musical experience. She said she had taken singing lessons from the nuns at the Feuillants convent in Paris during the exile of the English court.

"But no instrumental experience?"

Her brow furrowed. "Is that a problem?"

I smiled in a way to suggest it probably *was.* "What you say you want to do will be very difficult. It would require a great deal of your time, a great deal of sacrifice."

She appeared undaunted by this prospect.

Met with La Belle Lily today to discuss guitar lessons. She has the guitar Buckingham played a few times before giving it up for other amusements. I taught her how to tune it, and gave her a copy of Giovanni Foscarinis's guitar method. Foscarini makes assumptions about a student's general musical background probably not to be assumed in her case. I told her to study the introductory chapters and memorize three short exercises before our next meeting.

"Memorize them?" she said, frowning.

"Yes, one can't pay sufficient attention to what the left hand is doing while reading a score," I lied.

The pieces I am dedicating to Louis XIV are nearly finished. I double-checked them today to make sure there is nothing in them that might challenge his limitations as a player that I recall from my days at Versailles. The dedication will hopefully sustain his memory of me. This might prove valuable, should the Bible-and gun-toting Drury Lane barrel-makers, carpenters, and grave-diggers who regard King Charles as the Antichrist contrive to remove his head from his shoulders. The royal musicians would be put to flight. I would need a place to land.

Labouche tells me that Tuke is going about court and town soliciting subscribers for my collected works these days. I had understood that he was to finance the publishing personally. Perhaps he has discovered the costs of production are greater than he had imagined; or maybe he just enjoys the novelty of hustling about playing merchant.

La Belle Lily's first guitar lesson today.

I demonstrated the correct position of the right hand which requires a twist of the wrist at approximately a ninety-degree angle.

"It doesn't feel natural," she said.

"It can be painful."

"Does it become easier?"

I did not answer.

"If I had positioned my hand correctly, would the exercises have been easier?"

"Exercises are difficult *because* they are exercises," I pointed out. "The more of them one plays, the better."

"They're kind of boring."

"Good medicine may taste poorly."

"How long before one can play actual music?"

"Perhaps years," I lied

I proceeded to the subject of growing long right hand nails to pluck the strings. She held out exquisitely manicured nails. "These are not long enough?"

"No." I showed her the claws of my right hand. "As for the left hand, the nails should be shorter than yours are now, lest they cut into the strings."

"Very long nails on one hand, very short on the other?"

"Yes." This seemed guaranteed to offend female vanity.

I asked her to play the exercises I had assigned.

"I tried to memorize them, but I couldn't."

"Well then, read the music."

Even with Foscarini's pages open, she floundered. The exercises are too difficult for any beginner. She wanted hear me to play them. I played them at breakneck speed. She looked at me as if I were a wizard. I put my guitar back in its sack, and prepared to leave.

"Where are you going?"

"The lesson is concluded."

"But we have just begun."

"We can go no further until you have mastered the exercises."

Her lip quivered, and she looked contrite. "I'll try harder," she promised.

It was not the response I had anticipated.

The Russian ambassadors arrived at Whitehall this week. They entered the palace grounds in a grand parade of fine coaches, retainers following on horseback and in wagons bearing gifts to the King which included six ostriches and two caged lions.

Charles ordered the ostriches set free in St. James Park. "What does one feed a lion?" he inquired.

"Quakers," Buckingham suggested.

The court having departed with the Russians to Hampton for the horse races, I have been at liberty the past few days to continue polishing the pieces for Louis, and to enjoy long, uninterrupted hours of guitar-playing. This afternoon I had gone off to wherever it is the guitar takes one when a knocking at my door brought me back abruptly to Whitehall. La Belle Lily stood in the hall, guitar in hand.

At first I did not recognize her. She had her long hair tucked up under a Montero cap, the kind hunters wear, and she wore boy's breeches and a vest. Madame Labouche was peering at us from her doorway, I noticed. I invited Lily inside, but left the door open for Labouche's benefit. Lily surveyed my antiquated furniture, my old oak music stand scarred by age and travel, my unmade bed, my wash basin, and unswept fireplace.

"You didn't go to Hampton with the others?" I asked.

She had, she said, but she had been eager to get back to her guitar.

"How did you *get* back?"

"I walked."

That would have meant passing through some very

unsavory neighborhoods, I observed. She shrugged it off. She'd been working hard on the Foscarini exercises, and wanted me to hear what she had accomplished.

"I understood we were not to meet again until later this month."

She ignored my remark and seated herself on the stool before my music stand. She had mastered the correct right hand position, more or less, and trimmed her left hand nails severely as I recommended. Surprisingly, she had memorized the exercises. She did not play very well, but that she played them at all was remarkable.

"I was better when I was alone," she said.

Madame Labouche glanced into my room as she passed by. I waved to her.

"Did you see any improvement?" Lily inquired.

I said significant improvement took longer than she had been playing.

She was downcast. "I've wasted your time, I'm sorry."

Her diligence, and the progress she *had* made, were touching. I was on the verge of saying she hadn't wasted my time, but held my tongue.

She put her guitar back in its sack. I accompanied her to the door. She looked me in the eye. "I will try harder," she said. I watched her making her way along the corridor to the stairs. It occurred to me that her deepest longing, perhaps, wasn't to be adored and petted, but disciplined.

Madame Labouche, who was peering around the edge of her doorway, caught my eye.

"She's the new maid-of-honor from Paris," I said.

Madame Labouche smiled knowingly. "She's very pretty, isn't she? I wonder why she isn't at Hampton for the races?"

II.

I discover that it has been four months since I made my last entry here. The litigation my brother was pursuing in Naples to recover our parent's house vandals seized during the plague of 1656 required my presence. I had intended being away from London only a few weeks, but delays in the legal process prolonged my visit.

Madame Labouche informs me that during my absence "your Miss Lily" had disappeared from court, causing King Charles to lapse into melancholy, then poetry. Labouche had somehow secured a copy of one of his efforts which she showed me:

TO FRANCES LILY

O gods above how am I undone!
A heavenly goddess made her way to London
Our hearts to o'erwhelm. What'er she be,
She peerless is, as all men will agree.
In her are found as in Eve before the Fall
Beauty, virtue, innocent delight—
And absent now, absent too my light.

Believing Lily must have been kidnapped, Charles had enlisted the services of investigators. They had succeeded recently in locating the girl in a decrepit building at Aldgate whose other tenants were, in Labouche's words, "widows and other inconsiderable persons." Lily's neighbors there had taken her for a young man, because she had cut her hair short and always wore men's clothes. She had done nothing but play the guitar at all hours of the day and night, they said. A night watchman's having heard her playing at three in the morning led to her discovery. She had not been kidnapped, she was living there of her own volition. The Duke of Richmond owns the building. His son the Earl who manages the property, smitten by

Lily, had honored her request to occupy a flat secretly and had been delivering meals to her there personally.

King Charles went to Aldgate and pleaded with Lily to return to court. When she refused curtly to do so, he dispatched Dr. Hodgkinson to examine her and determine if perhaps she were suffering an imbalance of humours a bloodletting might remedy.

Hodgkinson found no natural explanation for her condition. He believed that only a witch's spell could account for her aversion to human society and her obsession with the guitar. (As Labouche imparted this last bit of information, she studied my reaction intently.)

Notes made at Dover as I await the Channel crossing:

I had not seen La Belle Lily since my return to Whitehall from Italy when she appeared at my door late last night, guitar in hand. The transformation in her appearance was indeed remarkable. She had very short hair. She wore loose, pleated britches, a short coat and a slouch hat. She looked like a boy. More than her hair and attire had changed. Her lips that had been full and rather pouty seemed to have contracted. The masculine firmness in the expression of her eyes, and the set of her jaw, spoke of prolonged, willful effort. That a witch's spell might indeed have produced such a transfiguration did not seem impossible.

I glanced down the corridor. Labouche was not on the qui vive for once, so I conducted the girl into my room and shut the door. Without saying a word, she seated herself on the stool in front of my music stand and began playing from memory, with precision and finesse, music I had composed in Venice years ago. That she could have accomplished this in so short a time was scarcely imaginable.

I could not conceal my surprise or withhold expressions of admiration, and the smile my approval brought from her was the sun coming from behind a dark cloud. I was standing by my window when she lunged toward me in an appreciative embrace that caught me off balance and thrust me back against the window. Then she packed up her guitar and left my room.

I was watching from the window as she entered the dusky courtyard below, guitar in hand. She had gone only a short distance when I saw a second figure issue from the shadows to confront her. When he pointed toward the window where I stood, and fixed me with a keen look, I realized he was King Charles.

I departed the palace under the cover of darkness with only my guitar, my manuscripts, and a few personal items in a carpetbag. Soon I will be aboard the ferry to convey me onto French soil. I can only hope that the pieces I have dedicated to Louis XIV meet with his approval.

NEW LIGHT ON THE BALL IN BRUSSELS

Lord Byron describes in *Childe Harold's Pilgrimage* the Duchess of Richmond's ball at Brussels in June, 1815. The Duke of Wellington, commander of the allied monarchical armies of Europe, and the cream of his officers, attended.

> There was a sound of revelry by night,
> And Belgium's capital had gather'd then
> Her Beauty and her Chivalry, and bright
> The lamps shone o'er fair women and brave men;
> A thousand hearts beat happily; and when
> Music arose with its voluptuous swell,
> Soft eyes look'd love to eyes which spake again,
> And all went merry as a marriage-bell.

That year Napoleon had escaped exile on Elba and cobbled together yet another army, and when it was learned during the ball this army was advancing on Brussels, Wellington's officers fled to their military posts. The next day at Quatre-Bras some died still wearing their dress uniforms. That battle was inconclusive, but Napoleon's final defeat at Waterloo came a few days later.

According to Byron, the distant roar of Napoleon's cannons broke up the party. In fact, a message to Wellington from Prussian commander Blücher had that effect. Byron was also mistaken in suggesting the sudden call to arms interrupted *dancing*. It is clear from the diaries of my ancestor Matteo Galante, a virtuoso guitarist, that it was the concert performance by him that was interrupted.

I had never paid much attention to Galante's diaries before inheriting them from my Aunt Margolia after her death. They had come down through generations of my family in

Europe and America as sacred relics. Old things, just because they're old, have a way of inspiring reverence they do not necessarily warrant. Matteo's diaries are cases in point. They *might* have been more interesting than they are, undoubtedly, had he been a person of wider sympathies and interests, because he was moving in the same Viennese musical circles as Beethoven, Schubert, and Hummel; and the Napoleonic wars were exploding all around him.

His references to his musical contemporaries are generally slight and contemptuous. He puts down that songbird Schubert as a fat fairy (*omosessualoi grosso*). His response to Beethoven's works was guitaristic: "crudely bombastic." (He had the same view of the French Revolution. Events associated with it seem to have interested him only when they disturbed his performance schedules and itineraries.)

On the other hand, there are tediously prolonged diary entries on the debate then current among guitarists as to whether the guitar should have six strings or more, alternate left-hand fingerings of certain difficult passages in the guitar literature, and remedies for muscular strains and aches he had encountered in his eight-hour-a-day practice regimen. ("The guitar is a delightful mistress," he writes, "but she requires a lot of attention"—*molto considerazione*.)

His account of performing at the Duchess of Richmond's ball is a rare engaging entry in the diary. He had been invited to perform in Brussels by the Duchess on the recommendation of Viennese Princess Caroline de Kinsky. An abhorrence of travel is a leitmotif in the diaries, and the trip by coach from Vienna to Brussels back then took about a week. His main reason for agreeing to suffer the ordeal of reaching Brussels seems to have been that the generous payment promised by the Duchess would free him f0r months from his "idiotic students."

There were delays en route to Brussels. A horse in full canter on an open stretch of highway dropped dead, nearly overturning the coach and breaking a wheel. Later, Matteo and other male passengers had to assist the drivers in hoisting the coach out of a mire.

By the time he reached the Duchess's palace, the ball was already in progress on a lovely, mild June evening with roses in bloom, and a full moon overhead. The abrupt transition from motion to stasis, coupled with the fact that he had eaten scarcely anything that day, lent a phantasmal aspect to the long-necked, pale-faced Duchess who greeted him at the palace entrance and stared at his muddy pants.

He was to perform during an interlude in the dancing before supper, she informed him. There was time for him to wash, dress for the occasion, and warm up the guitar, before the Duchess led him onto a low stage in a drawing room fragrant with wine and roses. She introduced him. He announced he would play three of Giuliani's *Rossiniane* (fantasias on themes from Rossini) and his own variations on "Folies d'Espagne."

Several times in the diaries he refers to the importance of a soloist being able to "descend into the well," as he puts it—achieve a state of concentration that eclipses awareness of an audience and prevents nervousness. That night, his longing for musical peace being intense after the ordeal of travel, such concentration was easy for him. The moment he began playing, the coordination of hands, music, feeling, and guitar was extraordinary. He found himself playing allegro passages faster than he would have ordinarily, knowing that he could. ("It was as if a nimble spirit had taken possession of my hands.") He played with abandon, eyes closed. Not wanting this ecstasy disturbed by applause, he proceeded directly, without break, from the crescendo and éclat at the end of the first *Rossiniane* into the second, and similarly from the second to the third, and then directly into the six variations on "Folies d'Espagne"—his run-on performance a prolonged fantasia impromptu. Having come to the end, "like a person reluctant to abandon the sweet dream from which he must awake," he remained seated with his eyes still closed, the guitar across his lap.

Applause was oddly delayed. He surmised that his brilliance had produced an awed silence.

At length, a single male voice rang out, “Bravo!”

Matteo opened his eyes.

The room was empty, except for a smiling elderly retainer leaning on a broom, an assortment of empty wine glasses on small tables, some overturned, and the furniture on which his audience had sat.

“That’s some guitar you play, sir!” the old fellow enthused.

Galante cleared his throat. “Where’d everybody go?”

“Well,” the janitor said, “what I hear is, the men’s gone off to fight Napoleon. The ladies is upstairs cryin’ and carryin’ on.”

Matteo wondered what portion of his transcendent performance the audience had missed. Their failure to enjoy the whole of it would have been tragic had *his* experience of it not been self-sufficing.

The sweeper went about his chores whistling the melody of the third *Rossiniane.*

Matteo leaned his guitar against the bench on which he had been sitting and stepped down from the stage. He made his way to the back of the room, feeling as if he were afloat on air. A delightful spicy, meaty fragrance wafted from an adjacent room on his left. He peered through the doorway at a long candlelit table covered with a white cloth, silver place-settings, and flower arrangements. An elaborate untouched buffet stood along one wall. He entered the room, selected a plate from a stack of china, heaped high lobster, and suckling pig in mustard sauce, and poured himself a goblet of red wine. Somewhere in the distance a woman was sobbing pianissimo.

Seated at the head of the table, he tucked a napkin into the neck of his performance shirt, and dug in with knife and fork. *Napoleon*? Last Matteo had heard, that French rascal was moldering on Elba.

V

A WEDDING IN ATLANTA

The dimensions of the church on Peachtree Street weren't those of Chartres or Notre Dame, but the design was studiously Gothic—nave, transept, choir, ambulatory, apse, stained glass windows—the works. The illusion of being in medieval Europe was fairly compelling. One look at the place would have brought from Frank Lloyd Wright his standard indictment of meretricious, allusive Victorian-American architecture: "Sentimental!" But like the shopping mall that mimics a "classic" American town center, or the sad-sweet prenuptial organ music we were hearing, the architecture expressed the perennial American yearning for transcendence of commerce and flux.

I recognized a few wedding guests from a party the groom and bride, Jake and Clarissa, threw when they were still living in our neighborhood. Most, though, were strangers to me, and probably to one another. Jake was from Little Rock, Clarissa from Indiana. Many of the guests were undoubtedly out-of-towners, and each of us was likely connected with the bride and/or groom only at some one point: familial, educational, vocational, recreational, or neighborly. We were a cast of extras necessary to perform the sacrament.

"Who gives away the bride?" the pastor boomed in a deep voice. (Historically, the rite had finalized an exchange of property.) Clarissa's father replied, "Her mother and I."

Clarissa's income as a television producer at CNN probably exceeded not only her retired father's, but Jake's. She was really quite capable of giving herself away—even buying herself a husband. But I suspected that deep-down Clarissa was just an old-fashioned girl. Besides, the language of the rite wasn't to be taken literally any more than the church architecture. A formal wedding was like reading *Paradise Lost* in an English class, or political candidates going on about "family values."

The pastor, having pontificated on the responsibilities of wedded partners, and the virtues of humility, sacrifice, and compassion that would disqualify most Americans for economic survival, he, Jake, and Clarissa made a symbolic retreat from the guests to the altar where Jesus hung dependably on his cross, to exchange of vows and receive Holy Communion.

Then the pastor invited "all baptized Christians" to the altar rail to receive Communion. Some went forward, some didn't. The pastor lit a "unity candle." Some melancholy group hymn-singing—and a vigorous organ rendition of Mendelssohn's wedding march spirited bride and groom out the back of the building.

Christine and I shared a table at the reception with a young Ukrainian couple, Dmitri and Judith, employees of a telecommunications firm in Atlanta; a reticent young Asian woman; and Myrtle, a plush, elderly black woman in a faded smock who revealed her home was in one of Atlanta's public housing projects. (Clarissa, Myrtle explained, had adopted her in the city's "Adopt a Grandmother" program. "It's a nice program.")

The Ukrainians had just returned from their first trip home to Eastern Europe since coming to the States as students eight years ago. They had spent some time with relatives in Poland. Christine mentioned our daughter was teaching English in Prague, and had visited Cracow, and the Holocaust Museum at Auschwitz.

"They think one of my great-uncles died at Auschwitz," Dmitri said. He brushed aside Christine's embarrassment. "It's as hard for us to imagine anything like that as it is for you." He raised his wine glass. "To world peace."

We drank to world peace.

The Ukrainians, my wife and I, discovered we'd all read the Russian classics. There was a conversation about *Crime and Punishment* in progress when Christine noticed its exclusion of the other guests at table. She changed the subject, observing how lackluster the hymn-singing at the church had been, compared with lively performances by the choir of the African -American Baptist church up the street from our house. She smiled at Myrtle.

"Tell us the truth, Myrtle," I said. "What do black folks think of white church music?"

Shyness and good manners made her reluctant to answer, but I egged her on until she said, "Well, they think it kind of drags," bringing appreciative laughter from around our table.

Dmitri glanced at his watch. "This has been fun. I regret leaving, but we have a second social engagement this afternoon—and since it's my boss's party…." He and Judith wanted to exchange e-mail addresses with Christine and me, and the exchange was made. I doubted we would see each other again, though. They lived in a northern suburb remote from our intown neighborhood, and the disparity in our ages, and lack of common projects, meant that attempts at friendship would almost certainly fizzle, I knew from experience.

As they got up from the table, the rest of us prepared to scatter, too. I commented on the all-American character of our group. The young Asian woman who'd not spoken but had been attentive to what others were saying, smiled.

Are you Japanese?" I asked.

"Half-Japanese, half Armenian," she replied, evoking valedictory laughter.

Christine and I were circulating aimlessly among the guests when we met up with Kim Lee, an academic colleague of hers. Easing away from the conversation they were having about a shared committee assignment, I linked up briefly with Jake the groom who introduced me to Clarissa's ministerial-student brother from Portland, an Atlanta Symphony musician obviously ill-at-ease with people other than his cello, and a downsized insurance company executive from Milwaukee.

I thought the contemplative black man with the full beard seated off to one side of the gathering an interesting specimen. When I approached him, he seemed at first unwilling to abandon his privacy, but I got out of him finally that he was a South African novelist teaching a seminar in creative writing at Georgia State University that summer. Clarissa had been taking a course from him.

He'd been raised in an African village and educated in English schools. "The textbooks were all English, of course. One informed us that David Livingstone had failed to locate the source of the Nile. When I told this to my father, he couldn't stop laughing. Our ancestors had known the source of the Nile for thousands of years."

The novelist was acquiring a new wife to add to his present collection of three. We discussed the relative merits of polygamy over against American-style serial divorce, and agreed that the former was probably less expensive in the long run.

He was funny on the subject of St. Paul's "lust of the eye": "I don't choose to feel desire. Obviously it exists for purposes that are not mine."

"With all those wives, you must have some children."

He smiled. "My friend, I have begun to lose count."

"What are they for, do you suppose?"

His eyes narrowed. "*For*?"

"I put the question, because we seem to be producing a great many more than our economy can support—and I know there are starving children in Africa."

"God, so to speak, requires children," the novelist said. "I feel this in my loins."

"To increase the quantity of misery in the world? Swell the number of beggars in the streets?"

"We never know what is in store for them. There are many surprises."

"They exist for purposes not ours, like the feeling in our loins?"

"Yes."

My wife appeared at my side. I introduced her to the novelist. "He has three wives, and he's acquiring a fourth."

"Your husband should have at least two or three," said the grinning African.

"That's cool," Christine said, "if I get a couple husbands."

"Might I be so bold as to apply for the position?" the African said.

Christine took a step back and studied him appraisingly. "Well, I *do* like a man with a beard." She turned to me. "I was telling Kim Lee about Sarah's travels in Europe. He said he couldn't believe we were old enough to have a daughter her age. I thanked him for the compliment. He said, 'Well, of course, in my culture I have just insulted you.'"

TEACHERS, PRIESTS, AND THE FATAL STRATEGIES

When male teachers hit on students—well, *you know men*. What makes recent reports of sexual liaisons between high school teachers and their students in America startling is that the teachers are women, and in some instances married women bearing no physical resemblance to the stereotypical old maid schoolmarm.

More amazing even than discoveries of teachers and their charges making out after hours in classrooms, or the backseats of cars, is that certain of these women want to *marry* their underage lovers, or have already done so.

As I am writing, *WorldNetDaily* has at its website a long list of these "predators on campus," along with their pictures. Dour police mugshots of women with bedraggled locks, mix with prim, smiley yearbook snapshots. In media accounts of these misalliances, titillation about balances outrage, an ambiguity that probably reflects public opinion pretty faithfully.

On the one hand, there is the inevitable male blogger quip, "Where were these women when I was in high school?" Otherwise, there is moral condemnation, combined perhaps with speculations about the psychological hang-ups of the offending teachers: their wish to improve on their own sorry teenage mating experiences, their eagerness to establish rapport with blasé students in any way possible, the pleasure they find in exerting control over the malleable young, or perhaps a need to compensate unfulfilling marriages.

The faculties of the public schools I had attended in the mid-twentieth century often comprised educated, unmarried women. They were the equivalent in a mainly Protestant town of teaching nuns, and it must sometimes have been provocative for them to be rubbing elbows with nubile young charges. (At a reunion of my high school class some years ago, there was talk of erotic overtones in the relationships of certain teachers and their students when we were in school. Max Wylie, a native of my hometown, described in a 1950 novel, *Go Home and Tell Your Mother,* what was rather obviously his personal early twentieth century experience of seduction by his buxom elementary school teacher. The local library kept the novel behind the librarian's desk, because every time copies were placed on open shelves they disappeared.)

In the past, though, the wall separating the intimate lives of the young and their their teachers was generally quite solid. If that wall were to have fallen to the trumpeting of lust, the results would likely have been ruinous both personally and professionally. That this remains the case makes very remarkable the willingness of so many women to pursue these relationships.

While media reports focus generally on the individual teacher's immorality and hangups, the number of these cases suggests a pathology of a more general, societal kind. There is a resemblance between relationships of female teachers and male students, and Catholic priests' seductions of the young, also much in the news. In either case, an exemplary cultural role is subverted. That subversion must, indeed, be critical to the *frisson* enjoyed by the offending teacher or priest.

Apropos, French sociologist Jean Baudrillard has written of "fatal strategies" operative in modern Western societies beneath their official rationality and positivity: a sort of collective death-wish. In Baudrillard's view, which resembles that of the historian Toynbee, societies, like everything else in animated Nature, are cyclical, periods of rising energies and successes followed by periods of decline and decay. Among the symptoms of decline Baudrillard describes in his *Fatal Strategies* is a "secret disobedience of a group to its own principles… profound immorality and duplicity, the principle of Evil active in all the great mythologies to affirm not exactly the supremacy of evil, but a fundamental duplicity which demands that any order exists only to be disobeyed, attacked, exceeded, and dismantled."

A willful de-sublimation of sexuality is one fatal strategy, and Baudrillard would certainly see seductions of the young by teachers and priests as cases in point. (Other fatal strategies include unregulated economic activity, let the chips fall where they may; the political indifference of the masses; public mockery of ruling parties; terrorism; the "lewd systems" of gambling, entertainment, fashion, and advertising; and the love of change for its own sake whether in political leadership, gadgets, or art movements.)

It is easier to observe "fatal strategies" at work in a society than to account for their genesis; and to explain what would motivate a specific female teacher or priest to become an agent of cultural subversion is no doubt usually impossible. But the numbers of people in positions of authority demonstrating enthusiasm for such subversion suggests that explanations focused on individual psychological difficulties or moral failures are inadequate. Considering the abundance of observable "fatal strategies" in societies like ours, such explanations smack of scapegoating.

CREMATION AND BURIAL

Americans increasingly prefer cremation to burial, an authority on these matters remarked in an interview on National Public Radio.

Why so? asked the interviewer.

There has been, the authority speculated, a change in the way Americans view the soul in relation to the body. In the past, they had been likely to think of the body as closely related to what a person *is* in the past. Lately, many had embraced a view of the soul resembling the Hindus', which emphasized the soul's distinction from the body.

Well, maybe, I thought. It seemed to me doubtful that an altered philosophical or theological outlook explained why so many now preferred cremation to burial. There was a better explanation in the fact that our society has become so radically mobile.

My mother in Ohio, who lived to be over ninety, spent her entire life in one Ohio town. As far as I know, she had never once considered cremation as a personal choice. I once visited with her the country churchyard near the town where four generations of my ancestors lay buried.

"There's your father," she said, pointing to a hunk of marble with Dad's name on it. I didn't feel that my father was "there"; and the idea of *my* ever being buried there amid my rural ancestors seemed preposterous. A mobile, urban American of my generation, I felt no affinity with that piece of ground and those people.

In fact, the idea of being stuck in the ground anywhere in particular seemed absurd. I mean, *why there*? The contrasting idea of having most of one's bodily substance dispersed into the air by incineration, if not exactly charming, squared better with the life on the wing I had lived.

An excerpt from a piece of mine the *North American Review* published some years back addresses the point: "A person moves around a lot. When he thinks of death, he does not think of joining the clan on the hillside, or of flowers being placed overhead by female relatives with nothing else to do Memorial Day afternoon because the menfolk are watching the Indianapolis 500 on tv. Appropriate that his final resting place should be a jar of ashes on the mantle which the wife or husband can carry about when moving. My Uncle Davis, who had traveled around all his life, through many states and wives, met his end in a sixteen car pileup near Johnstown on the Pennsylvania Turnpike. His first choice of a final resting place would have been the Medical College of Virginia, but the Medical College of Virginia was interested in typical specimens, so Uncle Davis was cremated, and his ashes fell into the hands of my cousin Libby in Marion, Ohio. She did not especially want them, or know what to do with them. While vacationing in the South, she emptied the jar in Pensacola. That was where Uncle Davis had lived for a time."

THE BUDDHAS AT BAMIYAN

In March, 2001, explosives destroyed two huge, ancient statues of standing Buddhas in cliff-side niches overlooking the desert near Bamiyan in Afghanistan. Al-Qaeda terrorists, believed to have had the blessing of the then-ruling Taliban, were responsible. Both groups were exponents of Wahhabism, Islamic fundamentalism. The iconoclasm of Wahhabism resembles that of movements that have arisen within Christianity from time to time to condemn idolatrous attachment to religious icons and relics. (Wahhabism also opposes image-producing communication technologies: television, radio, films, and the Internet.)

It was not obvious, though, why the Buddhas in the desert were attacked, since they were not objects of worship. Buddhism had not had a following in Afghanistan for a thousand years, and as far as locals were concerned the statues were just historical artifacts and tourist attractions. Equally mysterious was the fact that at about the same time the Buddhas were exploded, antiquities in a Kabul museum exempted previously from the Taliban's campaign against idolatry had also been destroyed.

Whatever the point of these destructive rampages, the Taliban clearly wanted the results publicized, because they loaded foreign journalists into an old government prop-plane in Kabul and flew them to Bamiyan to see the exploded Buddhas. Soon what had happened was all over world media.

What generally distressed Westerners was not the offense to Buddhism, but the loss of art treasures. Tut-tut-ing abounded. The United Nations Educational, Scientific, and Cultural Organization (UNESCO) issued a statement lamenting this "cultural tragedy for the world." Phillipe de Montebello, director of the Modern Museum of Art in New York, fumed, "There is no precedent for a country decreeing the physical annihilation of its historical patrimony." *Orientations*, an online magazine devoted to Asian antiquities, posted angry responses from readers at its website.

It had crossed my mind the target of the iconoclasts' fury might have been the First World's idolatry of the "cultural heritage," when I came upon a pointed little essay online ("Their Iconoclasm, Our Idolatry") by Crispin Sartwell, a professor of philosophy at Dickinson College, which argued exactly that point. "We in the West," he wrote, "have to some degree replaced religion with art." Art for us "is something holy that must be preserved: housed in fortress-like [temple-like?] buildings to which we make pilgrimages…. We have made of art a cult, and the work of art is our idol.... The Taliban know very well how to horrify us; they know our religion [of culture] and they know their own." The real issue was the conflict between the amoral aestheticism of the "arts community," and ethical Islam.

This interpretation was confirmed by remarks of Syed Rahmatullah Hashimi, a senior advisor to Taliban leader Mullah Omar at the University of Southern California shortly before the Buddhas were exploded. Hashimi described how the already great sufferings of the Afghan people after twenty years of war and drought had been intensified when the United Nations Security Council, goaded by Russia and the United States, enacted economic sanctions against the Taliban. Then, a delegation of moneyed Europeans, accompanied by a UN representative, appeared before the Afghan Council of the People offering funds to repair damage to the Buddhas at Bamiyan weather and vandalism had caused over the centuries. The Council's response was that if such funds were available, they should be devoted to saving children dying of malnutrition—not to repairing statues.

Hashimi described in pungent colloquial English what happened next: "These guys said that, no, that money is only for the statues. And the people were really pissed off. They said, if you don't care about our children, we are going to blow those statues. What would you do in these circumstances? You are under sanctions, and then the same people who have imposed sanctions are coming here to rebuild statues. I talked to my headquarters today. They said the statues have not been blown so far. But the people are angry. They are really angry, they want to blow them.

And so they did.

TRAVEL AND PURPOSELESSNESS

The traveler's vision of a carefree life on the road only lasts until he sets out, Samuel Johnson wrote. Then he discovers "the road is dusty, the air is sultry, the horses are sluggish.... The inn is crowded, his orders are neglected, and nothing remains but that he devour in haste what the cook has spoiled, and drive on in quest of better entertainment." (*The Idler*, 58)

Comparable unpleasantness attends modern travel. The tedium of superhighway driving, or sitting in a plane for hours on a runway awaiting takeoff, can be barely tolerable. Managing cash in a foreign currency requires constant doublethink. In online reviews of "luxury" cruises complaints abound. ("The menu choices were limited. I asked for an entrée without potatoes. I was told it could not be done." "There were little crawly creatures and cockroaches in the bathroom.")

People who relish traveling "for pleasure" will do it, nonetheless. Travel writer Lawrence Osborne's explanation of this in *The Naked Traveler* (2006) is that travel, by focusing attention on the "logistics of the journey itself in all their maddening detail and stupidity," relieves the mind of more serious concerns that require people's attention ordinarily.

Novelist Michael Critchton remarks in his *Travels* that when he was *not* traveling—even if only reading a book, keeping a luncheon date, or seeing a movie—he always had some purpose in mind. Traveling, on the other hand, was refreshingly whimsical. The Renaissance essayist Montaigne said the same: Traveling, he could forget the management of his French estate where something was always going wrong that required his attention. Itinerary and destination were virtually irrelevant for him as he gallivanted around Europe on horseback. He was never all that interested in arriving somewhere. Arrival was always a bit disappointing, in fact. He just wanted to where he had not been before, and nearly anything of interest could take him off his route. If the left hand road was bad, he took the right; and if he found his travels one day had been circular, returning him at nightfall nearly to his starting point in the morning, that was fine.

Psychologist Wilhelm Stekel described what he called "wandering mania," which isn't travel for pleasure but bears a psychological resemblance to it. He noted an ambiguity: Was an obsessive wanderer escaping from something, or pursuing it? My personal view, as a recovered wandering maniac, is *neither*. As long as wandering continues, the wanderer, who has abandoned the regimens and obligations life in time entails, is free of both past and future.

There was a woman in my Ohio hometown people called "Kit" who would be seen rambling the streets of our town at all hours of the day and night, eyes downcast, a large shopping bag in each hand. People had no idea who she was or where she lived. She never acknowledged anyone she passed in the street, never looked into a shop window or entered a restaurant. There were, inevitably, rumors and speculations. She was filthy rich and carried a fortune in the shopping bags; or she was dirt poor and homeless and carried everything she owned in those bags. She had an expensive car garaged somewhere and a chauffeur who drove her sometimes to distant places. The death of a child, or a broken marriage, had unbalanced her. All such speculations intimated that she was "crazy." I doubt if anyone in town entertained the possibility that she might have been a saint quite content with her rootless anonymity.

There is, though, is a certain similarity between a wandering maniac (also a person traveling for pleasure) and the wandering monks in certain cultures. Both East and West vagrancy has at times been associated with transcendence. Maribel Dietz, noting the many variations on the theme of the Christian's homelessness in Scripture, speculates in

Wandering Monks, Virgins, and Pilgrims: Ascetic Travel in the Mediterranean World, A.D. 300-800 that as the Roman Empire was disintegrating, construing the spiritual life as vagrancy must often have been a making a virtue of necessity. Mandaean Gnosticism celebrated the "alien" or the "stranger" for whom the material world was a foreign country full of danger.

Daniel Caner in his *Wandering, Begging Monks* (2002) mentions the case of an Egyptian monk who debated with himself the alternatives of wandering the desert or foreign lands, or locking himself in his solitary cell. In either choice the purpose would be to reduce involvement in the physical world nearly to the vanishing point, with the anticipation of spiritual rewards.

Ch'an Buddhist master Po-chang Hui-ha-i: "Should your mind desire to linger somewhere do not follow it and do not dwell there, whereupon your mind's questing for a dwelling place will cease of its own accord." In the monkish view, the trouble with dwelling somewhere was that it involved one necessarily in relationships, obligations, routines, getting and spending—*the world.*

If the non-dwelling life may have transcendent implications, it can also soothe the pain of not knowing what one's role in one's time and place is supposed to be. That was the case for me during a period of wandering mania in my late teens and early twenties.

At the time, Jack Kerouac and his friends, who were as uncertain where they belonged in the American scene as I was, had popularized "going on the road." It was their example, in part, that had led me to hitchhike three times from the Midwest across the United States—once to New Orleans, once to Denver, once to Cape Cod. My destinations were as arbitrary as Montaigne's. To be on the road, rather than somewhere in particular, was the thing.

A young man's footloose wandering naturally prompted fantasies of what Henry Tuckerman describes delicately in an 1844 essay ("The Philosophy of Travel") as "the cheering salutation of the passing peasant girl." I never experienced such a salutation, but I remember standing one early spring morning on the Main Street of Laurel, Mississippi with my thumb in the air as people on foot and in cars were rushing past to work or school. I was relishing the sensation of being the still point of the turning world when I noticed the smile of a teenaged girl in the passenger's seat of a car stopped nearby at a red light. It was not a cheering salutation, but a skeptical feminine response to my dubious, fleeting presence.

Similarities between travel, and experience of the literary and musical arts that move in time, have often been noted. There is a liberation of the psyche from fixity and temporal purpose in all such experiences.

Writer bell hooks [sic] preferred the "rigorous" mental journeying of authorship to physical motion; and novelist Jerzy Kosinski once remarked that since he could imagine countries as well as characters "a lot of travel seems to me a waste of time."

When Englishman Philip Glazebrook set out in the 1980s to retrace Victorian travel writers' tours through Turkey and neighboring lands, he took with him a number of the old travel books. Absorbed in reading one, he failed to notice that the train he was riding, having reversed course, was returning to its point of origin. When he realized what had happened, it occurred to him that he might have travelled with less trouble and expense in the reading room of a London library.

But not surprisingly, people drawn to literature or music may *also* be very fond of travel. Metaphors of motion in space figure in the language of musicologists and performers. Playing or listening to a musical work one passes "from a starting point through a series of intermediate steps to a destination." One is "pulled along" by music. It "transports one." Music "floats along," etc. The title of a guitar fantasia by Spanish composer Joaquín Rodrigo that meanders from one thing to the next is, "What a Fine Long Walk!" (Qué buen caminito!). Argentine concert guitarist Maria Louisa Anido described the mastery of her instrument as a universal passport: "I became an incessant traveler with the guitar on my shoulder, like the gauchos of my distant childhood." Travel spurred Mozart's creativity, and if long journeys were not in offing, he would change place of residence from town to suburbs and back again. Composer Hector Berlioz, in Rome on a fellowship, would wander in the mountains of the Abruzzi, guitar in hand, "strolling along shouting or singing, careless as to where I should sleep…sometimes hurrying, again stopping to investigate some ancient tomb, or to listen silently to the distant bells of St. Peter's far away on the plain." During these rambles he might be inspired to jot down a phrase for a symphony, or chant remembered passages from the *Aeneid* or the works of Dante, improvising accompaniment on the guitar and working himself up into a "pitch of excitement that ended in floods of tears."

For French author Stendhal, travel *and* music were dependable cures for his proneness to ennui, and they merge with authorship in his *Rome, Naples, and Florence in 1817*: a "helter-skelter chase pursued with impertinent flippancy," as one critic describes it. This fragmentary, diary-like work describing Stendhal's travels to opera halls in Italian cities combines notes from the road with reflections on music, dance, and literature. The casual drift from one thing to the next resembles not only the experience of footloose travel, but Rossini's operas which Stendhal admired.

Experiencing the refreshing liberation from fixity and purpose travel affords doesn't necessarily require crossing great distances. The first-person narrator of Sherwood Anderson's sketch, "In a Strange Town," is a college professor who sometimes boards a passenger train in his town and go a few miles down the line to some neighboring town. This would have been possible in Anderson's day when passenger trains made frequent stops.

The professor makes these little jaunts when "I have become dulled to the life of my own house, or my street, to the lives of my pupils." It is pleasing sometimes, he says, just to be "going about in a strange place, having no business there, just walking, thinking.... Being in a strange place like this makes me more aware. I like it. It makes me more alive." It also stirs the imagination, and the professor is a thin disguise of Anderson the writer. Knowing nothing of the people he encounters in a strange town, the professor finds himself making up little stories about their lives.

These mini-trips had originated for the professor after a student of his, a young woman, died in an accident. They had used to met in his office to discuss classroom matters, and there had been an erotic charge between them. The professor was considerably older than his student, and married. Nothing "improper" had occurred, but the meetings were temporary relief from the professor's routines, and allowed his imagination to roam a bit, as did the trips to strange towns which began, significantly, in the wake of the young woman's death.

There is a barber shop about a mile from my house in Atlanta. I walk there sometimes, and not only for a haircut.

I arrived one day just as a controversy had broken out among the barbers over whom the University of Alabama had played in basketball the previous weekend.

Vanderbilt, Horace thought.

Billy said South Carolina.

"I thought it was Tennessee," Cal said.

"I *know* it wasn't Tennessee," Billy said. "Get out your

schedule, Horace."

All haircutting now came to a standstill as Horace dug the Southeastern Conference schedule from his wallet.

A small Mexican boy seated on the board spanning the arms of Billy's chair was weeping softly over the assault on his person in progress.

Horace's nose was down close to the schedule. "They played Mississippi State."

"Bull *shit,*" Billy said—and, for the benefit of the Mexican boy's mother, a stringy-haired Georgia strawberry blond—"'Scuse my Russian, m'am." He plucked the schedule from Horace's hand. "You were reading the January schedule, dork! This is February. Look—it's like I said, they played South Carolina."

"Got to get me new glasses," Horace said.

Haircutting could now proceed.

The Mexican boy's cheeks were wet with tears, but he was no longer crying. "I think he's getting the hang of it," Billy said to the boy's mother.

"It's just his second time," she said.

"Why do kids get so upset by haircuts?" I put in—producing a silence, because while it was common knowledge that small children do not like haircuts, asking why struck them as odd. I had revealed my identity as a foreigner.

Billy covered for me by changing the subject. "How's your daughter doing in Minneapolis?" A native Minnesotan, he knew I'd spent a good many years up there, and that my daughter was there now.

"She's making good money as a waitress," I said. "Fifteen or twenty dollars an hour much of the time."

His eyebrows rose. "Where do I apply? He picked up his cookie jar full of lollipops in one hand, and with the other he shoved a mirror in front of the little boy's face. "Ain't you beautiful, Pedro?"

The boy would not raise his eyes. But he took a sucker

from the jar, and with that puffing his cheek, and the safety of his mother's lap recovered, he sniffled, sighed, and improved a little.

Now it was his sister's turn. She was a year or two older than he. Plump, black-haired, black olive-eyed, she hopped onto the plank ready and willing to be sheared by a big red-bearded Minnesotan. Vivacity oozed from her eyes, the pores of her skin. She was immediately the cynosure of attention in the room, inspiring a crazy wish to be associated somehow with this compact exuberance. Billy's expression of this was to take from his prop drawer a life-sized rubber rat and dangle it by the tail in front of her, inducing a giggling *frisson*. Then he put his latex skinhead cap on her head. "That's how you're gonna look when I get done with you, sister!"

"Oh no, I won't."

"Oh yes you will."

"No I won't."

"Yes you will."

"My Daddy'll kick your butt"—a turn so unexpected that Billy's hands holding scissors and comb fell uselessly to his side and laughter reddened his pale skin.

MOBILE

Sharon Bump calls me from Dalton, Georgia on Good Friday, 1998. She has an IBM electric office typewriter to sell for thirty dollars. Would I like to see it?

Yes, I would. It is 1998, and word processors have generally supplanted the typewriter, but long habit binds me to this machine I've used since a teenager. No one manufactures typewriters any more, but cheap used ones abound in second-hand stores. I like having two or three in a closet at all times. The type on them tends to go out of alignment, and repair is expensive, so when one starts producing dipsy-doodle lines, I just trash it and bring another from the closet.

If a second-hand store I visit hasn't a typewriter to sell, I'll leave my phone number with the proprietor and request a call when one is available. Sharon Bump in Dalton had been informed of my interest in old typewriters by her sister who runs a shop in Atlanta. Dalton is eighty miles north of Atlanta. I would not ordinarily drive that far to see an old typewriter, but wife Christine and I had talked about a joyride in the country Easter Sunday. Dalton would be as good a destination as any. I make an appointment to examine Sharon Bump's IBM Sunday afternoon.

My wife and I agree with the poet Horace who remarked (in Smith Palmer Bovie's memorable free translation) "We cruise around in our cars/ Or our yachts, pursuing our happiness. But what you pursue/ Is right here in Frogville, Swamptown, or Rattlekazoo,/ If you can just piece together the mind that accompanies you." Horace had modest getaways, though. (He speaks in one of his *Satires* of rambling about Rome to observe the shenanigans of confidence men near the Circus, and check out the price of veggies.)

On Easter Sunday, 1998, my wife and I are driving to Dalton, Georgia, to look at an old typewriter.

We go north out of Atlanta on I-75, leaving the freeway at an exit that, according to a sign, will deliver us to state route 19. The exit ramp ends at a crossroad. A sign there states that route 8 goes to the right—north, our intended direction—but nothing about route 19.

"That's crazy," Christine says.

Highway-repair equipment in a ditch at the intersection suggests that the sign for route 19 may have been displaced temporarily.

"Well, we're in no rush to reach Dalton," I point out. "We could just take route 8 and see where it goes"—my preferred method for navigating time and space.

"Drive over to that gas station and we'll ask."

My wife and I reversed roles years ago. A university professor who leads a disciplined professional life, she has an understandable aversion to faulty instructions that waste time. To expect her to abandon this habit of mind for a spin in the country would be unreasonable. I steer the Honda into the service station lot.

"You want to go in?" she says, pushing her luck. I give her a look over the top of my glasses. She leaves the car.

A Kentucky Fried Chicken restaurant is visible in the car's rearview mirror. Our daughter teaching English as a second language in the Czech Republic says that it's very prestigious in Prague to be eating Kentucky Fried Chicken while wearing Nikes and drinking Coca-Cola.

A line of four short, thickset, blue-jeaned Mexican men wearing cowboy hats and boots appear walking past the Kentucky Fried Chicken.

An article in the local paper described recently a woman in Atlanta calling the police after the Hispanic family next door tied a goat to the fence between her property and theirs. A cop had a little talk with the Mexican *pater familias* about zoning regulations that prohibit livestock in the city. The Mexican said the goat would soon be gone. The police had another call from the woman the next day. She was sobbing: "They butchered the goat and it's hanging from the children's swing set. They even offered me a piece!"

Christine's scowl as she opens the car door suggests that she has not found satisfaction. "It was a Pakistani," she says. "He'd never heard of route 19."

She chairs the committee for minority concerns at her university. "What did his being Pakistani have to do with it?"

"He was a dumb bunny."

I point to a convenience store across the road. "They might know over there."

I drive across the highway, and she enters the store. Two dogs evidently on serious business, tails in the air, trot purposefully past the storefront and disappear around a corner.

People dying are said to experience a swift review of their entire personal experience. The review couldn't possibly include *everything*, though. Some principle of selection must be in play. Or maybe the review is just a higgledy-piggledy mixture of what seemed significant and trivia? Maybe you'd recall the burglar coming through a window you shot dead, and then a slice of cold chocolate-iced angel food cake your aunt in Ohio served cold from the refrigerator on July 4, 1959, and then two dogs trotting past a storefront in north Georgia.

Christine returns to the car. "The woman says route 8 *turns into* route 19!"

Off we go.

Many miles north of Atlanta, new-looking accommodations for the swelling population of the region: shopping strips, schools, apartment complexes, suburban "ranchers," split-level houses with two car garages and satellite dishes on the roofs.

An abandoned driftwood-gray farmhouse and leaning barn.

An abandoned, ancient one-room brick schoolhouse in a farmer's field, hay bulging from raw window openings.

In one corner of a major crossroads crowded with fast food restaurants in hot colors, an old country cemetery overgrown with vines and weeds, vertical tombstones at various angles to the perpendicular.

At a curve in the road, a boxy little white clapboard church with a wooden cross draped with a purple cloth out front, and a hand-lettered sign on a stake, HE IS RISEN.

A bit further on, a Baptist church, a modern yellow brick structure with a soaring glass façade topped by a slender art-nouveau cross. The Easter morning service has just let out, and the scene on the plaza reminds me of small town Ohio in the 1950s: girls in pink and yellow chiffon dresses, white anklets, and black patent-leather shoes; boys all slicked-up in dress shirts, ties, and jackets with shoulder pads.

A family gathering on the wide, deep porch of an old country house near the road: people of various sizes, shapes and ages on a porch swing, steps, porch railings, lawn chairs.

"I feel like a Russian émigré," Christine says, "and I am thinking about that box of Triscuits in the back seat."

"Feeling like an émigré makes you hungry."

"Yes."

"Lao Tzu says when you're hungry, eat."

"I also have to pee. What's he say about that?"

"Tycho Brahe once had to pee in the worst sort of way."

"Who's Tycho Brahe?"

"Danish astronomer, sixteenth century."

"One of your Renaissance buddies."

"He observed the birth of a new star."

"But unfortunately he had to pee?"

"That was at a formal gathering. He felt it would be ignoble to go potty, so he held back. His bladder burst and he died. He wrote his own epitaph: 'He lived like a sage and died like a fool.'"

"Poor guy."

"He had an artificial nose."

"What happened to his real one?"

"He lost it in a duel with his cousin. They were arguing over the truth of a mathematical formula."

"Men!"

Condom-dispensing machines fill an entire wall of the men's room at the service station where we stop. Among the many choices is a "surprise package" (?). Messages engraved in the men's room door: "Fuck niggers," and next to that, "Sounds like fun to me."

"Kilroy was here, but left immediately."

There is no one in the compact downtown where I diagonal-park the car in front of a Richardson-Romanesque county courthouse with an impressively tall clock tower a la Milano or Firenze. In the nineteenth century one wouldn't have had to leave the U.S. to study European architecture.

We sit on a park bench in the courthouse green with the box of Triscuits and a thermos of iced tea. I contemplate a Triscuit at arm's length.

"You're going to quote Paul Goodman," she says.

I always do that in the presence of Triscuits. Goodman regarded them as the only under-advertised product in America:

> National Biscuit Triscuits—crunch, crunch—
> not so good as nooky or Vivaldi
> but—crunch, crunch—better than Ingmar Bergman
> or the academic friends that I—crunch, crunch
> crunch, crunch—made at the University of Wisconsin.

It has been some time since I tried to quote the poem, though, and I come up empty.

"Are we having a senior moment?"

Crunch-crunch-crunch.

In Dalton an hour before my appointment with Sharon Bump, we park along Main Street, and walk up a hill into a residential neighborhood of modest homes. In the front yard of one, there's a mound of clothing, shoes, and other personal items, and a crude sign scribbled on cardboard with a felt tip pen: YOU'RE NOT ALONE, HILLARY! THROW THE BUM OUT!—a reference to the ongoing scandal over President Clinton's dalliance with the White House intern.

The day is warm, and back on Main Street we're thirsty. I'm riffling through soda cans in a refrigerated chest at the back of a small grocery when I hear Christine chatting with a matronly black woman at the cash register, and a chubby white woman with a tangled mass of dirty-blond hair.

"A lot of people think I'm crazy. My husband does," the white woman says.

"He's never seen the ghost?" Christine asks.

"No, but he's seen the lights go on and off for no reason. He's an electrician, and he can't find anything in our wiring that would explain it."

"This is Carolyn," Christine says to me as I approach. "She has a ghost in her house."

"They like to tinker with electricity," I observe.

"You're just able to see what others can't," Christine says.

The black woman nods agreement. The white woman's broad face flushes with pleasure at the compliment.

"Would y'all come out to our house and talk to my husband?" Carolyn blurts out.

Christine looks at me. *Could* we?

"Sure."

"We'd be late for your appointment."

I shrug.

We follow Carolyn's faded red Beetle along steep, winding, rolling two-lane roads in the Appalachian foothills. There are forks in the road, and at one of them we lose sight of the Beetle, and I am not sure the choice of a road I have made is correct. It becomes obvious that it is not when we come to a sheriff's car parked sideways across the road. A deputy comes to my window. "We're cleaning up an accident yonder."

"Serious?"

"There are some injuries.... Where you headed?"

"Nowhere in particular."

He smiles. "Well, you're gonna have to get there some other way."

I make a U-turn, and drive back to the last fork in the road. We drive for some time looking for Carolyn's Beetle, but have not seen it when we come to a crossroads where a sign points to "Chatsworth."

"Want to go to Chatsworth?" I ask.

"Why would we go there?"

"You have a better idea?"

"What about your appointment?"

At this point. I have no idea where we are in relation to Sharon Bump's house. "There are a lot of old typewriters out there."

Chatsworth has a two-stoplight Main Street and a jumble of nondescript one- and two-story buildings. The streets are empty, but a neon OPEN sign flashes blue-and-red in the front window of the "Mexican Bar and Cantina."

The restaurant's busy interior—buzzing voices and clanking tableware and dishes—is a surprising contrast to the vacant street. Diners sit at small square tables arranged edge-t0-

edge in three long lines separated by aisles. There are a lot of Mexicans in north Georgia. The chattering clientele appears to be about half-and-half Indian and Caucasian stock.

The hostess seats us at a table beside a young Asian man just as a waitress places before him a crusty-looking brown concoction the size and shape of a baseball. He drives a fork into it. Vanilla ice cream oozes out, and he digs in with gusto.

When he comes up for air, Christine says, "Might I ask what that is?"

"Fried ice cream. Very good. Chinese dessert."

We strike up a conversation. He's a Thai who has been living above the Mexican Bar and Cantina while studying Technology Management at nearby Dalton State University. Soon he will return home to Thailand. "If I could take my Toyota to Bangkok I could sell it for many baht, but that is impossible. I must sell everything, or leave it behind."

He asks why we are in Chatsworth. I explain my interest in the archaic typewriter.

He smiles indulgently. "I have a word processor to sell. Very good machine. Fifty dollars—cheap."

"I'd like to see it," I say.

Christine's mouth falls open.

"My room is at the top of stairs. Come up, see word processor."

Christine orders the fried ice cream for dessert. "I understand it's a Chinese dessert?" she says to the Latino waitress.

"No, Mexican."

Climbing the echoic wooden staircase to the student's apartment, we can hear notes of an unfamiliar scale being plucked on a stringed instrument. The door to the apartment stands open. The Thai sits cross-legged on his bed playing a long-necked, almond-shaped, lute-like instrument. An oversized print of the famous Marilyn Monroe photo, skirts blown high by a draft from below, adorns the wall over his head. He lays the instrument aside on the bed, and comes to greet us at the door.

The word processor that stands on a desk looks to me like a typewriter attached to a television screen. He demonstrates its functionality. I give him fifty dollars for it, and with the word processor in the back seat of the car, we locate the freeway and start back Atlanta.

"You're really going to start using that thing?" Christine says.

"That's the way the wind's blowing."

THE DREAM OF THE IMPOSSIBLE

The dream is common: You need to get across town to Eden Avenue, but hoodlums have you surrounded in Downlow Corners. You want to put your shoes on, but both are for the left foot. The words of the sentences you try to write are jigsaw puzzle pieces tumbled from a box.

The Dream of the Impossible may occur when a sudden sound, or a bed partner flopping about, has disturbed sleep, activating the busybody mind's concern with some problem or project in waking life.

The Dream of the Impossible, servant of restorative slumber, comes to the rescue: "You can never succeed at what you are trying to do, you may as well relax."

ALIEN AMONG US

Marcel the cat, as I bend over his dish to replenish it, butts the food bag with his head, spilling pellets across the kitchen floor. He is big-eyed with astonishment at the unforeseen consequences of his action.

To make his water dish look like a stream flowing before he drinks, as ancestral voices require, he stirs it with his paw. If he had any idea what his paw deposits in that stagnant pool, he might have second thoughts about doing this.

To enhance camaraderie, he brings to our doorstep a bloody chipmunk, a beheaded mouse, a small shriveled green snake.

Lying against my chest, he claws the fabric of my new shirt affectionately. I respond by slapping him lightly on the top of the head, and he bites the hand that feeds him.

Making some repairs to our house, I measure and cut boards. Seated nearby in the meatloaf position, he contemplates warily my snaky retractable tape measure. *O brave new world that has such creatures in it!*

HOMEWARD BOUND

A huge banner stretched across the porch of a small house in my neighborhood:

YARD SALE TODAY

There are two card tables filled with domestic odds and ends in the yard. A slender young man seated on a porch step waves his arms about in self-parodic enthusiasm. "Yard sale! Yard sale! Prices drastically reduced! Everything must go!"

I go up into the yard.

"The best stuff's inside," he says.

I'm a little curious about the interior of this house in my neighborhood I've passed countless times over the years, so I enter. The house is more spacious than I had imagined. Most of the rooms are empty. There are furniture and household items piled in one room at the back of the house.

"If you don't like a price you see, make me an offer," he says at my back.

There's a deck of big, colorful A.E. Waite Tarot cards bent permanently by the shufflings of a serious student of the occult. The sticker says three dollars.

"Two bucks?"

"I'm easy." He takes the two bills I hold out.

"You moving?"

"Back to Alabama. The cards belonged to Mark. We were together—you know, married—eight years. He died of AIDS last month."

"Alabama's home?"

He takes a drag on the cigarette so profound his eyes close. They open as he exhales. "You could say that."

VACUUM CLEANER CHIC

A recent news item claimed that we are living in the era of the "designer pet"—the iguana, the king snake, the ferret. The Eureka Company is betting with its new line, the "Christian Kingspor Signature Series," that we are ready for the designer vacuum cleaner.

A photograph of Klingspor, an industrial designer with a Master of Fine Arts degree from the Royal Swedish Design Academy, and other impressive credentials, graces the cartons in which the new Eurekas are packed. The picture shows a tastefully-dressed, silver-haired, blue-eyed man in late middle age who could hold his own in a celebrity photo shoot with Geoffrey Beene, Bill Blass, and Ralph Lauren. A reproduction of Klingspor's dashingly creative, unreadable signature zig-zags vertically up the front of the new vacuums like some upwardly mobile graph line.

"The whole conception behind Christian's line is to give a more exciting, sophisticated and unique appeal to the product with a focus on elegance," according to the carton—as good an example as any of the curious modern market conflation of the interests of manufacturers with those of the clientele. (Simpatico consumers walk around in T-shirts advertising products, and drive automobiles with manufacturers' names emblazoned proudly across their sides.)

Eureka seems to be suggesting that if you have any class, you will want to have a Klingspor sucking dirt from your carpet.

I fell into conversation with a young woman clerking in Macy's housewares department who had noticed me contemplating the Klingspors. "What's new in vacuum cleaners these days?" I inquired.

"Not a lot really," she replied. "They're basically motors, fans, and bags. Well, I did hear that a Japanese company is coming out with one that talks."

"Oh? What would a talking vacuum say?"

She squared her shoulders, affecting robotic rigidity: "Please-change-my-bag-which-is-full."

I laughed.

"The Klingspors are basically the same vacuum Eureka has been making the past several years," she said. "The change in colors is nice. Last year's models were fire engine red, midnight blue, and pitch black."

The more sedate Klingspors are Dijon mustard-tan with accents of chocolate and emerald.

If the Klingspors are designed to please the discriminating eye, Eureka has not forgotten the fastidious nose. Every Klingspor comes with a supply of "scented fresh air tablets." Nature abhors a vacuum, and it seems that where the Klingspors are concerned, the feeling is mutual.

VI

EVOLUTION

My wife and I on our way from Georgia to Ohio left the freeway and entered Devil's Ledge, Tennessee for lunch. The Dinner Bell on Main Street was crowded with elderly men wearing military-style American Legion caps. There were no free tables, so we went back outside where three round tables with big shade umbrellas stood along the façade of the restaurant—but those, too, were occupied.

A portly man in a law enforcement uniform hailed us from one of them: "We gotta a couple seats over here, if you'd care to join us. Otherwise, you may have to wait around for dinner."

We accepted his offer.

"Crowd in there," I observed.

He nodded. "Buncha' old Legion boys chewin' the fat. They do it once a month." He introduced the woman at his side as his wife Peggy, then scooped up their menus and handed them to us.

"You the sheriff?" Christine inquired.

"Deputy."

Peggy fixed us with a squinty-eyed look as we pondered the menus. "You folks don't look like you're from around here."

The deputy shifted his substantial weight. "Oh Peggy, they could be from about anywhere, like the rest of us."

"We're from Atlanta," I volunteered.

Peggy smiled. She'd known all along we were foreigners.

"We're on the road to Ohio for my mother's ninetieth birthday party," I said.

The deputy smiled. "Big shindig, I'll bet."

"Relatives are coming from all over."

"That's wonderful. She'll never forget it."

"My sister and her husband live in Hillsboro, Ohio," Peggy said.

"I know Hillsboro," I said. "Southern part of the state. Hilly, like the name suggests."

"How'd Devil's Ledge get its name?" Christine inquired.

"There's a cliff down south of town some settlers fell off way back when," the deputy said.

"They was *shoved*," Peggy added. "It's haunted by Indian spirits."

"Some believe that," the deputy said. "The settlers were building over Indian burial ground."

"Where's your Mother live in Ohio?" Peggy asked.

"North-central, the part of the state the glacier leveled."

"You mean The Flood?"

"There are some very large rocks in my home county. Archaeologists say the glacier carried them down from points far north."

Peggy frowned skeptically: *How could anyone could possibly know that?*

Christine kicked my leg under the table.

A harried-looking waitress put plastic glasses of ice-water in front of us, and took our orders for sandwiches.

"We got mountains all around us here," Peggy said. "I been wanderin' around in 'em my whole life. Ever now and then, you come across sand the Flood left behind. Sand on a mountain! Wouldn't believe it if I hadn't seen it with my own eyes."

Christine tried to kick me under the table again but missed and hit the deputy, who flinched.

Peggy eyed me. "I suppose you believe in Evolution?"

The deputy scratched with a fingernail at two sets of initials paired by a plus-sign in the table top enamel.

I nodded yes, I believed in Evolution, and I guessed I did, although I'd never been able to connect belief (or disbelief) in it with anything that seemed to matter.

"Let me ask you something," Peggy said. "If Evolution is true, things are still evolving—is that right?"

I nodded hesitantly. Where was she going with this?

She smiled triumphantly. "Well, I don't see it happening—do you?"

GOING HOME AGAIN

My high school class reunion in small town Ohio was scheduled for the same weekend as my mother's ninetieth birthday there. My wife and I drove up from Atlanta.

A red light at the main intersection in nearby London, Ohio stopped us. Two teenagers appeared at the open window on Christine's side of the car to offer us a choice of pot or crack cocaine.

In my hometown it had always been possible to exit from route 42 into South Liberty Street, but the run of the highway had changed somehow since last I'd come this way. I would probably have seen in daylight what had happened, but now, after dark, I was at sea. A road sign:

DOWNTOWN>>>>

I turned the Honda into the curving exit road, and braked at a red light. The street crossing in front of the car appeared to be a main one—but which? I who had once explored every nook and cranny of this town on foot, or on bicycle, had no idea where I was.

The light changed. I turned right arbitrarily, and realized I was on William Street going the wrong way. I turned the car around.

Another light stopped us at the town's main intersection, William and Sandusky. Christine, looking off to her right through a big plate glass window at office cubicles and computer monitors, was horrified: "The L & K's gone!" The building had housed a restaurant we had frequented before we were married.

A car pulled alongside us, blocking our view of the former restaurant. A woman with a mop of Scotch-Irish sandy hair stuck her head out the window of the car and yelled, "Hey,

Georgia! Saw your license plate. I just moved up here from Dahlonega!"

"We know Dahlonega, Georgia," I called back. "We've been to the gold museum."

"Where you from?"

"Atlanta. Grant Park."

"I've been to the Zoo in Grant Park!"

The light changed. She was starting to say something else when a driver behind her honked impatiently. She waved, swept around the corner, and was gone.

"It's hard to imagine that your mother being anywhere but the old family home," Christine said, as we drove cross town. "You say her new digs are in a college dorm?"

"It used to be a college dorm. They've made it over into apartments for senior citizens."

Mother's apartment was roomy enough. My first impression, though, was of shocking compression: Items of furniture that had maintained comfortable distances from one another through decades in my family's two-story, four-bedroom family home appeared competitive for the available space.

Mother, too, as she showed us around, seemed smaller and more compact than when I'd last seen her. "So you're going to *two* parties this weekend?" she said, as we sat at the dinette around a pitcher of iced lemonade and a plate of cookies.

"Yep."

"You're going to be a busy boy."

That was how I liked it back home, because in these returns over the years I'd sometimes found myself wandering around the streets like the just-awakened, blinking Rip Van Winkle.

"Where's your daughter these days?"

"Prague, in the Czech Republic."

"What's she doing there?"

"Teaching English."

Mother appeared puzzled that Czechs would want to learn English. "It would be wonderful to have her here for my party."

"But Mom, she *is* coming. I'll be picking her up at the Columbus airport tomorrow." She was obviously surprised and delighted by the news, and I was about to say, *Don't you remember my telling you that?*—when I recalled my brother's warnings about her on-again, off-again memory these days.

She put us up in the apartment's second bedroom. By the time I was awake the next morning, Christine was already off to visit with her sister in Columbus.

Foraging in Mother's kitchen cabinets, I came up with a box of breakfast cereal, but the cupboard was nearly bare, evidence of an absent-minded failure to lay in provisions for guests unthinkable in the past.

Mother and I were drinking coffee in the dinette, when my cousin Dorothy stopped by. Dorothy had been researching our family's genealogy, and presented Mother and me copies of the short biography she'd written of William Williams, a Welsh ancestor on my father's side of the family.

"I recall Grandmother saying he was a character," I said.

Dorothy nodded. "They used to call him Billy the Baptist in Radnor village. If a bum came to his farmhouse door begging food, he'd get the third degree from Billy about the state of his soul."

"Would there have been a church in the village that early?"

"No. The Welsh settlers had prayer meetings in their homes at night. Billy never missed one, but it meant going home through woods in the dark."

"He probably figured he had divine protection."

"A pack of wolves followed him one night. He went up a tree and made enough noise to scarce them off. He thought his escape was providential."

Talking about William Williams reminded me of that time in late 1940s my father took my brother and me on a hunting trip in a small woods on my Uncle Bill's farm—William Williams' farm originally. My father, descended from a long line of Central Ohio farmers, was in advertising in Columbus, Ohio. We were going to hunt squirrels and rabbits, he said. We might even bag a deer, if we were lucky, because Uncle Bill had seen one in the purlieus of the woods that fall.

On a bitter cold November Saturday morning, we'd tromped across a choppy frozen field littered with dried buff-colored cornstalks leaning at odd angles, Dad cradling his Remington rifle, Bob and I our pellet guns. We sat on the exposed roots of a great oak and huddled together for warmth. The name of the game, Dad explained, was silence and patience. If the deer turned up, we were to leave the shooting to him. I was wearing layered socks under leather boots, but my toes became increasingly vague as we sat there. I tried to imagine what we were doing. Meat came out of packages in the supermarket, and who really wanted to eat Bambi or Thumper? Hamburgers were the real ticket. If you wanted to kill animals, shoot cows. I'd seen them on my uncle's farm, and they were sitting ducks.

My puzzlement about our hunting expedition resembled questions I had about the same time concerning stories of the Biblical Jews Mrs. Pierce told us in Methodist Sunday School. It was conceivably true that the Jews had been God's Chosen People, as she said, but He had obviously passed the torch, because the ancient Jews hadn't automobiles, electricity, or radio; and trying to imagine ancient Jewish plumbing conjured for me visions of the pungent, fly-infested, outbuilding behind the old country house of my Mother's ne'er-do-well country cousin Gertie.

Dinner would have been slim-pickings that night if we'd had to depend on our hunting. The deer hadn't appeared. Neither had the squirrels and rabbits. Dad had looked at his watch, and having evidently decided that his sons' lesson in manly endurance and silence had been prolonged enough, led us out of the woods back to our car parked beside Uncle Bill's barn. As he drove down the long, crushed stone lane to the road, he switched on the car radio. Remarkably, we'd reached the car at almost the exact moment Ohio State kicked off to Michigan in the annual Midwestern gridiron rivalry.

Years later, reading William Faulkner's *The Bear* in college, I realized our hunting trip in the woods must have echoed dimly some very old rural rite of initiation.

My daughter Sarah, when I met her at baggage pickup in the Columbus airport, looked a bit drawn and bedraggled after nearly a day in the air from Europe, but otherwise her tall, pretty, exuberant self. We wheeled her valises across the airport into the parking deck.

"God, everything in the States looks so *strange*."

"That Czech haircut of yours is a bit unusual, too."

"Like it?"

"Yes."

"I couldn't stop looking at all the fat asses on people when I changed planes in Atlanta."

"No fat asses in the Czech Republic?"

"Here, you see 'em on naturally skinny people."

A broad-bottomed, middle-aged couple waddled past.

"Do these people eat so much because they're unhappy?"

"Probably."

"*Jouissance.*"

"*Jouissance*?"

"Oh—that's Slavoj Zizek. It was shorthand for my friends in Prague."

"Never read him."

"You haven't missed much. I like *jouissance*, though.

Modern societies don't have much to offer in the way of big pleasures, he says. But there are lots of little treats: big ice cream cones, fatty steaks, shiny cars, big television screens."

I thought of Claes Oldenburg's monumental hamburgers and cake slices. My daughter and I discussing our native land always sound like a pair of cultural anthropologists.

We made our way out of the airport onto the Columbus beltline and from there onto route 23, and stopped at a convenience store where I picked up a dozen eggs, a loaf of bread, a gallon of milk, and a box of Wheaties, to restock Mother's larder.

The clerk, a buxom young woman in a polka-dot blouse with corn-yellow hair pulled back in a ponytail, and bangs across the forehead, was Al Capp's cartoon Appalachian blond, Daisy Mae. "Howya all doin'?"

Probably a native Southerner, too, judging from the accent. Since World War II there had been a steady flow of West Virginian mountain folk looking for work into Central Ohio

"They have coffee," Sarah observed.

"Want some?"

"It might help keep me awake until I find a bed."

"It's real fresh, I just made it," Daisy Mae said.

"We'll take one," I said.

"Two?"

"No, just one."

"I have decaf, if it keeps you awake."

"Just one, thanks."

Daisy Mae opened the spigot, coffee spilled into the Styrofoam. "Y'all Dad and daughter?"

"For life," I said.

She smiled. "Ah can see the family lakness.... You want a roll with your coffee, hon? They just came in. They're *go-o-o-o-o-od*. Don't tell nobody, but I had one a little while ago."

"I am kind of hungry."

"Yes, one of those," I said.

"Now, in Prague," Sarah said, as we got back into my car, "she'd have ignored us. The coffee would be stale, and she wouldn't try to sell the pastry. At the grocery in my neighborhood they threw change at you."

"Maybe because you were a foreigner?"

"They treat Czechs the same way! My friend Amalia said it's because all the store clerks did under communism was hand stuff over the counter."

"No one trying to please anyone."

"At the grocery in my neighborhood, they had Rice Krispies. I don't like them much, but they reminded me of home. I couldn't find them one day. I asked this old guy who spoke some English where they were. He said they stopped carrying them. They sold too many. The help got tired restocking shelves."

"That's something right out of Kafka."

"*Everything* in Prague is out of Kafka. You knew it was his hometown?"

"I'd forgotten."

"He seems more like a realist if you've lived there. There's a Hotel Kafka and a Café Kafka. Amalia and I went into the Café once. Two hot chocolates and two small pieces of cake—twenty-six dollars."

"An aptly named café."

"There was a guy in a corner playing flamenco guitar."

"A Spaniard?"

"Russian."

"Does Prague have supermarkets?"

"They're starting to, but most of the food stores are small and crowded. The wheels on the grocery carts are always screwed up."

"Oh? Why's that?"

"They're Prague grocery carts."

"Kafka karts."

She giggled. "The aisles are real narrow. People are always banging the carts into each other because of the wheels. They cuss and argue. There are also very long checkout lines. Czechs keep books in their pockets to read while they wait."

"So, there are long lines of people with their noses in books at the checkout, and behind them people are crashing carts and cussing."

"You'd like it."

"You heard that Aunt Elizabeth died?"

"Who?"

"The woman who always sent you the birthday cards with dollar bills in them."

"Oh yeah. Died, eh?"

I described Elizabeth's death in Florida. In retirement there, she'd taken up "bottle evangelism." She stuffed bottles with religious literature, corked them, and set them adrift in the Gulf of Mexico. She always put her mailing address in the bottles, and once she had a marriage proposal from an old fisherman in the Philippines. She had been on a boat out in the Gulf dropping off some more bottles when she collapsed.

"Are there a lot of religious nuts in your family?"

"A couple generations back there were. I *have* noticed a tendency for some of my generation to relapse into the faith as their consuming days wind down."

"This party of Grandma's is going to be a big deal?"

"They've invited a mob. It's all day Saturday."

"What do you do at a party that lasts all day?"

"I don't know."

"Will I know anyone but Grandma, you and Mom?"

"Well, your cousin Connie lives in Columbus. She'll probably be there. I seem to remember you two playing together as kids."

"Never liked her."

"I was thinking the other day of that time I saw her with her father right after his divorce, and mistook her for his new girlfriend."

"*Embarrassing*!"

"Well, I hadn't seen her since she was a kid."

"She has a kid of her own now, doesn't she?"

"A boy. Odd name. Quizno or Renfro—something like that"

"Uncles are supposed to know the names of their nieces and nephews!"

"So are cousins!"

We were both laughing.

Sarah had brought back the States with her the story of Rudolph, the Prague bricklayer who became suddenly a man of means.

Czech private wealth confiscated during the communist era has been returning slowly to its owners or their heirs since the Velvet Revolution in 1989. Rudolph hoped to use his inheritance as capital for starting a business.

Aided by a translator he contacted a California skylight company seeking European distributors for its products. He received in return an invitation to report on the prospects for skylight sales in the Czech Republic at a convention of the company's European distributors in Berne, Switzerland.

The meeting was to be in two weeks, so there was no time to lose, but Rudolph's translator could not be reached. He was in Poland hunting the red deer. With or without the translator, Rudolph would not have known how to write a business report, but he recalled that his neighbor's clever daughter Amalia was studying English at the university. He asked if she would write the report, accompany him to Berne, and present it.

Amalia hesitated. Her English was only so-so, and she knew no more about writing business reports than Rudolph; but the payment he was offering for her services was appealing, a trip to Berne would be amusing—and what did she have to lose?

Rudolph supplied her information for the report. She wrote a draft which she took to Sarah for criticism one evening. The report opened, "Good day, Sirs and Mesdames." Sarah figured it was going to be a long night, and it was, but by dawn the next morning they'd cobbled what she thought was a decent presentation. Amalia almost backed out of the project when Rudolph expressed his hope that while in Berne they might conceive the baby Jesus.

The first day of the meeting was a drinky-talky mixer. Rudolph, intimidated by all the men and women in business suits, retreated to his hotel room to drink vodka. The California executives found petite, blond, curvy Amalia's childlike-sounding English charming.

The second day was all business. Rudolph, a thin, slump-shouldered, gray-faced, presence in a stocking cap, sat beside Amalia at a long boardroom table. Amalia felt that either she was too short, or her chair too low, but the report she delivered seemed to please the American managers who were not interested in having Rudolph as their Czech distributor, but wanted to know if she spoke Russian—which she does. Would she consider representing their company St. Petersburg? She felt an American paw low on her back.

She was still considering this offer when Sarah left for the States.

In bed at Mother's that night, I read cousin Dorothy's life of Billy the Baptist:

> *Two of William's sisters died of influenza during the Atlantic crossing in 1809. The ship docked in*

Philadelphia, and William and his older brother David were, for reasons unknown, apprenticed to an innkeeper. Their parents went on westward over the Alleghenies to the Welsh community of Radnor in central Ohio.

The innkeeper in Philadelphia proved to be a cruel employer, so the brothers fled their apprenticeship over the mountains to Ohio on foot, one disguised as a woman. It took twenty-one days before they were reunited with their family, and shortly after that their father fell ill and died, leaving his wife and two daughters dependent on the labors of William and David. Then David died when a heavy timber fell on him during the construction of a barn.

Twelve year-old William ("Billy the Baptist") went to work as a hand on neighboring farms, often accepting food for his family as wages. By the age of twenty-one, though, he had acquired, in addition to land inherited from his father, sixty-five acres of virgin Ohio land. After each harvest he cleared and plowed a portion of this acreage. By the time he was twenty-six, when he married Margaret Davies (also a native of north Wales) he had become a farmer of substance.

Margaret bore him ten children in the next fifteen years. Five died either in childbirth or infancy. Margaret kept a garden, spun yarn to make cloth, sewed her family's garments, and rode horseback through the woods on trails marked by braised trees to trade eggs and butter for household necessities in the town of Delaware.

William and Margaret cared not only for their own children, but for three children of neighboring families left fatherless prematurely. All the children upon reaching maturity received substantial assistance in establishing households of their own. Margaret died at the age of seventy-six, William at eighty-one. The large attendances at their funerals attested to the esteem in which they were held by the community.

Laying aside the biography and turning out the light, I experienced in the dark a rush of shame for the flimsiness of my life, compared with my ancestor's.

But had Baptist Billy been dropped into the contemporary scene, he would have been a madman in short order—which I was not.

Christine, a native New Yorker, had no real interest in attending my class reunion and was still in Columbus with her sister Friday night as I made my way along William Street to meet my former classmates for a tour of our old high school. I was anticipating what lay ahead as eagerly as I once had the opening of a new school year.

I passed a large crow tugging hard on a length of intestine in a dead possum beside a curb. The bird fixed me with a beady eye.

Glancing around the crowd assembled on the plaza in front of the school, I recognized no one, and had experienced a moment of Rip Van Winkle terror before a plump, smiling fellow came forward from the crowd and extended a hand in greeting. "Carl Burston," he said, and I could see that this was indeed the current version of Carl: more gut, less hair.

Then a shyly smiling woman came toward me, identifying herself by tugging at the front of her baggy t-shirt that sported a reproduction of Lily Campbell's senior class picture.

Ellen Wyche, looking more or less her former self, gazed at me as if she had just seen a ghost. I'd never had much to do with her, but who was to say what role one might have played in others' psychic dramas?

A woman I took to be Cathy Hancock was actually Martha Lowery. "That's Cathy," Martha said, pointing. One had been prettier than the other as a teenager. This was still the case, but they had reversed roles.

Spencer Hammer, a chain-smoking teenager from the wrong side of the tracks whose physical resemblance to Elvis guaranteed high school popularity, had since acquired the double-chin and the spare tire of the elder Elvis and Spencer's factory-worker father—and a hacking cough.

Who was this smallish woman with the salt-and-pepper hair at the top of the short flight of steps leading to the school entrance? She had obviously recognized me.

A man with a Van Dyke beard stepped out of a car in front of the school and introduced himself as a history teacher at the school who was to be our tour guide. We filed into the building which, in the quiet, ironic way of buildings, had changed much less than those who had occupied it.

As we made our way along the halls, pausing here and there briefly to look at modifications to the interior made over the years, I realized why so many in the crowd out front had been strangers: They were people not of local origin my classmates had married.

Many more classmates appeared later in the evening at a bar-restaurant off Main Street where a banner stretched across one wall of a party room:

TOGETHER AGAIN, CLASS OF '58

The former classmates divided up more or less as they had before: the college-bound, mainly from the north and west sides of town, here; the others, there.

Pat Wiley, who had been in classes with me from the first through the twelfth grades, came through a door near where I stood. She didn't recognize me at first, but then did, and we called each other by the pet names we'd gone by as six year-olds. A lovely sweetness passed between us.

Don Longely remembered an elementary school pickup football game, East Side vs. West Side, in which we'd played on opposed teams.

There was talk about the recent death of George Townsend, who'd spent the last decade of his life in Mississippi after retirement from the Air Force building a room-sized miniature townscape through which he ran his collection of antique Lionel toy trains.

Someone mentioned six suicides among the 103 members of the class of 1958. "Seems a bit high," someone said, and it did.

Seated at a long table I realized the little woman with the salt-and-pepper hair I'd noticed on the school steps earlier was beside me.

"I feel as if I should know you," I said, "but the truth is, I don't."

"Donna Pippen," she replied, in that thin voice I recalled across forty years: an old flame of mine as a teenager—with whom I'd gotten absolutely nowhere. When I last saw her she had been a doll-cute teenager in wraparound skirts, cashmere sweaters, and neckerchiefs in the period style.

"You know, I always wondered why you never became a cheerleader, Donna. You certainly looked the part." (I actually said that.)

She found the subject congenial. "I wanted to. I was going to the tryouts my junior year, but I got cold feet. My family had just moved over from West Virginia. I was kind of overwhelmed by the city school and all."

"Is Stan here?"—our classmate she had married.

"He's over at the bar," she said, with a really nasty little curl of the lip. "You'll find him there most nights."

"Will I *recognize* him? I haven't been doing too well at that tonight."

"He's about the same—bigger gut."

"Well, I've got one of those, too."

She smiled at me as she wouldn't have in 1958. "You're better looking with more weight."

"Stan works here in town?"

"No, in Marysville.... You knew he and I aren't together anymore?"

I hadn't.

"You're in Atlanta?"

"Yes."

"Laverne lives in Alpharetta."—a northern suburb of Atlanta.

But who was Laverne?

"My sister Laverne? Married Frank Blair?"

I didn't remember either one of them.

"I get down to Atlanta most summers."

"Do you?"

"I'm going down week after next." That smile again.

Debra Miller, a rawboned, horsy teenager breezed into the room looking tall, blond, and fit in late middle-age. I'd seen her last at my father's funeral in the Seventies. Since then her sister Judy and one of my brothers had married.

"We're in-laws now, so we must have our hug," Debra said, so we had our hug. I'd noticed a lot of hugging that evening, a practice I could not remember being common among Central Ohioans. Had they picked it up from the hippies? The television talk show hosts?

Larry Adams approached to ask if I'd seen my cousin Louise Shaw, who was in the restaurant. I hadn't.

"Louise is your cousin?" said Donna at my side. "If you two are related, so are you and I, because Louise's sister Edie married my cousin Bobby."

"We seem to be getting kind of inbred," Debra observed with a smile.

"Soon we'll all be idiots," I replied.

Debra winked. "Could be a problem already."

Donna was sitting beside me at a table when Laura Dietz Preston distributed copies of a little booklet the reunion committee had prepared. There were brief bios of the classmates. I noticed in Donna's entry that she'd had four children.

A waiter handed Donna and me a menu to share. The small lined hand holding her half had performed a lot of chores for a lot of people over a long stretch of time. I solicited her advice as a local about what might be best on the menu. She recommended the club sandwiches, so we both ordered those, and salads.

Tom Scott, aware of my youthful interest in Donna, had an ironic eye fixed on this little tête-à-tête.

There was a conversation going about the controversy over fluoridating the local water back in the Fifties.

"That was nothing compared with the brouhaha over our band not having baton twirlers," Tom Scott said.

"Yeah, what was that all about?"

"Don't you remember? That mothers' group that made a stink about us not having twirlers when every other school band had them," Tom said. "They wanted their daughters' sweet little asses on display on there in front of the trombones."

"It was marketing," someone said.

"Why *didn't* we have twirlers?"

"Virgil"—our band director—"hated them," Tom said. "In that little book he wrote about organizing a high school marching band he refers to baton-twirling as 'an easily acquired dexterity with a rod.'"

General laughter.

Toward midnight I was preparing to leave the restaurant with Tom and Mary Scott when the waiter who'd served our table handed out checks for food and drinks. It was only as we reached the cash register I realized that the waiter, having taken

Donna and me for a couple, had put our food on the same bill. I looked around for Donna, who was nowhere to be seen. I explained to Tom and Mary what had happened.

"Well, you finally got that date. Now you have to pay for your thrills," Tom said.

Leaving the restaurant, we spied the silhouetted elder-Elvis gut of thrice-married Spencer Hammer disappearing into the shadowy parking lot with Darlene Brecht, not one of the three.

Back at Mother's, I opened the reunion booklet. At the front there were lyrics of a little ditty a classmate had composed, "We're Gonna Get Together to See Why We're Fallin' Apart":

We need to see each other
Just you and me.
To look at one another,
To see what we can see,
See why we're fallin' apart.
Now's the time to do it.
We're gonna get together
Fix trouble at the start.
Maybe you can tell me
Just what I need to know.
Help me recapture
My get up and go.

You tell me your secrets,
I'll tell you mine.
Hurry, cause there's little time....

Etc. It was nearly gibberish, but maybe that was the language appropriate for describing the obscure emotions these counter-clockwise gatherings stirred.

A reunion, by canceling the usual forward orientation of consciousness, resituated people momentarily outside time, psychologically. There was a certain resemblance between a reunion, and the orgiastic festivals of archaic societies that suspended temporarily work routines, social hierarchies and moralities. There had been myths of a return to the Chaos preceding the establishment of cosmic and social order associated with those festivals.

While a class reunion wasn't an orgiastic festival, there were some similarities between a return to aboriginal Chaos, and a return to that phase of modern life in which the ego was only partially formed. In either case, differences among peers that were socially significant ordinarily were dissolved. Like the primitive festival, the reunion promised revival and rebirth: a rediscovery of relationships in "heart to heart" talks, "fixing trouble," a recovery of "get up and go." (I made a mental note to discuss this comparison with my fellow cultural anthropologist, my daughter.)

As for Donna flirting with me, maybe no one ever forgets another's expression of desire, even if it had been unsolicited and rejected. The irony being that the rejectee, having shrugged off the pain of rejection, will have put the rejector out of mind long ago.

I was aware of my potential for cruelty in the situation.

Christine was back in town in the morning. Mother's party was to begin at noon. A photographer hired for the occasion would be taking pictures of the assembled relatives.

One of my brother's wives stopped by Mother's apartment with Xeroxes of a list of family members' mailing addresses. The far-flung addresses reminded me of a similar list in the class reunion booklet: Philadelphia, PA; Denver, CO;

Atlanta, GA; Georgetown, OH; Royal Oak, MI; Mason, OH; Athens, OH; East Sandwich, MA; South Kingston, RI; Hudson, MA; Richmond, IN; Chicago, IL; Minneapolis, MN; Easton, PA.—etc.

The relatives and friends of Mother were milling about in the dormitory lounge, a spacious, carpeted room with sturdy leather-covered sofas and armchairs, a crystal chandelier, and a grand piano. A paper banner stretched across a mantel above a fireplace:

HAPPY NINETIETH, MICKI!

The photographer had arrived, and a band was setting up in a corner.

One of my sisters-in-law marshaled relatives into pictorial groups: Micki and her sons, Micki and her grandchildren, Micki and her daughters-in-law. The idea of picture-taking as an icebreaker had seemed odd to me, but arranging and rearranging agglomerated kin for best photographic effect, and the associated tie-straightenings, locks-combings, and wisecracks ("Don, suck in your gut!" "How's he gonna suck in his double-chin?") were, in fact, generating familial vapors.

My daughter just back from Prague and her cousin Carrie, who had not seen each other since childhood, but whose physical resemblance had been noted in family snapshots, seemed to have connected.

"She had these big hooters," I heard Sarah say—and I knew she was regaling Carrie with the tale I had heard earlier of her Czech friend Amalia's grandmother who, after her husband's death, had at the age of sixty-seven realized a lifelong ambition to be a prostitute. "She was drinking a lot of vodka and walking around Old Town Prague in low-cut dresses. Crossing a street to meet an old john one night, she fell down, and a taxi ran over her head."

Carrie was in stitches. "End of Grandma!"

"Caput," Sarah said.

"Well, she died doing what she liked!"

"She *did*."

I stood at the end of the long table in the corridor beyond the lounge where two white-jacketed caterer's employees were serving drinks.

A small blonde woman, identity unknown, sauntered past, head tilted backward, a beer bottle angled down her throat.

Then came a tall, strongly built, dark-haired young man: "Hiya, Unc."

I raised my glass of white wine in greeting, and smiled. One of my brother's sons, I knew—but I couldn't remember which brother.

A rather solemn-looking dark-haired woman passed by. She took note of me out of the corner of her eye. She, too, was familiar but unidentifiable.

The band launched into a noisy rendition of "When the Saints Go Marching In"—not perhaps the best opening selection for a ninetieth birthday party.

A heavyset man with a fringe of hair approached. "How've you been?" he said. We shook hands.

"You know what?" I said. "I don't know whose hand I'm shaking."

He seemed startled that his transformation had been so complete. He identified himself as Ned, Uncle Bill's son, and introduced the woman at his side as his wife.

As the three of us retreated further along the corridor further to hear ourselves speak above the band, I recalled the breakup of Ned's first marriage with Betsy (or was it Betty?) which Ned's mother, my aunt, had once described to me.

B. had apparently been a model farmer's wife who cooked for the hands and tended her two children dutifully before, with Ned's permission, she began taking some courses at the local college. In my aunt's account of the matter, B. had fallen under the influence of a professor who "talked a lot of nonsense," and one day, without bothering to write a Dear John letter, she got into the family station wagon and drove off, abandoning her husband and children. They had never known what became of her.

"How long did you stay on the farm after Uncle Bill died?" I asked Ned.

"Not very long. He'd been just hanging on for years. The government subsidies helped a little, but..."

"So what have you done for a living?"

"You name it, I did it. I roto-rootered drains. I delivered Pepsi. I sprayed pesticide…."

"You were in Arizona?"

"Three years. Texas and Missouri after that."

My brother Bob joined us. His head, and Ned's, were identically bald on top with a surrounding fringe. "You know," I said, "I've got a theory about you guys balding as you have."

Ned's sister (my cousin Patricia) approached accompanied by the solemn dark-haired young woman I'd seen out in the hall who, I now realized, was Patricia's daughter, Margaret.

"The last time we talked," I said to Margaret, "you were leaving for New York to start a job in publishing."

"That was quite a while ago."

"Still in the business?"

"No. I was just out of college when I took that job. I was crazy about books. I got high sniffing new ones."

"An inexpensive addiction."

"Not really. I got over it when I saw my first paycheck."

"What's this about Ned and I going bald?" Bob inquired.

A young man with a Walkman radio appeared at Bob's side. "Ken Griffin, Jr. just homered," he shouted. "The Reds are up four-zip."

"Great," Bob enthused

"So what do you do now?" I asked Margaret.

"I'm in public relations with J.P. Morgan/Chase."

"I have one of your credit cards."

"I hope you're not a deadbeat."

"What's a deadbeat?"

"Someone who pays off his balance every month."

"I'm a deadbeat."

"I heard they were out there somewhere. I always wanted to meet one."

An elderly woman appeared at my side. "I want to talk to the tennis player."

"Who's that?" I said.

"You!"

"I barely remember playing—I'm wondering why *you* would."

"I saw you play once, you were good."

My brother Joe asked me for seventy-five dollars, my share of the bill for the band, and as I was digging bills from my wallet another elderly woman approached me.

"I know who you are, but you don't know who I am," she shouted.

"How can you be so sure?"

"*No* one recognizes me any more."

"OK, I give up. Who are you?"

"Charlene Virtue."

"So why are Bob and I going bald?" Ned asked.

The band was playing "Bye, Bye Blackbird."

A small woman, owlish in horn-rimmed glasses who wore a floor-length gingham dress and a sun bonnet joined us.

"This is my daughter Jill," Charlene Virtue said.

Jill and I shook hands.

"Jill's going across Ohio in a Conestoga wagon," Charlene said.

I smiled. "Why?"

"It was my editor's idea."

"You're a reporter?"

"I write for the Salem City *Times*. The wagon train is part of the Ohio Bicentennial Celebration. The roads are paved, but let me tell you, a Conestoga wagon is still a rough ride. I dream at night of my Nissan."

The woman who'd seen me play tennis was describing the nightly Happy Hour for residents of Mother's building.

"How happy do they get?" Bob asked.

"Not very."

"If I have to eat any more canned beans," Jill said, "I'll scream."

Roger Hart, a nonagenarian who'd gone to high school with my mother and father introduced himself to me.

"When Roger graduated from Ohio Wesleyan," Charlene Virtue said, "they gave him two degrees, one in business, and one in music, although he never took any music courses."

"How'd you manage that?" I asked.

"I played piano for a lot of campus musicals," Roger explained.

"I've gone potty in some places I never thought I would," Jill said.

"I spent most of my life in the Middle East," Hart said, "My friends have been mainly Muslims, some very devout, and I respect that. I even envy it a little."

"There's a wonderful sense of community in the wagon train," Jill said. "I was riding with a woman from St. Clairsville yesterday. 'Why did we ever let this go?' she said. I knew what she meant."

"What were you were saying about Ned and I losing hair?" Bob said—when Gail, one of my brother's wives, tugged at my sleeve. "You're on in about two minutes."

In the lounge, I read to the assembled guests a portion of the little biography of Mother I had written for the occasion. I was back in the corridor outside when Gail took me by the arm and towed me back toward the lounge to participate in a little ritual. The band was playing “Let Me Call You Sweetheart,” and each of Mother’s sons was to dance with her in succession.

I hadn’t been on a dance floor in about a half century. “I don’t think I remember how,” I confessed.

“Oh, come on, big boy, you’ll remember.”

If I had known I was going to have to do this, I would have practiced.

Bob and Mother were shuffling about. Gail shoved me onstage. I gave Bob a forget-it-bub-this-woman’s-mine tap on the shoulder, winning laughter from the audience, and assumed the position with Mother. That much I remembered—but that was all, and I froze. Mother tried to get things going by moving her feet, and wiggling.

“Think one-two-three, one-two-three,” someone coached from the sideline.

“I’m thinking,” I replied, “but nothing happens.”

There was laughter, booing. “He can write, but get him off the dance floor.”

The photographer appeared.

“Quick, get the picture!” I said. The flash went off, and I fled the lounge.

I was back in the corridor seeking a refill of wine when Gail passed by, gave me a sharp look and said, “What are you, an anarchist?”

Outside the building in the late afternoon, Christine and I watched Mother and her grandchildren step into a rented stretch limousine with an Afro-American chauffeur for a ride around town in style.

"Why are they doing that?" Christine asked.

"I don't know."

"Won't it be expensive?"

"Probably."

"Do we help pay for it?"

"Probably."

We set out on a walk around town.

"Talking with people was fun," Christine said, "but all that other stuff..."

"The *program*?"

"That, and the loud music."

"I suspect the planners figured that the party might not come off without all that."

"Like a kids' birthday party—if you don't have games for them to play, they just stand around sucking their thumbs."

"Exactly."

The Main Street of my youth was no more. Fred Bartram's Red and White Grocery that had opened just in time for the great town flood of 1913, but dried out to survive into the 1950s, was gone. No OK Hardware. No Watson's Drugs. Gone was Oscar Klein's Department Store. (Oscar once told a local reporter that his business had survived the Great Depression by continuing to stock bloomers for older women after younger ones opted for panties. "There were things women skimped on during the Depression. Underwear wasn't one of them.")

A person who came to this Main Street today in quest of groceries, an ax, work shoes, or a washing machine, would not find them in shops with inventories of scented candles, English toffee, exotic teas and coffees, used furniture, and antiques. As in a thousand other American towns, North and South, mall chain stores and the big boxes out and away had made off with the core businesses, leaving behind the crumbs of specialty store profits.

On an impulse, I tried the front door of the building on William Street that had housed the local *Gazette* since the 1950s.

I had worked there as a reporter in summers between college terms. Finding the door open, I drew Christine inside.

It had been nearly a half century since I was in the building, but to the right of the entrance the counter where business had been conducted was intact; and across the hall the publisher's office door stood open, as it always had, and I thought the man seated in front of a computer screen might have been Tom Griswold, a high school classmate of mine who inherited ownership of the paper from his father.

A woman appeared behind the counter. "Could I help you?"

"You could tell me if that fellow in there is Tom Griswold," I said, loudly enough so the man at the computer would hear. He turned toward us and smiled.

"That's not Tom," the woman said, "but it's his son Larry."

Rip Van Winkle had only missed by one generation.

"The good-looking one," Larry said, getting up from his chair to greet us. His face was a collage of features that had belonged to Tom Griswold and Helen Allen, the local girl Tom had married.

I mentioned having once worked at as a reporter for the paper.

"Shame you hadn't come in a couple months ago, you could have seen the old press."

"The one installed when the building opened in the Fifties?"

"It was still pumping out the paper a year ago. We finally sold it for scrap metal."

"You have a new press?"

"No press."

"How do you print the paper?"

"*We* don't. There's a plant in Marysville that prints for us and five other dailies in the region."

"You submit a day's edition to them electronically?"

He nodded.

"But how do the papers get back here?"

"By truck."

"Isn't that pretty slow? What if there's breaking news?"

"Well, that isn't really our game. We get beat by radio and television on breaking news. We're oriented more to feature stories and columns."

"Any possibility the *Gazette* might disappear?" The paper had been published uninterruptedly in town since 1813.

"It's not impossible." He reached to his left and opened the door to the room next to his office. "Remember the old newsroom?"

I looked through the door where there had once been a row of five grey steel office desks for reporters, each equipped with its sturdy manual office typewriter. Now there was a forest of chest-high electronic equipment.

"You need all this to send editions to Marysville?"

"No, we have a secondary business as a regional Internet service provider."

"So where's the newsroom?"

"Upstairs. Remember the old library?"

"I remember it being pretty small."

"You'd be surprised how much room there is with all those old bound editions of the paper gone."

"All on microfilm now, I suppose?"

"Yes."

"But why would you want your newsroom on the second floor?"

"Just to keep people from coming in off the street and hassling reporters."

People hassled reporters in small town Ohio? That was almost as surprising as kids selling drugs at the main intersection of London.

Larry led us down a hall and through a door into what had once been the "composing room" with its three "hot-type" Linotype machines: heavy-legged, ungainly-looking black cast-iron monsters, each with its vat of molten brass, and a keyboard at which a compositor sat. The molten brass made the composing room sweet-smelling and toasty warm on cold winter days, and so oppressively hot in July and August that men who worked there stripped to the waist. The Linotypes were gone. So was a lot of other composing room paraphernalia; and the concrete block wall that had separated the composing room from the press room was no more. The back two thirds of the building was now a huge empty room.

The old press was, indeed, gone. A complex apparatus forty or fifty feet long, maybe ten feet high, with hundreds of parts that moved in mind-boggling coordination during a deafening press run, it had seemed to me as a boy palpable evidence of the printed word's significance. All that remained was the well the press had straddled into which pressmen equipped with huge wrenches had descended to make repairs and adjustments.

The minimization of the *Gazette*'s operation reminded me of what computer technology had done to "print," "mail," "files," "folders," "documents," and "tools."

"What are you going to do with all this space?" I asked Larry.

"If you have any ideas, let us know."

The crowd at the reunion banquet in the hotel ballroom Saturday night was larger than the one Friday night at the restaurant, and a bit more formal in tone owing to the setting.

Before a buffet dinner, classmates with wine glasses kibitzed in cocktail-party clusters, and perused class relics arranged on long tables: old dance programs, letter sweaters, newspaper clippings, class rings and pins. Small tables for dining had been arranged in a semi-circle around a central dais. At each place-setting there was a souvenir mug ("Together Again, Class of 1958") commemorating the commemoration, and a "Together Again, Class of 1958" ballpoint pen.

A printed program specified the order of events for the evening.

After dinner, the program opened with group singing of our school's alma mater, a paean to our school flower, the Black-Eyed Susan, "tho humble flower it be."

Everyone was supplied a printout of the lyrics of "We're Gonna Get Together to See Why We're Fallin' Apart." The composer played the melody accompanying his song several times on the piano, in preparation for a stumbling, mumbling, group performance.

Three members of the class perched on tall stools to perform an intermittently amusing comedy-club routine salted with class reminiscences and jokes. George Winship, who had acted professionally, compensated weaker moments in the script by clenching a pair of dinner forks between nostrils and upper lip in his walrus imitation.

Aficionados of "line dancing," apparently the rage among the senior set in Central Ohio, took the floor. Arranged in widely-spaced rank and file like a marching band whose center was not holding, they moved about dreamily in slow, boxy patterns like fox-trotters who'd lost their partners. The master of ceremonies urged the classmates seated at their tables around the dance floor to join in, but since it seemed a neophyte line dancer might make a line-dancing ass of himself or herself without having the consolation of an equally befuddled partner, the dancing petered out.

Donna Pippen gazed at me across the ballroom floor. "Some enchanted evening, you will see a strange-e-e-e-er across a crowded room…"

The awards segment of the program came next, with gag prizes for the classmate whose physical appearance had changed the least, the classmate who'd lived in town the longest, the classmate married the longest, the classmate with the most children. Thrice-married Spencer Hammer took the prize for the most grandchildren. Accepting his award, he mimicked Oscar recipients: "I would like to thank my three wives..."

Someone challenged him to name all of his nineteen grandchildren in order of their ages. Spencer named three or four, before gazing skyward and trailing off comically.

I was not amused. A continuation of the previous night's freestyle camaraderie would have been preferable to our sitting there like television zombies as the "program" ground on, I felt. The similarity between the program and television-watching became an identity when a classmate wheeled into the center of the ballroom floor a big-screen television set with an attached VCR. The master of ceremonies explained that during renovations to the old wing of the high school, a workman had come upon a reel of fragile glycerin-based home movie film from the 1920s depicting local scenes. The film had been carefully preserved and reproduced.

The lights in the ballroom went down, and the television set came on. A small man with a mustache wearing the white summer suit and straw hat of the vaudeville song-and-dance man waved his hand frantically near the camera lens, then turned abruptly and walked lickety-split across Main Street. What appeared to be a jet-powered Model-T Ford filled with waving, grinning riders zoomed down the street past the camera. A man swung a ball bat and fired a bullet into center field, ran to first base in record time, and mopped his brow frantically. Four young women in short dresses with fringed hems and lampshade hats milled around agitatedly in front of the camera, then launched into a hectic Charleston.

The lights came up again. The master of ceremonies

announced that the evening would conclude with a group picture being taken in an adjoining room. I had lost count of how many group pictures I had posed for that day. As I took my place among classmates on a riser for another, it occurred to me that *this* one might be of value later as proof the class of '58 had in fact been "together again," lest anyone should imagine that he or she had only dreamed it.

VI

A WRITER'S BLOCK IN FICTION

Joan Acocella once wrote in a *New Yorker* piece[6*] of the absurdity of Americans probing writer's block with the aid of psychoanalysis, biological theories, and researches in brain chemistry. Europeans, she said, find the subject boring; and the English regard writer's block as just simply one of life's "regular, humbling facts"—not a syndrome.

That American writers brood on the mystery of writer's block has some connection probably with our historical association of hard work and productivity with virtue. Creative writing doesn't really fit into this paradigm very neatly, since no writer, regardless of talent, is likely to produce a constant stream of good work. There are, in the nature of the game, breakdowns, false starts, and fallow periods.

Of greater interest than a writer's inability to write at a given moment, to my own way of thinking, is an inability to produce work *in a specific genre.* That can be a revelation not only for the writer experiencing it, but perhaps for his or her culture. What has concerned me personally in this respect are difficulties in fiction. When I first got serious about writing in my mid-thirties, fiction was what I hoped to write, and over the years, I have produced a fair number of short stories and two novels. My fiction, though, has always veered in the direction of the mixed-genre work, and a lot of it might be classified as what is known these days as "creative non-fiction."

I once heard Maxine Chernoff, a good poet who was also writing some fiction at the time, say, "I don't know why I can't imagine anything *happening* in my stories." There have been

6 *June 14-21, 2004

times when *I* might have said that—or what Paul Goodman said in an essay, "On a Writer's Block" (1952):

> *There are productive authors who cannot imagine a story to tell. This is not an inhibition of writing as such. They may be productive, able to finish whole works that have a beginning, middle, and end. By writing, they can disengage themselves from "inner problems," and get them outside, in public. They can act through a lyrical work that includes conflict, surprise, climax (ambivalences, ironies, resolutions); or, again, they can carry through a dialectical argument and write criticism, sociology, and so forth. But the inhibition sets in when they try to invent a dramatic plot with characters. Nothing seems interesting enough to engage them in beginning; or they cannot make the action move, or the action loses its direction and dwindles away.... What is the block?*

For one who aspires to write fiction, not being able to imagine anything happening, or a "dramatic plot with characters," is indeed a problem. A reader expects something to happen in fiction, that one thing will lead to the next and that there will be movement toward an engaging and probable conclusion of some sort.

Plotting is not obviously the most difficult aspect of fictional writing. In a *Seinfeld* rerun on television, ten or twenty interesting things will happen and connect—crazily and improbably, but hilariously—in less than a half hour. Tired and at loose ends some evening, my attention will stray to a swift, densely plotted television police drama, and I will be diverted sure as shooting. Sometimes I am so excited my heart pounds. Am I getting too old for this kind of thing?

Man dies in armchair during police chase

My wife never sits down to watch tv, but if the sirens of my police drama wail, and one of the principals inquires, "How then did Mrs. Hoopoe disappear?" she will be in the doorway eager for word of the lost Hoopoe.

What is Hoopoe to her, or she to Hoopoe?

Generally speaking, plotting has not been the strong suit of modern "serious" writers, though, and modern criticism has tended to associate dense plotting with superficial entertainment. However, few weapons in the writer's arsenal are as potent as plot. Diane Johnson, who at the time I am writing this is interested in reinvigorating plot in fiction, imagines an airline passenger bored by the some thinly plotted "serious" work she is reading vaguely jealous of a passenger across the aisle flipping eagerly through the pages of a heavily plotted thriller by Sidney Sheldon or Stephen King.

The Marxian philosopher Georg Lukacs criticized the absence of plot in modern fiction in which "the real dramatic and epic movement of social happening disappears, and isolated characters of purely private interest, characters sketched in only a few lines, stand still, surrounded by a dead scenery." The realists Flaubert and Zola were favorite targets for him. (Flaubert in some poignantly tormented self-criticism of his *L'education sentimentale,* lamented that this work, while scrupulously faithful to life, was boring: "It is too true, and aesthetically speaking, it lacks the falsity of perspective. Every work must have a plot, a conflict, must form a pyramid [with a rising and falling action] but in life nothing like this exists.... Never mind, I believe no one has gone further in honesty.")

As far as Lukacs was concerned, the author who treats human existence as if it were a "constant, even-tempered stream" or as a "monotonous plain sprawling without contours" is the victim of a "subjective prejudice," because human reality *is* intrinsically conflictive and dynamic—always in motion, or about to be. It interested him that just when plotlessness had thinned the blood of much "serious" fiction in the nineteenth century there had emerged a vast, and vastly popular, "schematic" or "archetypal" popular fiction (detective stories and romances) consisting of scarcely anything but plot. Such writing did not depict characters in conflict with institutions, the forces of history, class barriers, or Nature, so it was not "serious," but by evoking the archetypes of dramatic form, the struggle of thesis and antithesis that runs along beneath all human immediacy, it engaged the imagination. *Pace* Flaubert, there was a sense in which it was truer to life than modern realism's flimsy narratives, detached narrator-observers, and stylistic refinements.

So why do "serious" writers have trouble developing plots? Goodman, contemplating the failure of the dramatic imagination (rather clearly his own) thought the source of the problem was the writer's inability to articulate conflicts in his "interpersonal relations." It was when those were clearest that the writer would be most able to create plots, and also to abstract away from personal experience in his writing. He proposed, as therapy, that a writer plunge into confessional writing, nothing held back. This would not be art, but it would serve to remind the writer of overlooked personal conflicts that could later serve as a basis for plotting: "Oh—but I see, I remember—if I tell this, and try to unify it dramatically, I shall have to mention—that. But I didn't foresee that!… Something unnoticed in the actuality has been brushed aside."

This might be good advice, I suppose, but the absence of plot in "serious" fiction has been common enough to suggest that factors other than, or in addition to, a failure to understand conflicts in "interpersonal relations" are in play. Lukacs would say that a writer who can't plot doesn't understand what history reveals so clearly, that human reality is by its very nature dialectical and dramatic. However, this fails to acknowledge that the energies for writing fiction arise not from a knowledge of history, but the writer's sense of participation in the life of his or her time and place; and the fact that modern, or at least recent, Western history has often not been dramatic or dialectical in any immediate, obvious way may have something to do with the difficulty "serious" writers have had with plotting.

Fluidity in "interpersonal relations" may have been a significant factor, too. Diane Johnson thinks the fact that Victorian lives were so often much richer in social connections and their attendant conflicts than ours, helps explains the density of plotting in Victorian novels: "You really had an uncle who might leave you out of his will. Your cousin was at hand to hate you. What you did had [social] effects, like the effects of a pebble on a pond." Then there was that intense nineteenth century conflict of ego and id that held Freud's attention. Whatever else might be said of these matters, there was drama in them to encourage storytelling.

A story by Alice Munro, "Oh, What Avails?" published by *The New Yorker* some years ago is an excellent illustration of how the fragmented, piecemeal character of experience typical in our part of the world today repels plotting. The piece is a *tour de force* rather than a story with a beginning, middle, and end. It follows a group of small town Canadians through a very long stretch of time, from childhood into middle age. Munro drops in on her characters' lives at intervals to show us what they are up to—nothing particularly interesting. Little happens in the story, but then little of importance is happening in their lives, either. They are "hanging in there," as we say. As the characters age they take up new addresses, vocations, lovers. False lights, vain hopes, and relationships without substance are as clearly facts of life for Munro, as they were for Flaubert. In one passage, a married woman, a latter day Madame Bovary, is anticipating an affair. In the next scene, set years later, we learn she has had the affair, gone through a divorce, and entered into another relationship. None of this is apparently worth detailed scrutiny. Mention of the woman's amours in Munro's flat, matter-of-fact voice are folded in with the carefully observed trivia of ordinary life of which the story largely consists. Given the long time span of the story, the trivia acquire a bizarre prominence—bright little balloons tossing on an ocean's surface. There being so few developments of consequence in lives across such a long stretch of time means inevitably that the story is thinly plotted; and since character in fiction is defined by reactions to challenges and conflicts, there isn't much of that, either.

Munro's story contradicts the expectation a reader brings to any story that something of interest will unfold in the lives of the characters. But the conventions of narrative bounce harmlessly off the lives depicted. As a response to the kind of human situation pretty common in the world as we know it, the story is both apt and ingenious—but a person reading such work might be forgiven for experiencing a longing for sci-fi or a detective story.

The only way a writer can determine what he or she can or cannot write is to write, and there may be surprises awaiting at the intersection of literary tradition, personal experience, and the times. Most literary experimentation occurs, I suspect, when a writer trying to imitate his forebears runs into a barrier tall, thick, and hard as a penitentiary wall. After beating his or her head repeatedly against that barrier, and making frantic attempts to surmount the difficulty, he or she is likely to conclude that trying something else might be wiser. It would not be too surprising if aspiring fiction writers, faced with the kind of dilemma I have been describing, were to begin producing work that, while it might resemble fiction a little by fits and starts, would turn out being something else.

James Gallant is an independent scholar, the *Fortnightly Review*'s "Verisimilitudes" columnist, and the author of *The Big Bust at Tyrone's Rooming House: A Novel of Atlanta* and *Whatever Happened to Ohio?* He lives in Atlanta.

Odd Volumes are edited and published for subscribers to *The Fortnightly Review* [fortnightlyreview.co.uk].

Made in the USA
Columbia, SC
01 June 2019